Conversations with George Luscombe

Library and Archives Canada Cataloguing in Publication
Conversations with George Luscombe : talking with a Canadian theatre visionary / Steven Bush.
Includes bibliographical references and index.

ISBN 978-0-88962-942-4

1. Luscombe, George, 1926-1999--Interviews. 2. Theatrical producers and directors--Canada--Interviews. 3. Theatre-- Canada. 4. Theatre. 5. Dramaturgy. I. Bush, Steven, 1944- II. Title.

PN2304.L88 2012 792.097109'04 C2012-901361-7

No part of this book may be reproduced or transmitted in any form, by any means, electronic or mechanical, including photocopying and recording, information storage and retrieval systems, without permission in writing from the publisher, except by a reviewer who may quote brief passages in a review.

Pubished by Mosaic Press, Oakville, Ontario, Canada, 2012.

MOSAIC PRESS, Publishers
Copyright © Steven Bush and the estate of George Luscombe, 2012
ISBN 978-0-88962-957-8
eBook 978-0-88962-958-5
book design by K. Daniel and E. Normann

We acknowledge the financial support of the Ontario Media Development Corporation (OMDC).

Mosaic Press in Canada:
1252 Speers Road, Units 1 & 2
Oakville, Ontario L6L 5N9
phone: (905) 825-2130

Mosaic Press in USA:
c/o Livingston, 40 Sonwil Dr,
Cheektowaga, NY 14225
phone: (905) 825-2130

www.mosaic-press.com

Conversations with George Luscombe

Steven Bush in conversation with the Canadian theatre visionary

Edited and Prepared by Steven Bush

Preface by R·H· Thomson

mosaic press

To George's students and Steven's students
and their students
and their students…

and

to Mona Luscombe (1929—2010)
who supported George and T.W. P.
for many many years
as George supported
the "Creative Work"

Table of Contents

Preface: *Roaring From The Roof Tops*

The last time I saw George was in hospital in Toronto. His leg had been amputated, his health was declining, the possibility of recovery was fading, yet from his hospital sheets he enthused about playing a one-legged King Lear, a modern Lear on a modern heath, howling from the office tower rooftops at the injustices of the world.

A life in art comes in three acts. Act I is discovery — the artist discovers the world, the world discovers the artist. Act II is ascendancy — a body of work is created, fired by the passions and observations of the artist. Act III is the descent, creating on the way to the exit.

I knew George during Acts II and III. His talent was part fire, part vision and part politics. George loved a robust theatricality rooted in the words of the everyman. He himself was part everyman, part bull. Everyday man and woman appeared in George's productions and sometimes everyday chaos as well. Kings, princesses, the priests, the powerful and the Presidents were not his preferred theatrical characters. Everyone else was.

The strength and dignity of ordinary Canadians interested George – working class Canadians as they were called in the 1950s when the politics of class still lingered. The politics of the powerless interested George. The feel of the street, the world of the factory floor, ordinary Canadians fighting fascism in Spain in 1937, and the unemployed men and women in the soup kitchens of Canada of the dirty thirties, all of these were George's passion. *Ten Lost Years* chronicled the hardship of ordinary lives impoverished by severe market failure in the Great Depression and it was George's seminal production. Inspired by the book created by Barry Broadfoot from interviews with those dispossessed Canadians, it placed everyday man and everyday woman at centre stage.

How a culture presents the stories of its citizens reveals who holds the power. Everyday man and everyday woman first appeared in religious plays of the Middle Ages. Power belonged to the Church. I played one of the executioners of Christ in the 'York Cycle' from the 15th century. My character, 'A Soldier', was an ordinary man tasked with improvising a method of nailing a suffering and prison-shrunken Jesus onto a pre-drilled cross with holes measured for a fitter Saviour. My character only existed within a religious story. The Church tolerated no other narratives. No scene dealt with The Soldier's arthritis or his troubles with his mother-in-law.

Shakespeare wrote about the common man, but never cast him in a major role. Power resided with the kings, queens, dukes and bishops. Shakespeare felt strongly about common man or woman yet kept them marginal. In *Henry VI, Part III* common folk are caught in a King's war: "Alarum. Enter a Son that hath kill'd his Father, at one door: and a Father that hath kill'd his Son at another door". In *King Lear*, a peasant servant of the Duke of Cornwall rebels against injustice and is murdered for it. Interesting characters, compassionately written, yet they are forever minor players. In the plays of the 17th and 18th centuries, ordinary folk are rarely found onstage. They re-enter by the end of the 19th century, but it isn't until the 20th century, when full political democracy has been achieved, that everyday man and everyday woman truly are given the stage. Everyone gets to vote and everyone can now stand centre stage. Narrative power parallels political power.

At Toronto Workshop Productions, stories of ordinary Canadians were firmly centre stage. And about time. The UN Universal Declaration of Human Rights in 1948 was not unconnected to the public appetite to see the failing salesman Willy Loman in *Death Of A Salesman*, the depression era men and women of Canada in *Ten Lost Years* or the homeless travelers in Waiting For Godot. Monarchs and bishops had almost vanished from plays in the 1950s and 1960s. Their power had disappeared and so were their stories on our stages.

George wanted to go further and tell the stories of those who questioned and challenged systems that had kept them without wealth or respect. The 1950s, which was George's Act I, acknowledged the rights and powers of ordinary men and women in an unprecedented way. After all, it was ordinary citizens who had fought two world wars, first in 1914 and then again in 1939. Teachers and farmhands, factory workers and retail workers, bank tellers, dentists and miners formed the armies that defeated Nazi Germany. Death was not guided by class distinction on the battlefield; it was democratically distributed, and surviving soldiers expected full democracy once they got home. Also the officer class no longer came solely from the upper class. Tradition had dictated that only those with social power became officers in the army. But now ordinary citizens became officers, not just the sons of the moneyed class. Unionized workers gained a similar respect and legitimacy. After all, if ordinary Canadians weren't going to be bullied by the enemy on the battlefield, why would they allow themselves to be bullied by the bosses back home? Yet all of this 'power to the people' played against the background of the post WWII 'Red scare' and the fear of possible Communist world domination. The Russian revolution in 1917 was about the rights and dignity of working class Russians and the overthrow of the corrupt ruling classes. But the Communist revolution soon descended into its own corruption and totalitarianism. However, post WWII, the genie of social rights and freedoms was out of the bottle. Canada attained the most equitable distribution of wealth in its history. The middle class expanded and the poverty class shrank. Life was fairer than it had ever been. The struggle for decent wages, safe working conditions and an old age that didn't automatically mean poverty had been won. This was the era in which George wrote and directed and ran TWP.

But financial fairness is deteriorating and we need new George Luscombes who will champion ordinary Canadians. Today, equality and fairness have become almost exclusively the domain of gender and racial rights, no longer concerning themselves with inequitable wealth distribution. For example, employees at Wal-Mart, or 'Associates' as they are called, do have racial and gender rights, but any attempt to achieve income fairness is ruthlessly stopped. In the few cases where the Wal-Mart employees have unionized, the owners have eliminated the stores. There are 7 billionaires in the Walton family and the family owns 48% of the Wal-Mart company.

Is this shift in power reflected in the stories we are told? I believe it is and, as in the Wal-Mart example, I suggest the reason is the drive for profits at the expense of social responsibility. I don't see the shift in our theatres, since the possibility of profits in theatre is a joke and, anyway, live theatre is now marginal and a small player in the story telling arts. However television and film monetize stories for profit and that drives the change. Yes, there are ordinary men and women in TV series and blockbuster films, but these are middle class and relentlessly glamorized. Glamour means more viewers, which means higher ad rates, which means more profit. The working poor are absent in mainstream story telling since there is no glamour in poverty. Glamour is the cleavage on women cops and the impeccable five o'clock shadow on the guys. Glamour is slim body types for women and compulsory muscle mass for men. Lighting, camera work, editing, sound, violence are all glamourized. Glamour turns our eyes away from the stories of ordinary lives. If the poor do occasionally appear, the grind of their lives is never told, they are politically neutered, they have good teeth, new clothes and, in America, they never worry about their medical bills. To monetize storytelling for profit means little interest in authenticity. Of course there are exceptions like the remarkable series *The Wire*, but they are marginal. Authentic everyday man and everyday woman have exited our mainstream stages once more. Power has shifted once again.

I want to mention George's hunger for authenticity. In 1980, I played in *The Mac Paps* at TWP. The play was about the Canadian men and women who were among the first to recognize the threat of fascism. They formed the Mackenzie-Papineau Battalion and in 1937 went to Spain to fight fascism. George assembled the play from the words of those who went. Fascism and Nazism were responsible for 60 million deaths in WWII. Some of the men and women who fought in Spain—first with their words, then with their actions and many with their lives—were present at the opening night of *The Mac Paps*. They were invited up on stage during our curtain call. I remember the steel in their idealist eyes. Both actors and audience applauded them. I felt humbled by the authenticity of ordinary-extraordinary elderly Canadians who were small in height but enormous in moral stature and who were among the first to stand up to one of the evils of the 20th century. And it was George Luscombe who made sure they were truly centre stage.

As I think of George's work, and the raging one-legged Lear he wanted to play, I wonder about the place of the ordinary workingmen and women in our country. Financial inequality is growing and wealth distribution in our country is slipping to 19th century levels. Collectivism is questioned and attacked. Who was the last Prime Minister who walked in the Labour Day parade? So next time I walk in downtown Toronto on a blustery day, I will listen for the roaring spirit of George Luscombe. It will be there, somewhere high on the urban heath of office tower roofs and hopefully in full ghostly voice.

Blow windes, and crack your cheeks; Rage, blow
You Cataracts, and Hyrricanos, spout
Till you have drench'd our Steeples, drowned the Cockes.
You Sulph'rous and Thought-executing Fires,
Vaunt-curriors of Oak-cleaving Thunder-bolts,
Sindge my white head.

R. H. Thomson
July 2011

Introduction

After I stepped off the bus from Ohio in February 1969, the first theatre I entered was Toronto Workshop Productions and the first show I saw was *The Good Soldier Schweik* directed by George Luscombe. Compared with work I'd seen and done in the States, Schweik struck me with its political content and also with its aesthetic – the design, the use of space and the way the actors moved. This was definitely not television put onstage. I knew this was a theatre where I wanted to work.

Shortly after, I came by for an audition. The story goes that, observing me 'loitering' in the adjoining parking lot, company manager June Faulkner said to George: "I think you've just found your Abraham Lincoln." I was indeed invited to play the role of Lincoln in the revised remount of *Gentlemen, Be Seated!*—soon to be retitled *Mr Bones*. I stayed with TWP for that show, for the trip to the Biennale di Venezia (with *Bones* and *Che Guevara*) and for the three productions of the following season. Later, I worked at TWP as co-author (with Richard McKenna) of *Richard Thirdtime* (which George directed) and *From the Boyne to Batoche* (which I directed).

Over the years following, George and I met from time to time to discuss projects. He asked me to act in *The Mac Paps* at TWP and I asked him to act in *Spring Awakening* at the University of Guelph, but we turned each other down. It wasn't until May 1996 – when I had the summer free from teaching at the University College Drama Program and George was at home rehabilitating after surgery – that we worked together again, beginning the series of conversations from which this book has been extracted.

* * *

In 1999 the late Urjo Kareda—theatre critic, dramaturge and longtime Artistic Director of Toronto's Tarragon Theatre—eulogized George as "Our Father." Now, over twelve years after George's death, many theatre students have never heard of him. But without Luscombe, Urjo suggested, theatre in Toronto would have developed very differently. George showed that theatre built on ensemble principles was possible. That producing new Canadian work in a culture historically dominated by British and U.S. models was possible. He inspired the next generation of theatre-makers to follow in his footsteps, or to consciously rebel and set out on different paths, or both. Certainly for many of us who subsequently formed theatre companies, George's example provided a benchmark, positive and/or negative, against which to evaluate what we were up to.

At the same time, Urjo noted, George and TWP were anomalies. As Hamlet said about his father: "I shall not look upon his like again." Think about it: A company led by a passionate director with a rigourously clear vision of the kind of theatre he wanted to create? Twelve actors? Training together? (Not just training students!) Employed for the whole season? Making new work? On sometimes current and controversial political topics?

For those not lucky enough to have seen George's shows, or studied about them in a university course, I refer you to the photographs throughout the book and the memorial tributes at the end, which give 'backstory' to our conversations.

* * *

Shortly after I'd attended a memorial for the director/writer Clarke Rogers, I mentioned my admiration for Clarke while noting that he seemed to have made some enemies. George responded: "If you don't make enemies, you're probably no damn good!"

Certainly George made some enemies. Indeed, some people who worked with him earlier in his career might not recognize the 'George' of these pages. Some adored him and others not at all. For some, he changed their lives hugely and for the better; for others, he seems to have inflicted wounds they still carry. In our reminiscences about the 'Creative Work,' George and I are probably describing it, at times, as it should have been rather than how it always was. And there are, very certainly, 'alternative versions' to some of the stories he tells in this book.

In fact, there are so many wondrous, inspiring, hilarious and (yes) painful stories from TWP's 30-odd years that I've encouraged other

TWP 'veterans'—many of whom clocked more hours there than I did—to record their recollections and publish them before we're all either dead or demented. There is much more to be told before we have anything approaching a thorough written account of the radically diverse experiences of working with George.

But this book is not that collection of memories from TWP alums.

Though it is full of personal anecdote, it is not an autobiography.

It is not a critical study of George, his methods or his social skills.

It is not a history of Toronto Workshop Productions: Neil Carson has covered that pretty darn well in *Harlequin in Hogtown*. (Note how frequently I lean on him in the 'Sources for Footnotes.')

And while there are many references to George's primary influences, and to other theatre-makers throughout the ages, it is not a scholarly comparative study.

But what the book is ... is George in his own words. And George in 1996—not 1966 or 1976 or 1986. And he's talking, primarily, about Actor Training and Ensemble.

On the other hand ... when George was teaching a performance class at Guelph, Maja Ardal (another TWP alum) asked him: "Are you training any exciting actors?" George replied: " I don't train actors. I train citizens."

That George is also very present in the following pages.

* * *

By the time we began recording, George had overcome his earlier qualms about making "another book on Acting." We knew full well, being who we were, that we'd frequently and happily digress to other topics; but training actors and developing ensemble was, from the start, the central narrative (or, in Stanislavskian terms, the "Through-Line of Actions") within and around which such digressions would occur; and our "Super-Objective" was to create a coherent account of George's training process. And I know that he wanted a book that, like his 'sacred text' An Actor Prepares, would be used – not just read and talked about.

Conversing with George was very easy and great fun. However, getting the conversations transcribed and edited, and finding a publisher as alert to the book's value as Howard Aster at Mosaic Press, has been a bit more challenging.

We had of course hoped that our book would be published while we both were still alive. Unfortunately for that hope, a major foundation we approached for minor funding to employ transcribers turned us down. Finally, after I'd followed another path that took up time and energy but ultimately led nowhere, our friend and colleague Robin Breon suggested that I apply for Work-Study assistants at the University of Toronto. Thanks to them, the eleven audiotapes (close to 13 hours in total) were finally transcribed.

But all these steps took too much time and, alas, in February 1999 George left the land of the living.

* * *

Paring the 550 pages of the full transcriptions down to the book's present length also took time. Throughout the editing process I've borne in mind Text Analysis according to Konstantin Stanislavski as transmitted by George. I've looked at each conversation as if it were a dramatic Unit and I've kept asking one of George's favourite questions: "What can the Unit not do without?" Answering this question led to Titles that, in turn, strengthened focus for each chapter.

Then: "What is the main Objective?" What were the 'characters' – the conversationalists – trying to achieve? What, in each Unit, was the main point we wanted to make?

Of course I'd often used this analytical method in play development workshops, the rehearsal hall and the classroom, but never with a "chapter book." However, George believed the method works for novels, fables, even for one's own life or a day in one's life, so why not for this?

This approach made it easier to cut material that didn't belong in one Unit – cut it entirely or move it to another Unit. Here and there I've done some 'cut & paste' because two versions of the same story 'read better' when conflated. Most of the conversations are printed in the order in which they took place, but some sections have been shifted forward or back simply because they 'fit better' in the new location.

Thanks to a conversation with George's daughter Karen Luscombe, I was reminded how much he hated "self-pity." While I don't recall George ever appearing or sounding "self-pitying," there were a couple of passages that—in print and without the reader having immediate benefit of George's tough, energetic and lyrical voice – could be read that way, so I've taken them out.

Beyond this, the working rules of the editing process have been:

Keep it "conversational." Don't turn our sometimes fumbling search for the right words into finely finished prose. Don't totally smooth-out the often meandering nature of real conversation.

Retain the particularities of George's voice.

Don't put words in his mouth: Edit, even re-position sections of text, but don't rewrite.

Make it "an easy read": The reader shouldn't have to work too hard to get what George and I were getting at.

* * *

Some books of conversations read as if the exchange had taken place in a limbo. In some, the transcription has been 'cleaned up' to the point where everyone sounds the same. I didn't want that. As a result, the "script" I've culled from our conversations may be more "naturalistic" or "documentary" than George would have liked. Had he lived longer – or had we been enabled to get transcriptions sooner – we'd have shaped the book together. However, since his passing, it has seemed important to retain a sense of the contexts in which we spoke. That's what my 'stage directions' are about. And also to alert the reader that, despite the gravity of some of the subject matter, our conversations were generally lighter in tone than the 'spoken' words on the page might convey.

Overall I've tried to stay true to our "Given Circumstances" and to our "Super-Objective." Indeed, the applied Stanislavskian method has helped organize our chats into a series of informal "lessons" that is at least close to what George had wanted.

As my very astute assistant Amanda Montague observed: "This text is not the final word, and the reader has only gotten a brief glimpse into the long conversation that has been the relationship between Steven and George."

Steven Bush
Toronto, Nunavut Day 2011

P.S. (United Nations Day 2011)—There has been no attempt to update these conversations. They happened from May to December 1996 and in 1996 they remain. Our reference points were determined by what we knew in the months we were taping.

George would undoubtedly have had something to say about the 9/11 attacks, the subsequent wars in Afghanistan and Iraq, the ascent of the Harper Gang to power in Ottawa or 'martial law' in downtown Toronto,

Summer 2010. And I am sure he would have been thrilled to see the 'Arab Spring' and 'Occupy Wall Street' movements spread their influence around the world. But he didn't live to see these events, so they're not in the book.

And certainly, if we'd been bless'd to be talking together today, we might touch upon the success of Soulpepper in establishing a year-round company with an ensemble core. We might touch upon Volcano, The Electric Company and other movement-inspired theatres that have developed across the country post-TWP. We might touch upon Viewpoints—a process I imagine George would have been enthused about as it bears relation to his Laban-based explorations of the actor body in space. But in 1996 neither George nor I knew about Viewpoints, so it's not in the book either.

But before you continue reading here's a strong encouragement to listen to ...

George's Voice

You may have picked up this book for any of several reasons: To check the index to see if your name or your favourite TWP show is listed; to flip through the practical exercises while preparing your next class; to find some factoids while cramming for an exam about Canadian theatre history; or to read the whole thing from cover to cover just because you're interested in what George has to say.

This book has been constructed so that you can use it in any of these ways.

But... before you continue reading, listen to the audio CD in the sleeve at the back of the book. At least some of it. Why? Because it will be helpful, I think, to have George's voice in your head as you read his words on the page. Attempt has been made—through editing and punctuation choices—to convey the tempo, the tone, the energy, even the stumbling-about of real conversation. But there was—indeed still is—a liveliness, lyricism and passion in George's voice that is almost impossible to convey simply through words on a page.

Happy listening! Happy reading!

The Conversations

Prologue: "God, send me a carpenter!"

May 10th 1996

GEORGE LUSCOMBE: Let's talk about twelve people, because that's usually what I'm dealing with. We even had a building called "Twelve Alexander." We thought that was a good omen, because I always talked about a company of twelve—and thirteen, in case you needed. So there was always one extra coming along and you didn't have to plan for that—that happened. That's the nice thing that happens in the arts—the one you don't plan for—but you have to have the ground ready for him or he can't come.

I remember one occasion uhhh I walked into the office and I was very upset. Nothing was getting done in the carpentry world and I screamed up at the ceiling: "God, send me a carpenter!" And wouldn't you know it? The fellow walked in.

STEVEN BUSH: … Immediately?

GEORGE: Immediately. *(Steven laughs)* Within moments. Everybody fell over 'cause the first thing he said was … "I'm lookin' for work; I'm a carpenter." I said: "Thank you very much. There's the theatre, here's the problem." And he stayed with us for a long time.

Then, of course, I made a big play of thanking God, being the atheist I am uhh so we had a lot of fun.

First Conversation: Getting Started

Scene—Here are the major "Given Circumstances": We recorded these conversations at George's home, both indoors and outdoors, in various weathers and with other life going on around us. Our moods, energy-levels and tempos vary from one conversation to another. Sometimes there's techno-trouble and the flow is interrupted. Sometimes the presence of birds is noted. Sometimes other humans appear.

GEORGE: When you audition people and bring them in after a couple weeks' audition, you still don't know a damn thing about them really. And the first steps are terribly important—like being there on time; leaving your bloody lunch behind; getting rid of the coffee routine. All that's cleared out and the theatre's treated far more like a sanctuary, I suppose. Because you want to inspire the spirit, as well as the mind, as well as the body, as well as, perhaps, things we can't put our finger on or can't describe. Therefore, those unknowns have to be free to work and they won't be unless you have a free body, a free feeling, and a good feeling about work.

the first steps: knowing where the fences are

I'm noted, terribly I know, as a disciplinarian, but I've always found that people felt good when they knew where 'the fences' were. They felt freer when there were certain behaviour patterns they had to adhere to. For the reason that you understood you and your neighbour were going to be in tune. How do you get in tune? This is very difficult... particularly so when you've got twelve strangers.

So it's terribly important how you start, and I always started physically because it's the easiest thing to do. I would ask them to get into a circle. Now we all know how important a circle is, and how many meanings it has—psychologically, spiritually, etc. "Be the same distance from the neighbour on your left as the neighbour on your right." And then people would turn their heads—overwork, you know, and immediately start to look all around. I said: "Wait, wait, wait. You can see out the sides of your eyes, to adjust." And they would giggle a bit, and that's good; and they would adjust, just a little, but that little attention to their relationship between the person on their left and on their right is very important.

exercise: forming a group

"Now you've done something; that's good. You came in here as separate individuals and now, all of a sudden, you have formed a group—only physically, but that's the first step, slowly taken. And when we ask you to come back up on stage again, *you* do the adjusting: Don't wait for me to tell you, because I won't. But I'll complain a lot if you don't know enough to get into a relationship with your neighbour."

I usually start with the first lessons of Laban and his use of an actor in space. Rudolf von Laban[1] was the creator of movement for the theatre, as far as we're concerned. He analyzed what the body could do and broke it up into what we call eight Efforts, each Effort having three qualities. The three qualities in their opposite pairs are light/heavy, fast/slow, and direct/indirect, and the combinations of these qualities *interchanged* make up the eight Efforts. Through the Efforts, we have been able to analyze the essence of the movements of the human body.

Rudolf von Laban and the Efforts

Laban was kicked out of Germany, had to run for his life—

STEVEN: In the Thirties?

GEORGE: In the Thirties, when Hitler arrived on the scene. In England we were fortunate enough to have him; that's where he continued his work. He was first hired, I am told, as a time… What do you call it? A *time* specialist: He'd go into factories and watch how they were working and then suggest to workers how they could complete the work with less effort, less sweat and toil, so they would get more done and be less tired. He did this for a living for a while, but his main study was how he could help people in the theatre by analyzing the movement of the body.

1. Rudolf von Laban (1879-1958) – Hungarian dancer, choreographer, dance theorist. Created influential system of dance and movement notation, now called Labanotation. (1)

controlling the body

I would ask the novice actor: "Walk to me. Walk to me as directly as you can, without going up with your body or down with your body." You know, in a normal walk, you go up a little and down a little and from side to side a little. You want to take away all those things and think of yourself as a bird. A bird travels directly without moving left or right or up and down. And people usually fail on the first step, because they're used to adjusting the hips for walking, which normally is all right, but we're talking about *controlling* the body now. *Completely control the body,* so that it's you that has made up your mind to walk from one point to another *directly,* without shifting. And after a few tries people would start to use their feet better. They would begin to adjust to the job at hand—which is moving from one point to another. They'd all be amused that such a simple thing is not so easy to accomplish and something they thought they *were* doing, they *weren't* doing.

And so it's *their* revelation that's important, not mine. They begin to see the light: "I *should* control my body better than that."

And then we take the next step. I would ask them to move as fast as possible. Now it becomes a real challenge, because if they move fast they're going to lose balance; and I suggest to them: "Only take one step, but move as fast as you can with that one step." We then suggest that it might help if they include the *rest* of the body. Why not let the arms be an *extension* of that step? The arms *follow* the Centre. It's the Centre of the body that's most important.

STEVEN: Explain 'the Centre'?

the centre

GEORGE (*reading from notes*): "The Centre. For the actor, everything begins from the Centre. When riding in an old elevator that comes to a sudden stop, that queasy feeling of change is first registered in the middle. When confronted with a dangerous sight, the Centre reacts in fear. When news of the death of a loved one is heard, the Centre responds before the mind can adjust, and keeps you from collapse. The emotional life is the starting point for the actor and that life begins at the Centre."

STEVEN: Mmhmmn.

GEORGE: Yeah, I would've explained to them that we're going to concentrate on the Centre. And then I would have explained

Laban's very important presence in the theatre company in which I was a part for so many years, Theatre Workshop.

STEVEN: Joan Littlewood?[2]

GEORGE: Joan Littlewood. And although I never met Laban personally, I worked with Jean Newlove[3], his disciple; she's still working. And it's through those people that I learned the Efforts. But I learned a great deal more when I came to teaching it—which I guess is always the way.

the thrust

If we had achieved the actor moving from the Centre, being *fast* and being *direct* and *heavy*—And 'heavy' doesn't mean noise, but 'heavy' means a *sense* of heaviness. I always gave the example of music: The funeral march. (*Hums Chopin's famous "Funeral March"*) You can feel the downward *press* of that. And if I want something light, I would then do my little ... (*Sings the most familiar circus tune*) That's a *sense* of lightness and a *sense* of heaviness. Not the *sound* of it, because the first thing you get is actors stamping their foot on the ground. So we would achieve then *directness, heaviness* and *fast* ... and we would do it one at a time, right around the room, and then do it all together.

voice & movement: never separate the two.

I have learned, through bitter experience, to bring the voice along with it: Never to separate the two. Can you believe that, in the early days of my teaching, I would work months on the Efforts, everybody being quiet, no voice at all?

STEVEN: Was that the way you were trained in England? Was a lot of the work silent?

GEORGE: Yes—must have been. All of a sudden, one day, the light went on: 'The two have got to be developed together!'

STEVEN: Do you think that's because a lot of Laban's original work was with dancers?

GEORGE: Yeah, I think that would have influenced it. Jean Newlove was a dancer and a movement teacher and therefore, I guess you're right, the emphasis would have been on the physical. And when we got into making sounds, we did voice exercises with Joan—which were lots of fun, very different! But I realized I had to marry

2. Joan Littlewood (1914-2002) – British theatre director and actor, famous for developing (in collaboration with Ewan MacColl and others) the Theatre Workshop, "a British People's Theatre."[(2)]

3. Jean Newlove (b.1929) – Articulated Laban's theory and practice in *Laban for Actors and Dancers: Putting Laban's Movement Theory into Practice* and (with John Dalby) *Laban for All.* [(3)]

the two together. And that was very important, because then you broke down all this nasal work—especially for Canadians, who are *so nasal* anyway—and get a sense of sound coming from the 'Centre'—our famous words again—so that, while you can "thrust"[4] physically, you can also make *sound* that is physical. Very often the voice will tell you you're not "thrusting" because the voice will waver or collapse or go down at the end. And I will point out to the actor that he is not "thrusting" either with the body or the voice. If we want to refute something, then it's important to be able to say "No!" and *mean* it. If we say "no" (*weakly*), it softens up. If the script suggested, and the actor decided that was a *final* statement, and *not* to be contradicted, he must be able to do that; and by knowing the Efforts, both vocally and physically, it gives us the tool to do so.

STEVEN: When talking with students, for the first time, about the 'Centre', what do you say?

fear of revealing ourselves

GEORGE: I have them stand well, because so many of us *do* not stand *well*—that is, the bones are not supporting the body. We're sloping with one shoulder down—that used to be a favourite where we've got a spine that is not upright—and we do other things because we're in *fear* of revealing ourselves. We hide behind the body. So we fold our arms in front of our crotch, or we turn our knees in a certain way. I do it with the actors on their first meeting—and I do the physical, embarrassed things, because then they get a *laugh* at it and realize that *all things you do* with the body are telling something.

The point is: Do you want to tell the right things? Well, in a play you must. You must tell what it is the writer has in mind, or as the actor have in mind, in your interpretation of that character. You can't do that with a body that won't behave itself, and you can't cover it up with costumes and makeup etc. And at this point I usually tell them the story of my return from England after so many years working with theatre, pantomime, repertory, touring and finally with Littlewood. And I came home so looking forward to seeing what Canada had produced in the years I was gone.

the level of work in canada in 1957

STEVEN: You were in England for 15 years altogether?

GEORGE: No, nearly six years. But then I came home. I took a neighbour, an older gentleman, and him and I went to the Crest—I

4. "Thrust" – One of the eight Effort Actions described and named by Laban.(s.b.)

think it was *Othello*—a certainly heavily-costumed play.

STEVEN: This was the Crest Theatre on Mount Pleasant?

GEORGE: The Crest Theatre[5] on Mount Pleasant, yes. It was very respectable work, and they were trying, and all of a sudden I saw my friend—I won't say his name, but an old actor friend—come onto stage. He was covered in makeup; he was covered in costume; he was playing a character so unlike himself, and yet you could identify him in a moment if you knew him: He was just playing the usual nice guy he was. I'm not saying to hide these qualities, but he had no powers of *adaptation*. He had no skill to project the person of great strength that he was playing.

The level of work in Canada in 1957 was abominable, and the idea of training wasn't present. It is now, and there's some good work done now, I think. But in those days, all you had to do was read English! You didn't memorize anything, but just came on and read from the book.

STEVEN: There were no memorized auditions?

GEORGE: No, very few. Nobody had a party piece, right? Although they might have a party piece and that was even worse.

STEVEN: Why was it even worse?

GEORGE: Well, because they had learned this thing by rote and it had no humanity; it didn't reflect anything of the person's personality, or what they were giving to the character. And, of course, they'd always try and make you laugh, which was another unfortunate business. So, I'm saying my friend wasn't the only one at fault. They had not taken a baby step forward, nor did they see the need for it.

starting theatre centre, workshop productions and national theatre school

I suppose that was why it was such a breath of fresh air when myself and Tony Ferry[6] began our school—which was Tony's idea, Theatre Centre he called it—and we had a summer class. Then that fell apart, because of financial conditions, which is always the case in this country. Therefore, I took the actors, at their request, and created TWP[7], called "Workshop Productions" at the time.

5. The Crest Theatre - Founded in 1953 by Donald and Murray Davis, it signalled the beginning of commercial theatre indigenous to Toronto.(4)

6. Tony Ferry - Originally from England, intensely passionate about fostering Canadian theatre. The students of his Theatre Centre became Luscombe's first 'company' of actors (5)

7. TWP - Toronto Workshop Productions created theatre for nearly thirty years - from 1959 to 1988.(6)

No one knew what it meant: They thought we were builders of tables and chairs. And I chose the name "Workshop" because we were going to work at our art, at our creativity. I put the name "Productions" on it because I didn't like the philosophy of *schools only.* I said: *"Every school must have a theatre and every theatre should come out of a school."*

That's why, in fact, we didn't become the National Theatre School, because when the movers and shakers of what happens in this little town found out what we were doing, they told us we could have all the financial support that we wanted and go right ahead with our darling work—which was, I suppose, more because Powys Thomas[8] was a part of us and he was something of a name because he had infiltrated Stratford. *Our* names didn't mean a thing—that is, Tony and myself—and all this sounded very good, and I said: "What's the strings?" And Powys told me 'the strings': It was that there would be no theatre. What we would do is train actors.

In the meantime, Powys got the nod—which was fine for Powys—to begin the National Theatre School. So he went off to Montreal, where it had to take place, and we decided we would begin in any case. Tony then went broke and had to go back to the Star[9] and, because I was doing television shows on occasion, I had more time and was able to get the basement of 47 Fraser. I began teaching the six people who survived the summer class and they asked me to carry on with them and I said "Fine. We will, as long as you don't expect a production. We will produce if I think that our quality is good enough, but we're not going to put a play on each year, or every month, or what have you. That's not the point." I made that perfectly clear to them and they were ready and able and that was the beginning of what became TWP.

STEVEN: Why do you think the funders would object to the School being connected to a professional producing theatre?

GEORGE: They saw the need for training in this country; they were wise enough to see that. I assume that they thought it was a wonderful thing to have something like a RADA—that's the

8. Powys Thomas (1926-1977) – One of the founders of the National Theatre School. Also founded the Vancouver Playhouse Acting School with Christopher Newton.[(7)]

9. The Toronto Star newspaper. [(s.b.)]

Chicago '70 (1970). Yippies toss money on to the floor of the New York Stock Exchange. Actors (l-r): Mel Dixon, Diane Grant, Steven Bush, Ray Whelan, Calvin Butler, Rick McKenna, Peter Faulkner & Jim Bearden) / *photographer unknown*

Royal Academy of Dramatic Art in England. There were 'Method' schools in New York that didn't produce a play, but they trained actors and were well-known at that time. I suppose they had something in mind of a similar sort.

STEVEN: As opposed to the Moscow Art Theatre[10] or the Berliner Ensemble[11] model.

GEORGE: No, that was too far to look. They didn't know who Stanislavski[12] was in those days, let alone Laban, but my determination was not to create another institution that turned out hot dogs and wieners and I say you only get creativity through both the teaching part and taking that into the real world of the theatre. One pushes the other. That's why all you fellas spent so much time being *taught.*

STEVEN: Those were the best things about being in the company.

GEORGE: Yes. Yes, it glued us together. But I would have a company together the first year and all the plays we produced were, you know, terrible. And the second year was a little better. And the third year, I'd go in there and hand all you fellas the scripts and you'd hand me the scripts and the thing would bubble and it needed very

training glued us together

10. Moscow Art Theatre – Russian repertory company founded by Konstantin Stanislavski and Vladimir Nemirovich-Danchenko in 1897.(8)

11. Berliner Ensemble – State-supported theatre company in the former DDR (aka: "East Germany") founded and directed by Bertolt Brecht from 1949 until his death in 1956.(9)

12. Konstantin Stanislavski (1863 – 1938)– Seminal director and drama theorist whose "system" has influenced actors, directors, playwrights and teachers all over the world.(10)

little work from me but as a bloody policeman. Those were exciting times—when one didn't have to explain to the actor *how to create.*

Then of course, all the other theatres would grab you fellas and pay you more and take you away. But that's all right, because the new bunch would come and it would start over—and I didn't *mind* the starting over again. People thought I did, I suppose, but it infused different people and different ideas. Each company had certain needs and wants and those were reflected in the plays that we did. When you were there, we did *Mr Bones* and *Chicago '70* and a lot of work criticizing the American state-of-being in our politics, and that was because of your influence—you as Steven Bush, and other actors.

We had a number of you there—I won't say why you were there (*Laughter*)

STEVEN: It's OK.

GEORGE: I don't know anymore.... Well, you were draft dodgers, and we welcomed you, and took advantage of you and used your brains. And when we had got you to a state of being able to contribute—that's what it's all about, being able to contribute—which you have done magnificently for so long—

STEVEN: You can't do that until you know the vocabulary, and work with it.

GEORGE: That's a very good point. To learn that vocabulary takes time. Well, that's what you have schools for, but the schools that we have—I only know the big ones because they sent people to me and I had to refuse so many for so many years. They didn't pass the audition. Which is a terrible thing to say.

TWP auditions

Yes, our *auditions* were different too. I always felt that the potential of the actor was not used. That's why I kept working with auditions: To enlarge my demands upon the actor. I let them do what they had prepared, then gave them improvisation challenges. One of my favourite ones was coming into your own room and then you realize that the lamp isn't working and you've closed the door and the room is absolutely dark. Now, you get the light to work and then you're finished. That improvisation I adapted from a play called *Faces* to see how brilliant the actor was and how much he pretended to see and didn't see.

STEVEN: You would have everyone do that?

GEORGE: No, no—I'd change it around just for my own sake. I'd have somebody live in a cave for a moment and then come out into the very bright sunshine, or something different, to see if they could sense nature's work upon them without hamming it up—to not do too much, but enough to make me feel the cold and to make me feel the sun when the whole body opened up to its warmth.

In fact, I used these techniques on New York actors when I went down there to cast *Faces*. I went through hundreds of actors who couldn't cope. The producers were very clever there; they made sure the actors had a lot of experience. But they couldn't cope with these small imaginative problems and therefore I was *weeks* casting the show.

STEVEN: Do you have any insight as to why the actors in New York were weak in this area?

GEORGE: They were busy trying to get work; busy running around; busy trying to be an actor. They'd bring you presents, you know, silly little things, trying to impress the director and all that sort of business. So many people get into theatre without the fundamentals and come in the wrong way. Models are famous for this; if they're a pretty model, they think: 'Well, I'll go into the theatre in order to get into movies.'

I remember this young man wanting to join the company, and I put him through the auditions. There was plenty of time in those days to invent improvisations, to get a good knowledge of the actor. When we were finished with this particular chap, I said: "You should go into films. You're a very good-looking young man, but you shouldn't try to come into the theatre. That's not what you want." And we had a little discussion about that and it turned out I was right. About a year later, I was called for a job at the National Film Board and I was playing, of course, the 'character actor' and while we were on break waiting for the fellas to adjust the cameras, a voice yelled out to me "Hi, George!" And I said "Who's that?" And he said "Remember me? I'm the guy you told to go into movies!" He was the star of the piece and I was just the 'one day wonder' who came on to his series. So I congratulated him and we had a good laugh.

So, one person did what I suggested. Which is rare, isn't it? (*Laughing*) Oh dear...

George singing while walking with school chums, c.1945 /*photo courtesy of Karen Luscombe.*

Luscombe's school days: a very unique club of people

STEVEN: One question I've been thinking about, George, is the first moment when you knew that you wanted to make theatre. Was there a moment like that?

GEORGE: No. I knew I had a place somewhere in the arts when I was very young. All through school—which I disliked with a great passion because of the memory work—you're rewarded for being quick rather than correct and these things made me very nervous and I was a bad student.

STEVEN: In Toronto?

GEORGE: Yes. I'm in a very unique club of people who have failed first grade. I loved to be with the other kids I knew on the street who were now in school, but when I got to be, it was misery there. I couldn't play. I had to sit still, and that was terribly difficult for me, as you may know, and I didn't grasp the idea of learning. There was no point to it and I came at the bottom of the class and had to repeat Grade One—which was just as well, I suppose, because I was perhaps a little more mature.

Maturity means that you've learned the pattern, you've learned how to cope. And I sometimes have said, facetiously, I would in my old age sue the Board of Education for having taken away my imagination for eight years. And it took me a long time to get it back.

STEVEN: How did that happen?

GEORGE: I got into a freer school. I went to a matriculation school which wasn't free at all: They had the system of 'ratting' on people. They had students appointed to discipline the younger students—I hated that too—and that was East York Collegiate. It was a miserable, fascist school—I wouldn't have known the expression at the time, but that's what it was. I got into a free-thinking area at Danforth Technical School[13] which allowed you so much choice—all the machine shops, which scared me to death—but I was fortunate enough to find an art class and it seemed like something I could cope with.

From then on it was a pleasurable experience and I graduated very well in high school. But I was also doing half a dozen other things: I was in an amateur drama class; it was political, created by the CCF[14], and my friends were in it. I was in the school band and worked my way as drum sergeant, so I was leading that; and I was doing all kinds of things that were healthy. Because there was a war on, the faculty didn't give a damn about us and I remember our top student demanding that we drop mathematics—which we did—so I'm dumb as a doornail when it comes to mathematics now. But we just had our own way, which was very nice, and left us free to follow our own things in life, like growing our hair down to our shoulders.

---

13. Now known as Danforth Collegiate and Technical Institute.[(s.b.)] [(11)]

14. CCF - The Co-operative Commonwealth Federation, founded in July 1933, wanted to reform society through placing value on cooperation over capitalism. In 1961 the CCF joined with the Canadian Labour Congress to become the New Democratic Party. [(12)]

Physical Awareness and Adaptation

GEORGE: May the 14th. Census Day. And a great big fine if you don't go along.

STEVEN: Is that true?

GEORGE: Yes. $500 fine, I think. You can got to prison if you don't uhh…

STEVEN: Better get home and cooperate!

GEORGE: We have to behave ourselves. We have to be counted. (*Steven chuckles*)

I take the people who have just come in the room. And the first thing I'd want to do was to help them understand how badly they walk, and that they *think* they're walking all right because the bad habits have become ingrained.

It used to be schoolgirls carrying books in one arm, until they had one shoulder lower than the other. I would cure that simply by asking people to lift up their arms and make their elbows even with each other. Since they can't see both elbows at once, they *feel* them. Once they're even, they put their arms back down, and their shoulders are straight. Strange, isn't it? You have to think about the elbows, not the shoulders.

exercise: dollar bill

I've invented a little exercise, a simple one but with a little fun to it. I have all the actors stand at one end of the room and I'm at the other. Now, in the old days I would put down a dollar bill, but they don't have those anymore, and two-dollar bills are going out now too, and to put a five-dollar bill is ridiculous I think, so I'll put something like a Kleenex on the floor with everyone watching. Then I ask them to close their eyes one at a time and come and pick it up. Some will walk to the left; some will try and pick it up before they get there; some will walk right by it and try and pick it up long after. It all reveals something about their nature and their character. They realize themselves that their judgement is wanting. It's a good way of beginning life with a new group: It breaks the ice. When I used a dollar bill, I said they could keep it if they picked it up, but I knew really that we'd go through the whole class, and not one would bend down and pick it up *with confidence*. Which is important. To walk down, deliberately bend over and pick it up and hand it to me. And if you can do that *without* the bill in your hand, you've *really* succeeded, because you've convinced me you're right.

feeling the centre

Then we would talk about Leonardo da Vinci. The actors would stretch out their hands, at my request, and try to form the shape of Da Vinci's Vitruvian Man[1] in the centre of the circle. If you achieve that, you realize that by putting your hand down in the centre, you find *your* Centre. You don't need calipers or tape measures: You know where your Centre is because you *feel* it; you have a sense of where it is because you're in the centre of the circle.

the thrust

Now that we've got everybody standing fairly well, we can begin with Laban's theory of the eight Efforts. The first Effort was "Thrust"—which was direct, fast and heavy—and we would have the accompanying vocal work, so the two were done together.

STEVEN: You wouldn't do all the Efforts in one class.

GEORGE: It's been my experience that three Efforts are sufficient, and *contrasting* Efforts works well. So, first class we would probably tackle "Thrust," "Press," and "Float." "Float" is a nice alternative to the *direct* Efforts. Later, we would introduce three more until we had covered all eight.

STEVEN: And would you review frequently?

GEORGE: Oh, every morning we would do the Efforts. Half-an-hour to an hour a day. As we got better at them, I would take longer with them and eventually they would self-initiate the Efforts. We would tell stories in terms of the Efforts.

STEVEN: One thing you stressed was the importance of people learning about themselves, so that not everything is coming from the instructor. How do the students know when they're 'getting it' or when they're not?

---

1. Vitruvian Man - Da Vinci's famous drawing of a nude man with outstretched limbs, inside of a circle. It is currently housed at the Gallerie dell'Accademia in Venice. [(13)]

GEORGE: As we're working, I will focus on if they are standing well, and if the two sides of the body are even and doing the same thing. These niggling things I would keep up, with the criticism coming from me until it is *internalized* in the actor.

exercise: physical adaptation

We'd have one person in the centre of the circle and another person would be their partner. I would say: "Harry, lead the way, and Dorothy, make the physical adaptation to Harry." That means keeping a short arm's length from Harry. She would maintain that physical space—not following, but *maintaining equal space.* Should he stop and bend over, she doesn't have to bend over, as long as the physical relationship is maintained. We keep it fairly slow because, if they rush it, they'll only end up in trouble. So he goes wherever he likes, in and around the circle, and she has succeeded when she maintains this physical relationship.

It's simple but it's hard to do, strangely enough, in the beginning. You have to watch that they don't expand like an elastic, or bump into each other by anticipating each other's moves. *All energy and thought is going into maintaining this distance.* But one knows as an actor that you make all kinds of adaptations during a play—psychologically, intellectually, vocally and physically. This is only asking one thing: To be *physically* related to the other person.

relationship: to see each other in space

Other things become obvious as the lesson proceeds: The leading person dominates the other person making the adaptation. Then we change leaders, so that Dorothy becomes the leader and Harry makes the physical adaptation; you switch back and forth. I would work my way through the whole class in this way, pairing them off.

Finally, when you get through the entire group, you add a third person. Who does the third person relate to? And you add a fourth in, and a fifth, and they realize they're *making an adaptation through the group*, not just through the leader anymore... although the leader will still be pushing. And we change leaders as we're going, and that's fun too because no one knows who the hell anybody is. So they have to look around, use their wits very quickly to find out who "Marian" is: *She's* now leading the pack. And everyone begins to giggle, they get to see the fun of it; but still, they're *learning to think on their feet*, with things changing quickly, and the rhythm changes and the pace changes, until finally you take a rest.

STEVEN: You don't use the word 'follower.'

GEORGE: The exercise isn't to teach people to follow, there'd be no challenge to it. The problem is... *to see each other in space.* Therefore, we balance the stage by working in terms of space. You must understand not just your position but theirs as well.

Probably at this point I would introduce another little exercise that I called "Getting to Know You," after that famous song. I would put a chair on stage—the first piece of furniture that's arrived, you realize—a good sturdy chair, which is important because the actor needs full support from it. I'd ask an actor to sit in the seat—the *hot* seat—and I would pick three actors to circle the chair, and put their left hand on his left shoulder, and then continue walking as the next actor did the same. And each time they touched the actor, they would call out their name loud and clear. So the actor in the chair makes a link between the *touch* and the actor's *name.* And when all three have made contact, the actor in the chair closes his eyes, and then the three begin again—but mixed-up this time. And as each actor touches him, the actor in the chair calls out the name of the person he is being touched by.

exercise: getting to know you

There are things for the director to watch. When the actor gets tight, he's not relaxed anymore. And this is why a good chair is important: It has to play the part of his muscles, so that he only has to take in information. The more he tightens up, the more likely it is he'll get the name wrong. Then he'll probably miss two more people. It's all a question of *staying relaxed under pressure*—which we all know isn't easy. Once we've spent a little time on this, we move on until each has had a chance in the hot seat.

STEVEN: One of the biggest challenges I've found is to encourage relaxation without putting additional pressure about how badly they're relaxing—"I'm not getting relaxed so I'm making myself tense about not relaxing!" How do you get around that one?

GEORGE: It's full of contradictions, isn't it? You're asking all the time for people to keep relaxed and yet do the most terrifying things. Such simple exercises are very good, because you can say... "Wait, be relaxed." And they'll refer back to that exercise when the two seemingly contradictory demands were made upon them.

Imagine trying to handle *Hamlet*. Oh my God! The moment before you go out, if you envisage the entire play of *Hamlet*, you'd freeze! You must tackle it one step at a time and gradually get your confidence. We have to be able to handle the *simple* steps ... which are never really simple.

exercise: the electric shock

Another exercise: I'd have all the actors in a circle and spread their arms so that only the fingertips were touching, and I would join the circle as well, to lead. So, once we all closed our eyes, except myself, I would give a little tap to the neighbour on my left and he would have to send that tap to his neighbour as fast as possible. We called the exercise "The Electric Shock." So it would go right around the room and back to myself and I would send it on again. You always can find somebody asleep at the switch, and so we'd all open our eyes and talk about it, then try again to see if we could get the effect going right around *without a stop*. Once we'd succeeded with that fairly well, I would send the shock one way, then send another the other way, so usually some poor fellow was hit on both sides at once and then have to figure out, very quickly, how to pass it on. That's always fun and wakes everyone up.

child's play

STEVEN: So much of the work—both that I've participated in with you and also seen on stage—has a great sense of wonder in it, and circus, and clowning around in umm ... Yeah "child's play." You want to talk about that a bit?

GEORGE: It seems like that, Steven, because you're dealing with the very beginnings of everything. You're beginning to touch, to move, to walk. And the more fun you can have at it, the better of course—like "The Electric Shock"—giving them little labels so you'll remember them when you're tackling more difficult jobs.

So when we come to mime, we'd start out with *"The Glass Ball."*

exercise: the glass ball

We'd sit in a circle and talk about a glass ball they each have in front of them. We let them imagine their own ball. It has to be something that they can pick up, and handle, and look through. So they describe it—where they got it, where it came from—so that it becomes very real.

Then I would ask them to handle it—and I *wouldn't* say "Carefully!" ... because different people would handle it differently. Some would just pick it up and not care about it, which reflected how they thought about the ball. It would give the ball a certain

Summer '76 (1975)—Here Richard Payne is the monkey on Grant Roll's back. /*photographer unknown*

life, which they had to maintain: They couldn't all of a sudden get more interested in the ball than they were in the beginning. And they would ask themselves: 'Do I want to pass it to my neighbour? Is my neighbour knocking it about now? Is that causing me problems?' We would pass the balls around, so everyone had touched one that was not their own, and a lot of time is spent on this, so that the thing becomes important to them.

Eventually then, I'd ask them to put the ball behind their back and we would deal with *a basketball.* We'd stand up and throw it between us, and we'd watch to see who would then step on the ball behind them because they hadn't seen it well enough. And we would go on to different balls until we managed to envisage *one ball shared between the entire group—a big air balloon.* Everyone would put their hands on it so that now they're feeling a ball that belongs to others as well. And once everyone is feeling and seeing it, I would make the appropriate whistling sound, and the balloon would dissolve and they would all fall down on their faces *together.* You wouldn't have to tell anybody because they're so used to working together by this time…

STEVEN: In terms of classes, what would be an average time?

GEORGE: With a group of actors in a theatre, we'd break for lunch after three or four hours. In university, I found it was about the same.

Konstantin Stanislavski, 1918 /*photographer unknown*

“The Foundations of Creative Work”: Purpose and Given Circumstances

GEORGE: OK. Purpose. This is Stanislavski’s first step in the making of an actor. *Never be on stage without a purpose.* The Purpose must be related to the demands of the Given Circumstances, or the demands of the improvisation at the time.

What I usually do is ask people to come up and sit in a chair, and tell them nothing, and those excruciating moments in the chair allow them to educate themselves about the difficulty of being on stage without Purpose.

exercise: a play called *Waiting*

(*George reads from his written notes on “Purpose”*) “ ‘Come up and sit in this chair, we are going to perform a play called *Waiting*. You are the only character in this play. I will act as your stage manager. When I say “Curtain up,” the play has begun; when I give the word, the play has ended. We will begin. “Curtain up!”

“All is quiet. Steven has been on stage before, he is not a novice; and yet after a few moments of what seems to be a rather forced smile, the legs cross with a snap and hold the lower limbs in a self-made vice. The smile has weakened and has become confused, and before long the legs do another snap and reverse position. All of a sudden, both arms make it for the back of the chair. There is the smile again, only this time revealing more teeth. I relent. ‘Thank you, Steven, come down.’

“ ‘Maria, would you come and take part in our play, please?’ The moment Maria sat in the chair, the head went down, the hands came up to cover it and we all looked at the nape of her neck for the minute and a half. ‘Thank you, Maria.’

“‘Donald?’ Donald was confident: He had read the chapter on Purpose in *An Actor Prepares*. He was prepared to wait with a purpose. As he sat heavily into the chair, I said the magic phrase. Immediately his head spun left, and after a moment to the right, this time followed by his whole body. When the same time had elapsed, all of Donald swung front. A whole series of definite movements followed—up, down, across, then finally front again. We began to know when the next move would take place. Yes, we could guess when he was going to move again; the time between each move became fixed. 'Thank you, Donald.'

"So it continued the rest of the afternoon. I'd keep the play going for two, maybe three minutes, especially when I had doubts as to what's going inside them, or if they did seem to be succeeding and holding my interest and I became curious as to how long they could sustain my interest.

"When all had had an opportunity to perform the play, I then explained Stanislavski's great dictum: Never go onto the stage without a purpose. Not the general purpose of being in front of an audience, but *a strong*

that gives you the right to be there. Today, students—through the movies and television—have by the time they are five picked up a great deal of knowledge about play-acting. Indeed they are very perceptive about what the adult world expects of them and are able to deliver a whole range of stereotyped behaviour patterns. The uninitiated might mistake them for the real thing."

STEVEN: And here you're talking about 'acting in real life'?

GEORGE: Yes. I'm saying that their influences are so great now from TV and movies that they pick up behaviour patterns by watching... which they are not necessarily aware of. But to propose that as the truth is a real problem. Because indeed you've got a weak blueprint of an 'original' that was a blueprint itself—if you're talking about movies and television. So *where is truth*? This is why it's a difficult lesson; and it's difficult for the teacher to be responsive to things that are valuable but also to recognize clichés that don't belong there.

(Returns to reading) "On top of that, the actor/student is asked to perform in a play that is deceptively simple. In front of his peers, he is not about to fail and thereby make a fool of himself, if he can help it. So, they are going to do *something.* Now you and I must consider: Am I watching this actor because I *must*, or am I truly

caught up in what's going on in the progress of his thoughts?

"After a moment, I scan the class: Already one has his eyes closed, another is playing with his shoe and a third is watching me for my reaction. There is nothing as exciting in this world as one human being for another. When you place that being in the circumstances of a play on centre stage, then the power to hold our attention is enhanced, enhanced tenfold. Yet, after a minute the minds wander, seek interest in mundane things about us. If the actor on stage has not a firm hold—meaning a grip that cannot be loosened—then the audience too cannot hold. You may do all the analysis of the play and the character you like; you may spend a fortune on costumes and sets; you may stack opening night with your friends and relatives. If you do not have a strong Purpose on stage, the coughing, the shuffling will begin. *You will not hold our attention since you cannot hold your own.*" (*George concludes reading.*)

STEVEN: Why do you think it's so hard for a young actor to hold his own attention?

GEORGE: Well, I know that, before the heavy influence of television, this was still a difficult class to teach. You're the centre of concentration for an entire audience. When students are up there, if it's their peers who are watching, who wants to fail in front of their fellows?

STEVEN: In all the times you've done that "Waiting" exercise, have you found someone just able to ... be there without a lot of overworking?

GEORGE: Oh yes, yes. Some were very good; usually the actor who's spent some time and is enjoying the spotlight.

After we've done that to everybody, then we bring them back on stage and choose *a purpose related to an imagined set of circumstances*—maybe trying to cope with excruciating pain while waiting to see the dentist—and the stronger that purpose is held onto, the stronger the work becomes. And they stop noticing how their arms or legs are going, all the external things, because they are concentrating on the reason for being there.

The Given Circumstances. This is forgotten so often when actors are working after a few years: They work intuitively, they respond as they think they should. But, had they taken the *details* of

given circumstances

the Given Circumstances, it could have given them other roads to go. The Given Circumstances make them more aware. The Given Circumstances are, first of all, given to you by the writer: The place, the time, the epoch, the furniture. They are conditions given to an actor that he *must not ignore*. If he plays Given Circumstances that are not accepted by the other actor—Disaster afoot! He's in a different play! If one actor creates a wall, the other actor is obliged to accept that wall. If somebody can float in mid-air, then the other person accepts that. So, Given Circumstances are essential to an actor in developing a character.

STEVEN: If circumstances are *given*, how do they grow or develop?

GEORGE: They grow on the *basis* of what is given. Otherwise you have anarchy. When we move into improvised work, there are still Circumstances that we accept; any that are introduced must take into account those that already exist. The Purpose works *upon* those Given Circumstances; it can't change them.

"Purpose + Given Circumstances = Inner Stimulus": A nice little formula of Stanislavski's. And it's the inner stimulus we are trying to work towards, and work from.

STEVEN: Given Circumstances: What do you include?

GEORGE: Everything that you are given as an actor. That includes the stage; that includes whether we are inside or outside; that includes whether you're on the thrust stage or the proscenium arch—because your sense of space changes between those two.

All that you are given, including all the trap-doors and all the wheels and all the whistles and what-have-you on the stage ... which I tend to do without.

Except I would have loved to have had trap-doors at TWP. I'd have loved to have used another area of the imaginative world ... the underworld.

STEVEN: The underworld.

GEORGE: And as it was used in the medieval stage—the Devil's place to be. We *had* the upper areas. ...

Given Circumstances from the play's point-of-view: Everything that the author has given you. You contradict this at a great risk—especially those directors who love to update the classics and put them in another age ... perhaps out of boredom. What a shame to be bored with life and bored with the classics, so that you have to change the time and place. It *may* be useful, but I've seen it damage the play terribly. Guthrie[1] used it in *Hamlet* once; I saw it at that theatre in the States …

STEVEN: Minneapolis.

GEORGE: Yes, Minneapolis, and he had it in the Napoleonic Age, I think. He was using guns and every time they talked about their swords, it was a contradiction; it didn't live in the play; it was a bump so that it reminded you of what they had done… rather than integrate the change, easily.

I think Stratford's faced with that all the time, our own Stratford, because they repeat the plays so often that the next director says "Well, what can we do with this (*Steven laughs*) to make it different from the last fella who did it?" Right? (*George laughs.*) So those are really hardly the ideas that should move you to do the play.

STEVEN: Rather, why do we want to do this play and what is it saying?

GEORGE: Exactly, exactly.

The Given Circumstances are so often ignored when it comes to improvised work to find your way into the play. Which is what improvisation should be about. And *then,* sometimes it can be useful in rehearsal period, if you are *stuck* on a problem—I have done this many times… *Change the Given Circumstances but hold on to the same Objectives.* So you may be having difficulty with Richard III and you put him and Anne in a phone booth, but (*Steven laughs*) you *hold on* to the Objectives and it becomes a very different play. Now you don't have to keep that imagery when you come to rehearse—because, again, you'd be corrupting the play, I think—but you have made *discoveries* that have *enlivened* the text which has become boring to you and your own mouth.

But, again, to be able to *change* the Circumstances you have to *understand* the Given Circumstances. So often actors who know a little of Stanislavski will say 'Oh yes, I know my Objective in this Unit' and will be playing an Objective without consideration of the Circumstances that that Objective lives in. *It must live in the Circumstances of the play which are agreed upon by everyone.* So in Analysis, when we ask 'What are the Given Circumstances here?',

1. Sir Tyrone Guthrie (1900-1971) – An English stage director and producer influential to the 20th century revival of interest in classics. Guthrie was a co-founder of the Stratford Festival of Canada in 1953, where he reintroduced the Shakespeare "thrust" stage to modern theatre. Founded the Guthrie Theatre in Minneapolis in 1963, where George saw this production of *Hamlet.*[14]

the entire cast has their two cents' worth. And when we name the Units eventually, everybody agrees on the name of that Unit, and *your Objective comes from the name of the Unit.* Otherwise you are playing your own play. And you wonder why you see twelve different plays on the stage.

Even with actors who have been with me for three years, I've had to go back to the Given Circumstances to remind them ... because they have skillfully chosen something that seems right, but it's slightly out of step because it's not taking into consideration the Given Circumstances. (*George exhales*)

the playing of results

STEVEN: One of the toughest problems is to resist giving *result-oriented directions.* I think, primarily because of your influence, I will resist giving that kind of direction as long as I possibly can. But there's a lot of pressure from actors, particularly as opening night approaches, or if they feel like they're adrift.

GEORGE: Well, Steven, you're absolutely right. The playing of 'results': It's a dangerous thing and bloody awful to be falling into. It's cold and unresponsive; it doesn't even work with the other actors. In our 'Creative Work' we expect them to be alive *all* the time and responding to each actor. Results are safe. That's why you get young actors going for results, because they will be praised for it. And to ask them to throw that away is to ask them to go into a very dangerous area, where they depend upon the Given Circumstances, all the time, and on *their own responses* to those Circumstances. And to trust those responses are going to be correct. They may not always be flashy, may not get the laugh you want, but they will be honest, and a human response is what we're working for. Difficult to do.

a man is his circumstances.

STEVEN: Years ago, I was agonizing over some question of so-called "Characterization" and your response to me was ... "A man *is* his circumstances." This is something I frequently quote to students.

GEORGE: Especially for young people, they'll want to build character immediately and they'll tell you things about what they do and about their mother and grandmother—which is sometimes very useless and is overloading ... and especially at the beginning.

We know nothing about character in the beginning. We are naked in our approach to a work. That's how I would like to approach all plays.

And you go, layer by layer, *building* this character. And one very important layer is Given Circumstances: Is he in a war? In a hospital? What Time is he in? That is a *slow* process; that's *why* we have long rehearsals. Each time, you put on another bit of clothing; you don't get it all at once. I think that's our problem: We're *anxious* to get ahead, *anxious* to know them *without the building.* To find the Given Circumstances and to find Purpose will be the *beginning* of Character ... without us having looked from the outside in, but from the inside out.

The *Float*, the *Press* and Some Uses of the Efforts

In the garden. Birds chirping and other sounds of ordinary life on a quiet side-street of a noisy city on a bright warm day.

the float

GEORGE: We've previously talked about "Thrust" and it's time we introduced the next Effort, called "Float." And again, standing well, relaxed but good posture, we would remind people of moving from the Centre. "Begin to imagine 'Float'." … To *consciously* move the pelvis is quite all right and this will *affect* how the upper torso is moving—so the Effort is *indirect, light,* and *slow.* And then the arms will be inclined to move, out of necessity to balance the body. "Imagine floating in air, floating in water, and the entire body will begin to lift very lightly. *All* the body floats: the *nose* floats, the *ears* float, the *hair* floats, *everything* floats." That's how we go on, berating people—quietly—as we 'float' across the stage. It can have direction but its direction will be *indirect,* so "it may take *years* to get from point A to point B—although your Objective is to get *to* this point—because 'slow' is as slow as you can move without stopping. … The 'light'—we talked of music before—upward (*sings something sprightly and balletic*) Da da *da*—da da *da*—it's upward … to try to imagine what is 'light' as opposed to 'heavy' … (*humming Chopin's "Funeral March"*) hum ba pa bum … and therefore as *slow* as you can move … and 'indirect' means the *entire* body is indirect."

The "Float" is a nice Effort to put next to the "Thrust" … which is so strong, so heavy, so direct. And the "Float" has just the opposite effect. And there are people who are, believe it or not, natural-born "floaters" and others who find the "Thrust" is their way

The Mechanic (3rd production, 1965-1966)—Grappler (Edward Kelly) observes his daughter Lucinda (Yvonne Adalian) 'floating' on a chair / *Photographer unknown*

of extending themselves. People who are good boxers will love the "Thrust" whereas others who are more indirect, like myself—I know I was very excellent with the "Float." Littlewood pointed this out to me: I would 'wrestle' my way out of a problem, I'd never 'fight' my way out of it. Until I became aware that this was an easy Effort for me and then concentrated on the *work* that was needed on the *direct* Efforts.

STEVEN: So, in seeing something about the Effort that we move into easily, we're also seeing something about our own natures.

GEORGE: Absolutely, absolutely, goes back to that question of *walking*, doesn't it? Why some people walk in the sense that they were hiding something, or some people walk 'cause they're trying to knock down the door they're going through. It's fun to sit in a restaurant and watch people come in and analyze them quickly for their *dominant* Effort.

In the years I was with the Theatre Workshop company, every day there were a few hours on the Efforts—*even when* rehearsing a play. You mustn't get caught up in the fact that you've only got so much time to rehearse so you must *get at it!*

exercise: Littlewood coaching Luscombe using the Efforts

My own experience in using the Efforts in a rehearsal situation was in *Richard II* with Littlewood's company and I was having difficulty with the character of Mowbray—not just remembering lines because I was scared as hell of Shakespeare—but capturing the *nature* of the man. Joan had me on my own this one day and asked me to analyze the entire speech using the Efforts, which I found easy to do, and I found great relief in doing so. It made a lot of sense to the speech.

STEVEN: In the Mowbray speech, how many Efforts might you employ?

GEORGE: I think about four to six. I would take the first three or four lines and bracket it if I thought that was a "Press," and then bracket the next if I thought it was a "Float." It gave great contrast in the speech, and you would choose the Effort that gave the greatest contrast and also supported the intellectual idea. Of course within the Given Circumstances, you could choose Efforts on one, two, three *words* and make your point. It would in fact enhance the *emotional* content of the work. It did succeed with me, that little exercise.

STEVEN: It sounds like a way to keep a speech from falling into 'mood-playing,' or flattening out.

GEORGE: Yes, indeed, that analysis doesn't leave you the next day: You keep it in the script. And while you check on it, you can *change* it. And you will do it instinctively 'on the night' if you all of a sudden feel that it's a "Slash" instead of a "Press." And it's exciting.

STEVEN: The names for the Efforts are all good Action words.

GEORGE: Yes, I suppose… Yes they are.

the press

The next one we call "Press." I sometimes don't tell the name of the Effort to the actors when we first introduce them. I have fun telling them the *qualities* of the Efforts, and they attempt to carry them out, and I ask them how they felt, what they thought it should be called. Which is a good game to play and keeps everybody on their toes.

Each Effort has three qualities, and these qualities are changed around until you have every movement the human body can make in a pure way. There's "Thrust," "Float," "Press," "Flick," "Dab," "Glide" umm… The last one is "Slash" but I think I've left one out…?

STEVEN: "Wring."
GEORGE: Wring... Wring!... Wring!!
STEVEN: One of my favourites.
GEORGE: Yes, it is a favourite, "Wring"... and then "Slash."

We'll tackle "Press" at the moment, because it's a variation on "Thrust" in that it's direct and heavy, but *slow.* I suppose it's like pressing a wall. When you work on this with actors you find them shaking, or wavering. All this has to be corrected by the instructor until you are able to move in a *direct* manner from one place to another.

STEVEN: It was a hard one for me; I always tended to wobble.

François-Regis Klanfer (above) appears to be "pressing" Len Doncheff (below) in this moment from *The Captain of Köpenick* (1975). / *photographer unknown*

GEORGE: Yes it's an interesting Effort, I think, because it is so often required in our speech—the control needed—I know the "Press" is great fun vocally. We work the voice along with the body so when we're "floating," the voice is going up and down the scale very lightly, it has freedom to move all around. When we "press," it's one direct sound moving forward. It doesn't matter what scale, and it can change, as long as that change is *direct.* It can't be like a slide trombone, as we're so often guilty of in everyday speech: We drop off at the end. A lot of new actors will do that. It's like in "Over the Rainbow"[1]: It's so exciting when you go from (*George*

1. Judy Garland famously sings "Over the Rainbow" in the movie *The Wizard of Oz.* (a.m/s.b.)

sings two notes) “bong, bong”—you jump a whole octave. Judy Garland was marvellous at it.

STEVEN: Yes. It’s startling though.

GEORGE: But she goes up a complete octave and there’s no in-between; it would destroy the effect. This is why “Press” is important to learn, so we can control that and move into another register. You fellas would be trained for six to eight weeks, eight hours a day. It was so important to get to the point where the Efforts were second nature.

STEVEN: It’s a technique that needs time to be absorbed into the actor’s system.

GEORGE: Absolutely. It pays off for the actor, and for the audience, but ‘Show Business’ can’t wait that long for an effect. A lot of people have never experienced the excitement of *developing the body* as a theatre worker. Good God! Who wants to mail order for a couple of lessons on how to act! (*Steven laughs*) Or it’s like those ads on the back of matchboxes: “Send this in and you’ll be playing Chopin in a day!” Well, nobody plays Chopin in a day; nobody acts Lear in a moment. You spend years developing this work. You don’t have to tell dancers this: Dancers work very hard and they couldn’t go out on stage at all if they didn’t keep their bodies in shape. That’s why we work on the Efforts; we work as hard as any dancer. The body can’t do what we want it to, or what the playwright wants it to, unless we have control over our faci … facil … faci … facilities (*Both Steven and George laugh*) … our body—unless we have full control over all aspects of it. That’s why the Efforts are so important.

we work as hard as any dancer.

STEVEN: It’s thrilling to see people who have worked with the Efforts for some time: I think of Ray Whelan[2] or Peter Faulkner, the facility they had—

GEORGE: Remember Ray Whelan in *Arturo Ui*[3]? He began life in the gutter—literally our gutter around the edge of the stage—and I didn’t let him out of the gutter ’cause he was playing the part of Hitler. He had to move like a rat and he analyzed a rat movement with the Efforts.

2. Ray Whelan (b. 1941) – TWP member in 1960s and 70’s. Played title roles in *The Captain of Köpenick*, *The Good Soldier Schweik* and *Arturo Ui*. Co-founded Toronto’s Open Circle Theatre (1973–1982) with Sylvia Tucker, another TWP alum. Directed *“I” The Impeachment Trial of George W. Bush and Richard B. Cheney* in California in 2008[s.b.] [15]

3. Brecht’s *The Resistible Rise of Arturo Ui*. Presented as *Arturo Ui* by TWP in 1971[16]

Arturo Ui (1971)—Ray Whelan as Ui, with Barry Wasman (l) and Donald Meyers (r) in background. / *photographer unknown*

That's another thing we should talk about: Taking birds and animals, analyzing their dominant Effort. They're not trying to mimic—which is different entirely, mimicking the animal—they're trying to find the *essence* of his movement. We shall come to that eventually; I think we will. (*George laughs*)

STEVEN: Hearing you talk of the Efforts reminds me why theatre from Quebec in the last ten or fifteen years has impressed audiences a lot more than English Canadian theatre. And it has to do with longer rehearsal times—because of their contractual arrangements—and also uh... the way that many of the groups embrace physicality.

physical theatre in Quebec

GEORGE: I've not seen very much at all of the Quebec groups, but I would agree with you.

STEVEN: I would think that if you'd seen Lepage[4] or Carbone 14[5] or... ahh Édouard Lock[6], that you'd see an affinity with the work you were doing at TWP.

GEORGE: English Canadian theatre has been so dominated by Shaw

4. Robert Lepage (b. 1957) –Theatre & film director, dramatist, actor. Still based in Quebec City with his company Ex Machina, Lepage has directed theatre all over the world and is hailed for his innovative visual/intermedial approach.[(17)]

5. Carbone 14, based in Montréal until its dissolution in 2005, produced a style of physical theatre that was formalistic, imagistic and avant-garde. *Le Dortoir*, its most popular show, toured the world for 4 years between 1989 and 1991.[(18)]

6. Édouard Lock (b. 1954) – Director and choreographer based in Montreal noted for a harsh, high-energy style of dance with a heavy emphasis on gestural detail. His company is called LaLaLa Human Steps.[(19)]

and Coward. At one time all an actor needed to know was how to hold a cigarette and a wine glass to get a job in Noel Coward, and the body meant nothing. In those days they discounted anyone who was moving with great energy on the stage. They thought it amusing, but entirely out of place.

STEVEN: It was a class position.

GEORGE: Eh?

STEVEN: A British class position.

GEORGE: Yes it is.... Which is interesting because Littlewood took years to break that down. *Didn't* break it down until after *Oh What a Lovely War!* and *The Quare Fellow*, such works as that....

STEVEN: Hmmn.

GEORGE: As you know, I believe that rehearsal is a discovery period, not a time for playing the show. It's a time for searching, to come out with the honesty on the stage. What is honesty on the stage? It's a thing you sense, and the audience knows it: They believe you or they don't believe you. For a while they can be hoodwinked with clever tricks, with obvious pratfalls or what have you—I shouldn't say that 'cause I like pratfalls!—but the obvious behaviour pattern becomes boring. *The actor who works honestly is never quite sure what the next moment brings.* He's in control of it because he's in control of his technique and his analysis of the play. All this prepares him for the moment of inspiration, and we're damn lucky if that comes in for a moment or two any night.... But you have to be prepared for it when it comes.

honesty on the stage

Relaxation and Voice

(Still in the garden, with birds. A crow makes a statement from time to time)

GEORGE: One of the preparations is relaxation *before* the show. How do you do that? In this world of ours ... which is helter-skelter, going from one thing to the other, everything is nerve-wracking ... the actor has got to find time, and certainly before a show, to completely relax *the body first*. The mind itself will follow the body, if you give the body a chance to settle down.

exercise: relaxation

And our exercise for that is to lay flat on your back on the stage. And then try and convince them that they don't have to worry about the telephone: "If it rings no one's going to answer it. No one's going to interfere with us for the next few minutes. And no matter what you have to do later in the day, it cannot be done now, so *give it up*! So give yourself an opportunity to relax *completely* for this few moments that we're here together."

And I will continue to talk this way as we begin, to relax from the bottom of the feet to the top of the head. "Think of your *feet*, think of the *arch* of your feet, let it go." And it's all you need to say. "You may not know it, but you've been straining in the feet.... The *ankles*, picture the ankles, let them go." And you continue this right up the body: The large muscle of the *leg*; the *knee cap*—which is always jumping about. "And now let it go and try to sink into the floor. Let the body *sink*, don't force it down. All those muscles that you need to walk upright—that's why we're lying down at the moment—are free: You don't need them." We'll get ourselves up to the *hips*, up to the small of the *back*: "And try to imagine it touching the floor. It won't but *imagine* it does." And up the back, where the big muscles are, then the *shoulders*: "Allow them to sink, if they will, *down*. And back to the *head*." ... And when we had short haircuts, all the men used to usually hang to one side; but when you've got long hair, sometimes the hair will support your head in an upright position. "Let it go.... What you're letting go is the *neck*, of course, and the head can be where it's most comfortable. And work yourself down the *arms*, and to the *biceps*, down to the *elbows* and down to the *fingers*. And you find the thumb already *stiff* and think of the *thumb*, so it relaxes."

And you have to *think* of each area of the body until, perhaps, you are in preparation for sleep—"But don't sleep! So that you're still aware you're doing all this." They can still hear the instructor, walking about, seeing if everybody's right... picking a leg up once in a while and letting it drop on its own... picking a hand up and letting it drop on its own. If it will. And you often find that it's still tense and is holding up in the air.

We used to do this exercise with Carlo Mazzone[1], the Italian mime and actor. We did it outside in the field, and I saw him walk over the bodies of the people with great long chunks of stone. If they got excited that they were going to be crushed to death, he would blame them for having taken notice of him with a great boulder in his hands.

working on the voice

I don't play such tricks. It's enough to keep talking, and checking on the bodies... and the eyelids, you know, which sometimes remain staring open... until they realize that there's an eyelid there that can be relaxed. The jaw will slightly fall open...

"Now is a good time to do your breathing exercises and to allow your voice to come from the Centre of the body."

If you do a lot of shouting—which we would never allow in our theatre, if you remember—you'll wish you could replace the voice-box. Shouting and screaming are not natural things to do with the body. To catch the *essence* of a scream takes a lot of discipline... for which we use all the tools that we're going through now.

1. Carlo Mazzone-Clementi (1920-2000) – Student of Etienne Decroux, performed with Marcel Marceau.[(20)] According to Luscombe, the Stratford Festival hired him "and then didn't put him to work. He taught us this exercise about the Life Cycle. He also had expertise at the 'mime walk' and I had my actors learn that."[(21)]

Having got to the point where we are relaxed, it's fun then to work on the voice, because you're breathing like a baby, as you should.

I find, especially with college students, that their voices are trapped way up in their face. They've made vocal adaptation to psychological problems, making it very ugly indeed—ugly because it contradicts the nature of the body and *it's not their voice.*

So you go back to the Centre of the body, and breathing with the diaphragm properly as a baby does. The diaphragm muscles are like your arms pushing a bellows; the bellows is the lungs pushing out the air; and the spout is the mouth. You don't do anything with the spout at all, you just use the bellows; so your diaphragm muscles do the work, pushing the air up through the voice-box and out the mouth. Once they find it, they can whisper and be heard; they can speak without getting tired; they are no longer ranting and raving for effect; they are pumping air through with the diaphragm, and using that for effect.

STEVEN: A criticism we often got in the time that I worked with you was that our vocal work wasn't at the level of our physical work. Often.

criticism of voice at TWP

GEORGE: Yeah and I think that that was bad judgement by the critics.

STEVEN: Yeah?

GEORGE: They were so enamoured by the physical work, so knocked out by it, that there had to be something else that wasn't satisfactory. I certainly can't remember not understanding.

STEVEN: In the training, the Laban Efforts was ongoing—either your senior actor or you would always conduct those sessions—but vocally, there didn't seem to be anyone to continue that practice with the company.

GEORGE: No, because there weren't that many Charles Jordans[2] around. He had purposely re-taught himself to speak, and to sing, because he felt that what he was doing was artificial; and I had Charles working with me in the early days because I thought he was talking a great deal of sense. Because I didn't believe in 'placing' the voice, that 'elocution' stuff that people were so fond of. 'The less thought-out the better!' I thought. To free the voice and

2. Charles Jordan (1915-1986) – Singer and voice teacher. Performed in numerous CBC radio broadcasts of operas. Began teaching voice in 1947 and continued for more than thirty years.[(22)]

to let the voice be a part of the size of the person seemed to me much more important than saying 'Put the sound up here and over there.' And also, in so many opera singers, they seem to be very dis-associated with the body. And that was just the opposite of what I was trying to do. So I, as a result, probably left it to the actor, once we had freed the voice.

I can also remember them saying at one point: "Oh, Luscombe has finally got everybody speaking well." I think it was *Shelley*[3] or something and they "understood everything!" I always felt they *should* have, if they were listening.

STEVEN: It may have just been because of the writing. I mean, she wrote under the influence of Mary Shelley so, as I remember, the script has that quality.

GEORGE: Yes, well you'd think that would be a script that they would criticize us on, but on that occasion they didn't. I don't say that we were the paragons of virtue, but I think sometimes they were so unused to seeing people move, that's all they could see. They stopped listening and then they said: "Oh, what great movers you are!" Well yes we were, but we thought *everybody* should be. (*Steven laughs*) We thought that was what theatre was about.

STEVEN: Actors move.

disassociated acting in Canada in the 50s & 60s

GEORGE: There was a great tendency, especially when I was just beginning, for all the rest of the theatres to be concentrating on the lines. That was why I had such trouble with writers. A friend who was a writer and actor at the CBC informed me that, when he went to the theatre, he closed his eyes, sat in the back, and listened to the words. That way he could understand the play and he wasn't bothered by the physical, whatever was taking place on the stage. Well, there was very little, in those days, taking place on the stage.

STEVEN: Not much to watch.

GEORGE: No. You just listened. And this was the kind of thing that was going on in the theatre when we started in the 60's.

STEVEN: At that time I think there was a stronger tradition in radio drama than there was on the stage.

GEORGE: Yes there was, just because in this country there was *so* little stage. And any of the actors were radio actors.

STEVEN: That's actually one area where we have made some progress.

3. *Shelley; or, The Idealist* by Ann Jellicoe, produced at TWP in 1971.[(23)]

I think of the work that Kristin Linklater's[4] done. David Smukler[5], Michael Connolly[6]—some of the people I've worked with—emphasized a lot of the same points that you're talking about.

GEORGE: Glad to hear it, because when I started, Charles Jordan was the only person I'd met who had re-thought his training, and he threw it all out the window and began again with the kind of voice exercises we're talking about.

changes in voice training since

STEVEN: Was there any reason you didn't continue your collaboration with him?

GEORGE: No, no, we always kept in touch. You want your teachers in the atmosphere of the theatre and uhh…I suppose it was because it was *separate*, Steven, and all things in the theatre are best kept under one roof.

STEVEN: And unfortunately it almost never happens.

GEORGE: Never, except when you'd create it yourself, as we did. And you have to have a roof to begin with.

4. Kristin Linklater – Creator of the internationally influential actor-training practice 'Linklater Voice,' based upon the essential connection of language with breath and voice. Author of *Freeing the Natural Voice* and founder of the Linklater Center for Voice and Language.[(24)]

5. David Smukler – Director of the National Voice Intensive, held annually at the University of British Columbia; co-founder of the Graduate Theatre Program at York University. Smukler was part of the first group trained by Kristin Linklater.[(25)]

6. Michael Connolly – Student of David Smukler and a voice teacher in his own right at University College Drama Program, at other schools and in workshops for professionals.[(26)]

Working with Space

GEORGE: It's one o'clock now.
STEVEN: We can go for another ten minutes if you feel up for it…
GEORGE: OK.
STEVEN: Or… *(Noting paper that George is holding)* Well, this looks like part of your lesson plan.

exercise: space

GEORGE: It is "Space," yes.

We'll take two people in the centre of the stage. As the instructor, I usually do this myself with one actor, but I'm not sure it's a good idea: It's kind of like showing what's expected.

So… take two students into the middle of the stage, standing facing each other, arm's length apart, and just sit there quietly watching until one feels the need to fill the space left by the other. Now they might stand there for a long time. But one person moves, even so slightly—a movement of the head, or a slight shift of the body—and as soon as that happens the other person moves into the space allowed them by the first person's movement. So, very often it starts with a head movement, slightly to one side; and the other person moves in with an arm into that space that's become available. So *they're looking at the space, not the actor.* And as *that* actor moves, he himself—or she—has created another space for the *first* actor to move into.

So you get these two actors moving as if they were mercury in a thermometer, or it's… like oil and water perhaps. Two things in water that keep finding each other and keep finding the space available to them. They must try and *maintain the rate of speed* at which they began, which is very slow, because it helps them see if they're *with* each other. So they're moving *to* each other but they're working in space... Nice contradiction.

STEVEN: Do they make eye contact?

GEORGE: None, except in the very beginning. It's very difficult to stand in front of somebody and not look at them—which I think would be a mistake, too artificial—but in that movement, even as you're now nodding your head, you give me space *behind* your head. If we were then working slowly, we would lose eye contact and the *space* is what I'm looking at then; and I continue to *look at space, not at the body.*

STEVEN: So one of the purposes here is developing that sensitivity to the space between you—

GEORGE: Without that old thing of "look at your actor," we all know about that, but the—

STEVEN: We can easily get locked into that—

GEORGE: Sure. But there is another dimension: *The space the actor takes up.* That space is part of the stage.

exercise: filling the space

And it's important that these people remain moving *slowly*; otherwise, they become like a whirling dervish and lose control of the exercise. If it moves slowly, you can *enjoy the fun of seeing space that is created by the other actor* moving in order to fill your space—adjusting with the legs sometimes, moving down and up, stepping quietly in order to use their torso to fill a space they see available.

Of course, we then do our old thing of adding a third. The third person stands back just for a moment, and he adapts to the rhythm of the other two, so as to not speed it up or slow it down. So now you've got three people, not touching physically, and sharing the same space as the two were. That's important: *You do not expand the space;* you try to share the only space that's available. When you get a third person in, there's always a chance to move in between someone's legs, and then come up the back. I remember one of our actors used to love doing that.

Soon we'll add a fourth, and another, and another, until all the class are sharing the same space. It's something to see, because it's a group of new people who don't know each other, and they're creating a mass without bumping into each other. *It creates a sense of everybody in control on the stage at once...*

Then, I would suggest that they've got a foot and a half more space than they've had and they must *fill* it.

STEVEN: It's been quite cozy up till now.

GEORGE: Very, very close. Now they've got an extra foot and a half, and they move out slowly... but still keeping this relationship with each other and using up all the space that exists now. And it's *their* judgement, what a foot and a half is.

exercise: balancing the stage

Then I'll move to the entire stage: "But keep up this relationship. You must fill the area that you have taken." The movement often becomes quieter with more space to work in. There's no threat of bumping into each other now, so they can enjoy the space with greater ease. Yet, *they still must identify the space that they're in*... now with the entire body. So that means *moving from the Centre*.... We'll go to the largest area and still retain this contact—which is not physical but *an understanding of the space they have to share.* In that moment, I settle everybody down and point to them, where they are: They have *balanced the stage.*

If one actor stepped out and moved to one side, without anyone else moving, they'd upset the balance of the stage. I often use the picture of a... plate supported by one point in the centre: If you step off the edge of the plate, you will tip it and then everybody will fall. So, you must take into consideration other people so that everybody has the same amount of space. When someone makes an adjustment, everybody at that moment will be forced to adjust to *them* because they've changed the balance of the stage.

A nice exercise. And I have never succeeded to my satisfaction with people *moving very quickly* in this, because they lose their sensitivity. It's always better to do this slowly.

STEVEN: But, eventually, you want to be able to move in different tempos.

GEORGE: Oh yes. But the next step is to say, in the next class: "Come on stage, please. Balance the stage." Just this one phrase alone will let them choose wherever they want to be in relationship to the other actor without my saying "You stand here, you move over there"—which I never do, you know, and would discourage any such foolishness. Say: "Balance the stage!" and the actors will create that setting for you.

STEVEN: If they've done Lesson One with you.

Hey, Rube! (1972-73)—Actors—facing the camera (l-r): Peter Millard, Jeff Braunstein, Ken McEvoy & Candace O'Connor, Geoffrey Saville-Read (above); partly hidden: Durango Coy; backs to camera (l-r): Terry Schonblum, Barry Wasman, Grant Roll & Krysia Jarmicka-Read / *photographer: Robert van der Hilst*

GEORGE: If they've done this lesson, they will know immediately. "Balance the stage and begin work!" As quickly as that.

And I'm introducing the Given Circumstances of, say, the existence of a boat on stage; and they're smart enough to build their own boat, as long as they know *who's* in the boat. They will make the decision for themselves.

STEVEN: Working together.

GEORGE: Yeah.

STEVEN: You talked about encouraging the actors to relate to the space rather than to another body. Can you say a bit more about why?

GEORGE: It's because we ignore space so often. We see the other actor and we start acting with them, but I say the other actor is *taking up space* and he's *creating other spaces* by his presence.

intuition… and things you didn't expect

There's a lot of things happening in this exercise: There's intuition, there's a feeling for each other, there are relationships that are best not talked about… in the sense that you talk about something and it disappears. (*Steven grunts approvingly*)

Go back to the first lesson in Space … one actor making an adaptation to another as they travel across the stage. You're sitting—I've seen this a dozen times—looking at them and you'll say "Ahh there's the boss, and there's his helper moving around trying to take instructions." Just from the way their bodies look.

STEVEN: Without consciously building the scenario.

GEORGE: With no words, and the two actors weren't even thinking of that. That's the other fun. They've created something physically and so, like a good piece of poetry, it can be read and mean anything … even the opposite of its intentions, on occasion.

STEVEN: When the actors are at all attuned with this kind of work, it's beautiful to watch.

GEORGE: Yes, indeed, it's a great joy, isn't it? It's a shame that I see people ignoring these basic exercises.

STEVEN: So many student actors, people 18 to 25—almost all their reference points are the 'talking head' acting they see on television, which is a completely false picture of what the actor's work *on stage* is.

GEORGE: Yes, yes, and also it's so incredibly limiting. You have a situation where you must handle human emotions and thoughts and you leave it all to a few words coming from the head. Our bodies are *always* responding, good or bad; these exercises make sure that the body responds as the actor wishes it, not by accident, and not deterred by the physical handicaps that we all start out with.

why no physical contact?

STEVEN: With this exercise, why no physical contact?

GEORGE: Because the minute you put your hand on the other person, you're no longer seeing *space* and uhhh … (*George laughs*)

I went through a stage in TV where it seemed to be the thing to do for any actor who was working with you to grab hold of you—usually around the shoulders—and that was making contact, or so they thought. But of course it was the farthest thing from contact.

STEVEN: So much of the energy between the actors, the bodies in space, is lost by too much contact.

GEORGE: Of course, yes, yes it is.

STEVEN: Will you intervene if you feel they're taking up too much space too quickly?

GEORGE: Oh yes! They *usually* start speeding up, especially when a third person comes in, and it's my job to keep them at the same speed and give them good reason for that. If they are missing the possible advantages of space, I will say: "Oh, look at this space here, it's open. Look there." And some will feel like they must remain somehow upright all their lives and so I encourage them to use all of space—up, down, around.

Early on, I will encourage them to use *the 'table plane'* of space—about the level of a table. So they place their torso at the level of a table. Then I'll encourage them to go into *'Hell'* down below, and make friends with the stage, with the wooden planks under you, so that means using it and using it with all of your body. Then finally using *the 'air'*—the sky, the largest area—so they're aware of the *dimensions in space*: the great outdoors, the middle plane, and under the world.

exercise: Dimensions in space

STEVEN: How did your work change when you worked outside?

GEORGE: It just opened up. You had such ... more room, and you saw the actors more relaxed as they worked in the open air and reach for the sky—the sky was up there! *(Steven chortles)* And the earth had a smell to it.

I remember performing outdoors once, with *Before Compiègne*, which was the story of Joan of Arc. And we were up at Stratford, in the park, and it was a tryout to see how we did, and if anybody would turn up, 'cause we had no publicity at that time. (People *didn't* come, by the way, when they saw us in the park!) God was our lighting man and when Joan was cursing God, or speaking to It, the sun would come in and out, and it usually worked *right*, and it was really exciting!

experts at handling space

And I could imagine why there was such favour in Greece playing outdoors, where you didn't turn the bloody lights out and have a blackout because you wanted to change scenery. You know that I never use blackouts, just because I despise the technique; it's so off-putting. And what's wrong with seeing actors change into their next character, or whatever they're doing? I think the stage can survive without the running on and off with heavy equipment.

It's how you handle space. This *is* what we work with. We should be *experts at handling space*, but too often we're not.

imaginary fires

It's very like one director who, when we rented the theatre, asked: "Was it OK if they had a bonfire on stage?" I said: "My god, no!" I said: "Read chapter something or other of Stanislavski: 'It's your *imagination* should burn, not the fireplace!' You'll burn the theatre down, and we won't have a theatre!" Nevertheless, he managed to slip in a little flame, much to my annoyance, but he couldn't fathom doing it without. This is a shame; this is the lack of imagination.

STEVEN: I can't remember how Stanislavski achieved those uhh fire cues. There must be fireplaces in those Chekhov plays, with those naturalist/realist sets, which in the photographs look terrifically—

GEORGE: Yes, but they are papier maché sets. If you try building a fire in it, you'll soon have problems. They should have been *imaginary* fires... if Stanislavski followed his own teaching. Which sometimes teachers don't. (*George and Steven laugh*)

STEVEN: The initial exercise you described: Would you say that's your invention? Or did you draw that from Laban?

GEORGE: Oh, my own work. I've been doing it a long time. I even did it out in the Haliburton area where we held summer camp. I guess it took me a while to relate that work to balancing the stage. When I expanded the space, I realized 'Ahh we balanced the stage: They're all where they should be.' I've used it as such ever since. So a lot of these things you find out as you do the exercises.

The *Dab*, the *Flick* and the *Ninth Effort*

GEORGE: So we're going to talk about what I like to call cousins … "Dab" and "Flick." "Dab" is *direct, light*, and *fast*; and while practicing this, I'm always reminded of a chicken, or some other animal that moves quickly and pokes its way through. So we have a lot of fun with that. When everybody is trying to "dab," I try to get them to talk to each other with sounds, just sounds, that are direct, light, fast. the *dab*

Then we go to "Flick" and the only difference here is it's indirect; it's *indirect, light*—and *fast*! We can be very close together and "flick" without banging into each other. We're *in control* of the body parts, but we're *not directing* it. We're not saying: "Move your arm out here; move your hand out there." We're saying: "Move from the Centre!" And if you "flick" the Centre, the arms and the head will follow, and become—"flick!"—become light. It's an extraordinary movement when done by twelve people on the stage. the *flick*

STEVEN: I was amused many times watching Ray Whelan, who was a master of the "Dab" and the "Flick," I thought.

GEORGE: Oh yes, yes, he was incredibly good. I would cast him for his light Efforts … the light Efforts of a rat "flicking" through the stage.

STEVEN: How much did your work with the Efforts change as you worked with your own company in Canada?

GEORGE: Well, I got to know them better and use them better as a director. They can be used as long as their application is *no longer an exercise* but indeed used directly in the work—and subtly enough that the audience isn't aware of the source. They only see a person move well, and are surprised at that. In Canada, at least.

STEVEN: I never heard you really say what the "*Ninth* Effort" was.
GEORGE: Ah. . . .
STEVEN: Could you define that mysterious "Ninth Effort"?
GEORGE: Yes, I could. It's simple.
STEVEN: Is that against your belief?

the ninth effort

GEORGE: No, no, I was happy to find it. All it is . . . is that *outwardly* you seem to be still, but the Effort is *inside*. One must never be truly immobile on the stage. Say, oh, you're a statue: "No no, statues are without thought, without movement!" Everything moves and changes—I'm a Marxist on this point—everything changes in the world, no matter how slowly. Even rocks change and eventually become sand. Even if you can't see it, everything in life is changing. So, the "Ninth Effort" is immobility like the hand of a clock: It's moving, but you can't see it. You must be moving inside.

And that's a little illegitimate, you see: I never learned the "Ninth Effort" in Littlewood's company; this was our own invention.
STEVEN: So Laban wouldn't claim the "Ninth Effort"?
GEORGE: I don't think so. *(Both laugh)* I don't think so.

Part of the auditorium and stage at TWP, 12 Alexander Street. / *photographer unknown.*

Community, Ensemble, Live Theatre and Technology

STEVEN: OK. And we're talking on Tuesday June 11th 1996.

GEORGE: On occasion at TWP, in desperate need of money, I used to bring in the political movers and shakers of Toronto, and hope they were going to say something nice about what they had seen. And these were politicians who were used to being in front of everybody. But you recall our stage was so set up it had the audience on three sides, so what happened on one side affected the people on the other side. So you had to control the whole house, and how do you do that? And these politicians surprised me sometimes: They were nervous about being in front of people—when you'd think really they were the most assured—and it was fun to see them shiver and shake.

thrust stage vs. proscenium stage

STEVEN: Maybe afraid of the questions the audience might ask.

GEORGE: Perhaps. Yes. But *they felt in touch*, you see. That's the great thing about the Greek theatre, I think, as was originally built—not out of stone, but a hole, a pit out there out of town. *And our own stage, you worked from the centre.* So what happened on that stage affected the fellow on the left-hand side, and he would perhaps feel angry or giggle and laugh; and this would cause the person on the right-hand side to respond—not only to the actor but to the reaction of the fellow on the left-hand side. So you got a permutation which could only happen in a theatre built that way.

STEVEN: That's an experience we don't have, either as actors or audience, with the proscenium arch.

GEORGE: If you get the proscenium arch, it's like the royal box. We mistakenly called that "the traditional theatre" in this country for years. The traditional theatre was Shakespeare's, of course, and it was a bull pit where people were surrounding the stage.

All those things matter, don't they? Again we're talking about *balance... including the audience* in our balance.

STEVEN: I think that the proscenium stage was an attempt to eradicate that connection with the audience.

GEORGE: Well, it did eradicate it, but it was brought over after the Restoration and the actors went to the King—there's a letter in the British Museum about it—and pleaded: "Could we have our theatre, please?" In other words they had to ask permission to play, the actors did—always begging, things haven't changed very much (*Steven laughs*)—and the King said: "Yes, you can, as long as you play in the proscenium arch." Didn't use the word 'proscenium arch' but—

STEVEN: Picture frame?

GEORGE:—as he had enjoyed it in Europe when he was exiled during Cromwell's takeover and revolution. The king could sit at the front, the best seat, dead on. Everybody else had secondary seats around him, and it was like the movies. That *became* the movies: The picture frame, the little lights. So he insisted this be a part of the English theatre. But the change was incredible. The highest paid member of the theatre was the scenic artist.

STEVEN: The proscenium stage was a triumph for the designer and for the technical aspects of theatre.

GEORGE: Absolutely.

STEVEN: But a loss for the playwright and the actor.

GEORGE: Yes yes, and to follow that through to our own age, when technology dominates productions... especially those in which people are willing to spend a lot of money. They've taken their cue from the movies: Crashes are very important, helicopters land on stage, chandeliers fall down.

when technology dominates

There's nothing new in that: Inigo Jones[1] (*Steven laughs*) did the same damned thing after Shakespeare died. Inigo Jones had turned the theatre into a movie. Eye-popping things were going on which the people loved. And that was the end of language. The end of English theatre as we knew it. As they knew it. And it never came back. It was wiped out by technology.

And they've got the Drury Lane Theatre built with all those trap-doors and wheels. You go backstage there, as I've heard from

1. Inigo Jones (1573-1652) – Renowned English architect, employed by King James VI and I to arrange the masques of Ben Jonson.[27]

some directors who've tried to use all that equipment, it's fantastic. It is a great deal of fun-and-games to play, but it has nothing to do with the imagination; in fact, it defeats the imagination.

STEVEN: Because it lays everything out.

GEORGE: Yes, and you bring horses and elephants on stage—as they did, evidently, in the Drury Lane Theatre—

STEVEN:—and had been done before in Roman theatre.

GEORGE: Absolutely, absolutely, yeah. But the more you emphasize one element *only*, you lose the other. The way Ewan MacColl[2] would treat a play, and Joan Littlewood—they were attempting to return us to a play that had music, drama, spectacle... but none dominating the other.

Speech is not a natural endowment to the human species: It evolved out of a great desire to communicate sensations, desires, knowledge that could not be transmitted by a grunt. But the grunt came first. Speech still has to be taught...

STEVEN: And you're saying that it happens first in the Centre, and then a lot of other responses, including eventually speech, kick into motion?

GEORGE: Yes, but these things come later. I think, in creating a play, *speech is the last thing to concern yourself with.* The things you are concerned about are improvised and developed with a writer present. He's taking notes and eventually, hopefully, is putting words to those experiences that the actors have explored in his presence. At least a number of plays have been created that way—not *all* of them, nor is that the only way to create a play.

play development with a writer present

The emphasis in *our* effort was to create a Canadian theatre that spoke to the people from our experiences in this country at this time. It didn't matter that some of the actors were from Africa or America or somewhere else, but while they're in this city, and being unjustly discriminated against for one reason or another, then these things were studied. We were fortunate when you fellas[3] came along; we were able to extrapolate your experiences and put them onto the stage, because it felt genuine.

2. Ewan MacColl (1915-1989) – British singer, songwriter, playwright, director. Began his collaboration with Joan Littlewood in 1934, leading to the formation of the Theatre Workshop in 1945. Wrote plays for the company (including *The Travellers* and *Uranium 235)* that Littlewood directed.[(28)]

3. Referring to several actors, including myself, who came from the United States, resisting the war in Vietnam.[(s.b.)]

STEVEN: So often what has happened now is, the playwright's over here—

GEORGE: In another house.

STEVEN: In another house. He may come in now and then for a workshop, but he tends not to work hands-on with the director and designer and actors in the space. Some great work has happened that way, but I think we've lost a lot, because that separated model is more common now than the integrated model that you are talking about.

GEORGE: It's cheaper, and it takes less time, but the writer's work can be flatly turned down on the basis of *what it is at that moment*... and it seldom gets an opportunity to be explored again.

As you know, *we changed the economy of the theatre.* We did our best to let the front office raise the money and we spent all our time in rehearsal, so that we could expand on ideas.

Chicago '70

I recall one famous time—you were involved—we were scheduled to do a European play on police. It was a lovely play, full of fun, and it was meaningful in its criticism of the gendarme. So we did read it, but after a while we got a newspaper about the trials of the Eight in Chicago after the Democratic convention[4]. I'll never forget the picture of you, Steven, sitting on the bar—'cause we couldn't go on stage, there was a set there already—reading the Ginsberg[5] speech. Then another actor looked over your shoulder at the newspaper and read Judge Hoffmann's words, and so on. We were all leaning over you to pick up different comments.

STEVEN: We had one copy to read from.

GEORGE: We had one copy, yes! And it was an underground paper, wasn't it? Anyway, it made us laugh and it touched a sense of truth. It was a satire of the court system, which I felt was not only American, but applied to the courts probably in all the world—certainly in this country. We sent somebody to Chicago, Jack Boschulte[6], to cover the trials. So he wrote it all down and conveyed by telephone his impression of the trial and we were

4. Trials of leaders of organizations that staged protests at the 1968 Democratic National Convention in Chicago. Usually referred to as the 'Chicago Conspiracy Trial.' (29)

5. Allen Ginsberg (1926-1997) – Famous outspoken Beat poet who testified on behalf of the defendants at the trial. (30)

6. Jack Boschulte (1938-1997) – A native of Chicago and frequent actor/musician in the TWP company.(s.b.)

still getting the underground press: It had the day-by-day verbatim account of the courtroom—which to our eyes was hilarious. We forgot about *Police*[7] although I thought if we didn't get enough material for a full night we could do both plays—and after a couple of weeks in rehearsal of *Chicago* we gave up the idea of *Police* because we weren't rehearsing it. We were improvising on the newspaper work, and it was a valuable lesson for us all and ... a great entertainment, which we finally took back to New York.

STEVEN: It was a great experience, working on something that had just happened.

GEORGE: It was still happening! You recall that? It hadn't ended.

STEVEN: It seemed to be one of those events that opened up a whole bunch of other issues of the day and—

GEORGE: Absolutely. We got in the Vietnam War, of course, through the My Lai horror, and the torture—

STEVEN:—and racism.

GEORGE: ... of racism was there.

STEVEN: The ecological disaster was here and there in different testimony.

GEORGE: We had so much material, some we didn't use.

STEVEN: I was struck, when I'd watched the movie that Kerry Feltham[8] made—

GEORGE: Which we were not terribly happy with, no.

STEVEN: The film still has a lot of power—primarily because of the things that were said through the trial—but *that great sense of fun* was, to a great degree, edited out.

GEORGE: Yes, I agree. Yes, I'm sure you're right.

I had a discussion with Nancy Jowsey[9]—we were up in the lighting booth, her and I—and she said: "George, you know if you succeed in this work you will create a revolution against yourself 'cause you're the leader!" And I said: "I think you're probably right, but we'll do that if we succeed!" And sure enough, part way in, you all got together and sent me on my way. I'll never forget, June

---

7. *The Police* by Slavomir Mrozek[(s.b.)]

8. Kerry Feltham (b.1939) - Canadian director and producer. Directed the movie adaptation of *Chicago '70* released under the title *The Great Chicago Conspiracy Circus.*[(31)]

9. Nancy (Jowsey) Lewis – Resident designer at TWP from 1963 to 1973. Designed *The Good Soldier Schweik, The Tempest, Chicago '70* and many other productions. [(32)]

Faulkner[10] saw me in the middle of the day walk out the front door—and I don't do that! You remember? She said "What's going on?!" She was very concerned about the theatre. Anyway I went out for half an hour or so and Peter Faulkner[11] said: "You'd better come back in, George." It was anarchy all right but it had lost its direction—not just because of me, but because nobody was able *to take hold.* The anarchy had to be there but it still had to have direction—which was a real juggling act. I'd call a coffee break and that was against the idea of anarchy!

So we had wonderful discussions out of that experience, which reflected itself in the play. And it became very successful—except for one critic, Mr. Cohen[12], who wanted to see an Agatha Christie goddamn trial.

STEVEN: Is that what he asked for in his review?

GEORGE: No. Nearly, nearly!

STEVEN: A more naturalistic presentation?

GEORGE: Yes, he wanted to see the trial and we gave him a circus and we said: "The trial *is* a circus."

He missed that point altogether, wasn't interested in it really. He had his flaws too. He wasn't ever quite part of the Sixties.

STEVEN: A great nurturer, though.

GEORGE: Oh, absolutely. People believed him when he spoke. We went to New York on the basis of Cohen's reviews, often. I said to the producers down there: "C'mon, I'll pay your way up here to Toronto to see the show. I think it's good." And they said: "What did Cohen say?" And if he had approved, they would take the show unseen—that was the kind of power he had. You know he was offered a job at *The New York Times* and didn't take it; he recommended Clive Barnes who did take it.

STEVEN: Clive Barnes gave us a good review in the *Times.*

GEORGE: That's true.

And here we are talking about reviewers and we're supposed to be talking about Stanislavski, but *we live in a community, which*

---

10. June Faulkner (1926-2010) – Business manager for TWP (1967-79) and close collaborator with George for 15 years. (32) At June's public memorial in March 2010 one speaker proposed that, without June, there would not have been a TWP. [(s.b.)]

11. Peter Faulkner – Worked many seasons at TWP. Outstanding performances included *The Good Soldier Schweik, The Tempest, Chicago '70* and *Ten Lost Years.*[(33)]

12. Nathan Cohen (1923-1971) – Influential theatre critic who reviewed (and often supported) TWP productions.[(34)]

Chicago '70 (1970). Actors (l-r): Ray Whelan, Rick McKenna, Neil Walsh, Jim Bearden, Steven Bush, Diane Grant, Mel Dixon, Calvin Butler (directing traffic) & Peter Faulkner (foreground, on bicycle) / *photographer unknown*

community and economy

affects our economy. We in small theatres with 300 seats had to depend upon newspaper reporters, those who would encourage the public to come to our work. In the Seventies it was costing a great deal of money; the cost of the tickets had hardly risen, but the baby-sitter and the few drinks before the show or the few drinks after—

STEVEN: Those cost nothing as compared with the mid-Nineties though.

GEORGE: No, today it's an extraordinary event. I have no way of understanding the economies of the theatre now. They are bottom-line money-based and it shows in the work, I'm sure. That's the great thing about theatre: Everything you do on the stage is reflected—

STEVEN: It reflects the world you're in.

GEORGE: It reflects your behaviour, the way in which you work. If you are dishonest, you can't give an honest performance. I'm convinced of it. Dishonest as an artist, I mean. On the stage, you are under a magnifying glass. That's why Purpose is important, because you feel—if you're new to the stage—the isolation of yourself among a group of people. There's a great deal of pressure on you to behave: That's why you quickly move your arms or something. You try to solve a problem which you think may exist, but doesn't, therefore creating another problem.

STEVEN: One of the things we're robbed of, in these ridiculous short rehearsal times that are the norm now, is just that opportunity... to find that out through having enough exploration in rehearsal—

GEORGE: Also, the patience of the people involved to give you time to discover the truth of the moment. Remember in the Shelley play?

STEVEN: I saw it, but I wasn't in it.

GEORGE: Ann Jellicoe's play *Shelley,* which is a beautiful thing. Ray Whelan was trying to play the Everyperson—

STEVEN: General Utility Man.

GEORGE: He was an actor of mine for many years at this point, and we talked and talked about the role, and we were failing. I knew that this was very important to the play, that it must not fail, and I didn't know how it was supposed to solve itself. One lunch hour, which we usually spent in the Parkside Tavern—

Ray Whelan in *Shelley*

STEVEN:—your other office—

GEORGE:—I took Ray aside, and I told him some things that I had recognized about his work, to free him of the burden; and when we came back that afternoon, he just took up the idea marvellously, to the point where—Oh damn it! It was a dress rehearsal, we were that close to opening and we hadn't solved a main problem like this. And Nancy had made him a strange kind of skirt and a top, and he came out on stage, opening night, and curtseyed to the audience! He said: "Look at this: I've been here six or seven years, and here I am playing a runabout in a skirt!"

STEVEN: Yeah, I remember that speech.

GEORGE: It wasn't in the script at all: It was improvised. It made a wonderful beginning for the play, which played *against* it, because all the rest was a very true story—mostly of Mary more than Shelley. So Ray was flitting in and out, doing the jobs that he had to do, and he was pressed into being a baby and he made all the baby sounds—just wonderful! We were *willing to wait* to the last minute, with an actor who knew his stuff, and it all worked. *Plus* the costume lady.

STEVEN: Working together, part of the ensemble.

GEORGE: Sure, she was very aware of what was going on. I must point out that the costume office was just to the left of the stage, so the door was open and she could hear all the rehearsals, and all the problems, while she was working.

STEVEN: You can't do that if you're off in another building.

GEORGE: No, of course not. I must tell you about the lighting man since we're on to this kind of a story.

STEVEN: It's all part of Ensemble.

GEORGE: It is. The actors work all day, the lighting man works all day too: That was our theory. At one time he took exercises with us in the morning: He had to know what the actors went through physically, because he was also the stage manager. He would come to me and say: "George, I think you had better let them go." This was his sensitivity to the problems of the stage, which are emotional, physical, intellectual...and to have him around was a great help.

designers, stage managers and technicians in the TWP ensemble

On one occasion down on old Fraser Avenue[13], he was in the little box that we'd built for him, rehearsing *Before Compiègne*, and we'd done it a million times I think. And while *we're* working, John's working, creating lights that were helping the actors and moving them to a performance that I hadn't seen before. And when it was all finished, I turned around and thanked John in front of the actors. And he was delighted, of course, because I'm very short with my praises, you know. It comes when there's something really exciting; then people value it. I pointed out to the actors that they were good because John was better, and he had been following the play all along and he was experimenting, as we were, with the nature of the lighting.

...and John Faulkner on lights!

STEVEN: This is the wonderful John Faulkner you're talking about. I've never known anybody who could play a lighting board the way he did. He never had a plot, I gather.

GEORGE: No, we didn't make plots.

STEVEN: He would improvise with the actors every night.

GEORGE: Not only did we not have lighting plots, but we didn't have a lighting *rehearsal*. We didn't do what they all do in the theatre: 'Today's lighting rehearsal,' so everybody's bored: 'Oh God!' You know? And they all have to stand around being lit—

STEVEN:—having their energy drained—

GEORGE:—and hating the play, defeating the purpose—

STEVEN:—rather than moving things forward—

GEORGE:—defeating the purpose because you're only a moment from opening night and *you kill the play*. It's the same reason that, as you know, I don't block.

13. 47 Fraser Avenue, TWP's original theatre space, before the company moved to 12 Alexander Street.[35]

STEVEN: I wanted to talk with you about that troublesome word, "blocking."

GEORGE: What image does "block" convey to you?

STEVEN: Uhhh a brick wall.

GEORGE: Yes, exactly, a square head, a brick wall, something very static; and before television, we never said the word "block" … 'cause I was in theatre before television, believe it or not. You "blocked" in the television world because the important thing is the cameras and the cables, not the actors, as you well know. (*Steven chuckles*) The actors are "blocks" that stand there and take certain positions on tapes—which I never used, as some people do, in the theatre. You see, they've invaded—the *technology* has invaded the theatre without anyone examining it or knowing why.

blocking

But you see *words are important*. In the days before television we never used the word "block." We used to say: "Well, we'll do our moves today"—which was bad enough, you see—and I had an old director…(*laughs*) He used to open the script and put pennies on the page opposite to the lines, you see: He'd move the pennies around instead of moving us around. "The pennies look good on the page!" (*Steven laughs*) And therefore we'd be all right. We wouldn't be *blocking* each other.

How to arrive on the stage without standing in front of someone else? That only shows how you don't know how to use the stage. The actor understands space. He understands relationships. These things remove the need for what they call 'blocking.' The word is terrible, isn't it?

STEVEN: Terrible word.

GEORGE: It's "blockhead," you see. You don't *think* and that is what they want in the T.V. and the movies—that you are a puppet … for the most part. The whole setup is money-oriented. The bottom-line is what's important. They like to use the term "industry" in theatre. And I object to that strenuously.

STEVEN: No, another terrible word.

GEORGE: And the difficulty is, the bottom-line is *profit*. And *our* bottom-line is something else. It's called *"finding the most exciting interpretation of our existence."* So it's not an industry…

the bottom-line

STEVEN: What other negative things has the theatre contracted from television besides 'blocking' and the notion of being a part of an 'industry'?

GEORGE: It is this interpretation of everything in terms of Naturalism or Realism. The *behaviour* of the people is realistic: People grunt and groan according to where the hell they grunt and groan. You can scream at people in Realism. In my theatre, people never scream. I wouldn't allow it. It destroys the vocal cords. It's unpleasant to the ear. But an *interpretation* of that scream can be reached with sound. It's like poetry: You get the essence of the scream without the scream. And therefore you learn more about what it is.

the interpretation of everything in terms of naturalism

STEVEN: Hmmnn.

GEORGE: I thought of *the theatre being used as a theatre*. Not an imitation of a technology which we don't have our hands on—that is, television cameras, what have you. We use them on occasion, but they must adhere to *the rules of the theatre* when we do that. As I did with *Names*[14] and with several other plays.

Why I make a point of it ... is that terms have evolved from the needs of the television. Like 'cheat.'

STEVEN: Define "cheat" for those of us who don't know.

GEORGE: If you say "cheat" in television, they are asking you to move in a certain way to favour a camera angle that the director or the cameraman would like. Instead of moving the goddamned camera! (*Steven laughs*) You know, why not move the camera around the actor? Let the actor be the centre and then get the best shot you can of that man when he's creating truth. But they say: "Can you cheat this way please? You're talking to her, but don't let your head face her, face up a little bit so I can get something of your face."

cheat

The need for a face. You know that on the stage you don't need a face: *We have a body*. (*Steven laughs*) You can act with the back; you're responding with your entire body. The face is only one part of it uhhh beautiful as it may be; the *body* beautiful is just as beautiful. The sense of a person's failure is seen in his hips. In his feet. In his arms. But in a TV camera, where the fella wants a close-up, he's not seeing your head and arms and legs. He's only seeing an eyebrow, or something, and wants that particular bit.

on the stage you don't need a face ...

STEVEN: How did Joan Littlewood talk about this question?

GEORGE: We didn't "block." She never explained to us why she didn't but I think we all just knew instinctively that that wasn't what we did, because we found our own moves, our own physical

14. *Names*, performed in 1983 at TWP, used TV monitors to explore issues of disguise and reflection in the McCarthy Era hearings.[(36)]

relationships, through the analysis of the play applied on the stage. And if you had the wrong Objective, you'd invariably find the moves you were making were wrong.

STEVEN: What do you do when you're almost meeting the public with your production and there's one actor who always seems to find himself in the wrong spot? He doesn't seem to have that 'body awareness' of space. What do you do?

GEORGE: You fire the actor.... You've got a problem with some people who shouldn't be actors and at some point you have to say: "Look, I don't think this world is for you, but the front office needs a business manager." That isn't said often enough.

we're not all actors.

In my experience, I once had.... This was terrible, it was in the days when drama was thought of as therapy, and I found myself with a person who'd been sent by a doctor—which I only found out later, when she'd been there for a few weeks and her husband told me—in order to be cured of her problems. She had some talent for dancing and all of a sudden this doctor decided that a good place to send her was Workshop Productions.

The story was that eventually I had to ask her to leave. She was really quite out of control, had no idea of discipline and thought everything was in service of herself. You can't build a theatre that way.

So that was somebody that was impossible to work with. Which is a long way to go to answer your question. It may be simpler than that. You may have needed to re-examine his Objectives, or if he was playing the Objective *against* the Given Circumstances. Had he *forgotten* about the Given Circumstances? Because if that's the case, you can't play the Objective.

STEVEN: I recall very occasionally in rehearsals you would say to myself or another actor... "Allow yourself to be found here." Now I could tell that you hated to say that, but it seemed to be a way of nudging me—

allow yourself to be found here.

GEORGE: Oh yes, I would do that. I would find all kinds of ways to encourage the actor to achieve his Objective if he hadn't succeeded in finding it himself. But that is a time problem, that's economics. And it requires the skill to do it without destroying the initiative of the actor, which I hope I avoided doing for the most part.

STEVEN: I have experienced, quite often, that actors will panic if they don't have "blocking" by the end of their second week or so.

GEORGE: Oh yes, yes. Of course, you have to be very strict, and you have to give them the responsibility to solve that problem. It's not yours as the director, because you're using their interpretation of the Objective in the terms of the Circumstances. Again, it's *their* truth that matters. If they do *your* truth, it's not the same because they're playing what they think you want. That is hard for directors to understand 'cause they think they're God Almighty and the truth only belongs to him or her.

STEVEN: We fall so in love with our concepts.

GEORGE: Of course! Yes! They spend all summer working it out and then find an actor doesn't want to do it.

STEVEN: (*laughing*) I wonder why.

GEORGE: That's why the fun of it is—and I say the fun 'cause it's like diving into deep water, learning to swim and coming up—to *eliminate our pre-thinking*... so that it could come fresh from the actor.

In *The Mac Paps*[15] I had a concept of what that thing was supposedly going to be. I tried to convey this to six or seven different writers, none of whom I eventually used, because they kept writing it from their experience and not the Mac Paps' experience. It wasn't until I got the tape recordings of the men's own experiences that I had the play, because *it was their words*. This was like *Ten Lost Years*; when we did that, I said: "Now I know how to do the Mac Paps." And I searched out the tapes at the CBC building. Bob Allen allowed us access to the archives and we spent all summer correlating the tapes from 1936-1939 and numbering them. They'd been sitting on the shelves since Mac Reynolds went across the country to interview the people—

The Mac Paps: it was their words.

STEVEN: Early Forties?

GEORGE: It was in the early Forties that he went across the country, I'm sure it was, yeah. They are great stories, and when I put the right actors together—and I say 'the right actors' 'cause they were enthusiastic and they wanted to learn, even though some I hadn't trained—like R.H.[16] and Tom Butler—and a few of my own actors

15. *The Mac Paps* – Story of Mackenzie-Papineau Battalion of the International Brigade, which fought in Spain from 1936 to 1939. Script written by Luscombe and Larry Cox, derived from CBC producer Mac Reynolds' compilation of oral histories. Performed in 1980 and winner of the Chalmers Award for Best New Play.[37]

16. R.H. Thomson (b.1947) – Acclaimed actor of film, television, and stage, as well as a theatre director. Author/ performer of *The Lost Boys*, drawn from 700 letters of his five great-uncles who fought in WWI and from their family in Brantford, Ont.[38]

like Jack Boschulte and Iris[17]—

STEVEN: I remember R.D. Reid in that show.

GEORGE: Yes, and the stories were so good that they created a wonderful life on the stage, which was again improvised by the actors. Human beings do the strangest and most predictable things sometimes. And yet unpredictable in the sense that they surprise you.

I remember the story in *Mac Paps* when the boat was sinking. And one person observed another fellow who got up as high as he could on the mast, so when he dove off, he would miss the structure of the boat below. But before he dove, he quietly put his shoes together in the bedroom. He didn't want to wear them in the water, but put them side-by-side in his bedroom, and then dove when everything was neat and tidy. (*Steven laughs*) And you couldn't write that, you couldn't.

STEVEN: No.

GEORGE: … I hope we haven't strayed too far afield.

STEVEN: No. Do you have any other comments on "blocking"?

GEORGE: Of course, people are frightened of doing away with it and they've been so intimidated by the electronic media. We'll be taking words from the Internet soon, you know. But we want to be careful about that. Their purposes are different than our purposes and we will lose the reason for the theatre.

the reason for the theatre is because it's live.

The reason for the theatre is because it's live. … And that's an experience that's going to become more and more important in the future, I believe. We're in the doldrums now, but *in the future we'll need to bolster the soul*—if I can use that expression, if an atheist can use it—in order to enhance our living experience. We need this people-to-people communication 'cause there's so much technology getting in the way of it. I'm one of the very old-fashioned people: I don't like to use the telephone because I can't see the person. I can't carry on very long without seeing their eyes. And this is true in the theatre. It goes back to "blocking" again because *if your "blockheads" are "blocking," you've lost a search for truth, and it shows in the eyes.*

17. Iris Paabo – Performed in many TWP productions, notably *Thieves' Carnival*, *Ten Lost Years* and *Summer '76*. Devised the score for *The Mac Paps*[(39)]

Applying the Efforts

STEVEN: We've talked a lot about the Efforts. They seem to be really valuable as training, but can you give some specific examples of how an actor might use the Efforts in building a role?

GEORGE: Yes we can. The actors have to have learned the Efforts. And hopefully it's their second nature; they can respond to an impromptu situation with an Effort that works... even if they think it over and change it later. After you've had a group of actors for several months doing this every morning for an hour at least—

STEVEN: We're not talking about a weekend workshop, a 'crash course' in the Efforts.

GEORGE: No, no, no way. Nor is it work for students in university, where you only have them twice a week.

STEVEN: You're talking about a professional situation, ongoing ensemble work, where you have them daily for months.

GEORGE: Yes. Then you find that the actors are moving better. It may not be obvious to the audience that they're influenced by the Efforts, but they're recognizing *the economy of movement* that the actors have achieved.

I saw this in *Before Compiègne*. A woman said to us: "My goodness, who's your choreographer? Those actors move so well!" "There's no choreographer, because we don't 'block'." But the actors had been working *for months* on the Efforts; even during performance, every day, we would have a session on the Efforts.

directing *The Mechanic* with the Efforts

So I took those same people for our next play. We just stole the plots of Moliére to create a Commedia dell'Arte company playing this play we called *The Mechanic*, because we updated the problems so the doctor became a garage mechanic and was brought into the house of a rich man who misunderstood his reason for being there. It's all Commedia dell'Arte stuff which is still amusing after all these years 'cause there's nothing new in comedy.

Each character was dominated by an Effort. That doesn't mean he couldn't make other Efforts, but he was dominated by an Effort. So Grappler—the Father who was always being cuckolded by the Mechanic—he was a "Dab," you see. It was Ed Kelly[1], who was magnificent in "dabbing": You didn't know where the next direct move was going to be, but it was clear and precise. Marvellous. He even got himself caught in the tuba, so his ass was in the tuba—and he still "dabbed," trying to extract himself from the tuba.

And the Maid was a "Flick"—which she got from dusting—introducing all the actors to Brubeck's music "Take Five." The Maid, by dusting off the characters, introduced them and they came alive in their dominant Effort. The lovely Mother... who never looked after her daughter, but was always interested in the next man coming into the house... she was a "Glide." She "glided" across the stage in a marvellous way. Nobody *walked* across the stage: Everybody was working *in pure Effort.*

It has given our actors a confidence to do things that they wouldn't have the courage perhaps to attempt. The influence of the Efforts is always there, when the actors have had enough time to learn them—because they move better, they look better, they can carry out their Objectives better.

Uhhh I feel like a salesman for the Efforts. (*George laughs*)

the Efforts in realism

STEVEN: *The Mechanic* was before my days in Canada, but it certainly holds a place in people's memories as one of your great shows. Would it be possible to apply the Efforts to *The Cherry Orchard* or *Enemy of the People*?

GEORGE: Well, when I played in *Enemy of the People* for Littlewood, Harry Corbett[2] played the Uncle and used the Efforts in his hilarity and his extraordinary behaviour, but nobody knew it. It's not seen as a strange kind of movement; it seems like part of the character. I think in that way you would use it in Ibsen or Chekhov.

STEVEN: Question of *scale* in terms of the surface realism of the writers: What would be a fair way to talk about that?

1. Edward Kelly – Member of the TWP company in the 1960s. Noted also for his performances in *Before Compiègne* and *The Death of Woyzeck.* (40)

2. Harry H. Corbett (1925-1982) – Performed numerous roles at the Theatre Workshop during the 1950s and achieved international fame in the TV series *Steptoe and Son.*(41)

The Mechanic (3rd production, 1965-66). Actors (l-r): Adrian Pecknold (holding tuba), Donald Meyers (in glasses) and Edward Kelly (stuck in tuba) / *photographer unknown*

GEORGE: It's the demands of the play, 'cause you don't want to cover the language or substitute for it. You want to enhance it.

Sometimes actors would accuse me of not allowing their character to evolve as people in the training period. "Well," I said, "I don't like you as a person." (*Both laugh*) Well I didn't say that, but that would be the feeling. I would point out to them that if this is the person, he's only using half of his body; he's not exploiting all of the possibilities that he has. That's why you are learning the Efforts. It's not to turn you into robots, far from it. It's to give you control over all that you are.

STEVEN: It's to expand your range?

GEORGE: Yes. You do it anywhere else, but in the theatre when you do it, you're making robots of people ... according to some.

STEVEN: This can be more extreme now, as we've had another couple of generations that have seen very little, if any, theatre, but a lot of 'talking-head' acting framed by the camera.

GEORGE: Yes, yes, yes. Well, that was comparable to my problem in the Forties when I was on my way to becoming a radio actor, and my teacher—Ann Marshall—wisely steered me away from it as a career, because it wasn't theatre. The radio actors of the day tended to use their heads and voices only and their bodies weren't involved.

radio acting: their bodies weren't involved.

So it's like the mill-workers of the nineteenth century, working on the looms with their right hands. And their right hands became enormous and strong and their left hands were fragile, and hardly usable. This actually happened in the early Industrial Revolution: People were changed by the work they did.

STEVEN: Would you do that work now, if somebody phoned you up from Radio Drama? Or would you find the form too constricting in terms of time?

GEORGE: No, I would respond positively to it.

STEVEN: It's terribly fast, doing radio work.

GEORGE: I don't know whether I *could*, I have no idea, but I always enjoyed sound, you know, in the theatre. When I started the theatre, nobody cared a damn about sound: They'd wear street shoes on the stage, you know—clunk, clunk, clunk—because they didn't have any idea about moving. People don't put enough emphasis on the sound (and I don't mean just getting recordings, but) the sound of a human being walking across grass or walking across sand.

sound in theatre: *A Christmas Carol*

I was a sound man for *Christmas Carol* in Joan Littlewood's company. We all took turns doing the technical work; sometimes we were lighting men, sometimes we were something else. I was the sound man and I played about three different parts in the play, and I had old Scrooge there going up to bed and I wanted a sound when he got on the steps. I couldn't get a sound I could control. I tried every bloody thing with it and I hadn't created a satisfactory sound for these steps. The steps had to come alive and fight the old man—who was Howard Goorney[3] by the way—and in desperation, one last rehearsal we were having, I grabbed the mic and went "Kweeeek." It was a *vocal* sound, and I kept this funny sound up, and changed it. Howard loved it; he loved playing with it.

STEVEN: That's much more fun than a recorded, 'correct' sound cue.

GEORGE: And then one step didn't make a sound, and he wonders why, and he comes back to make the step make a sound. So we had a lot of fun with it, and the kids had a lot of fun with it.

STEVEN: So you had improvisation happening—

GEORGE: Yeah and it happened every time in performance. Well—

STEVEN: Talk again on Friday?

GEORGE: ... Yes, I think that's time.

STEVEN: Thanks, George.

---

3. Howard Goorney (1921-2007) – British actor of both stage and film. Author of *The Theatre Workshop Story*[(42)]

The Last Three Efforts: *Wring*, *Glide* and *Slash*

GEORGE: Well, we're going to do the last three Efforts of the eight, and then it will be complete. We will have covered all the pure Efforts; these are the dominant movements which the human body is capable of.

"Wring"—W-R-I-N-G. This is a favourite Effort, of mine at least. It's indirect, heavy, and slow. 'Slow' means as slow as you can move without stopping. 'Indirect' means the entire body is indirect all the way out to the extension of the limbs, but the limbs take their cue from the Centre. That's the most important because otherwise we would be flailing about and the arms would be doing one thing and you think you're working with the whole body but you're not and the movement is *eccentric*. the wring

Ummm when we wanted to create something really quite ugly—the results of the atom bomb for instance... and the people who were left over—the actors *combined* the Efforts so they were quite crazy: Part of their body was doing one thing and part was doing another. So the body was contradicting itself in the pure form of the Efforts. Theatrically, it was very effective and still it had the... Oh, how can I say this? The success of *creating ugly sights without being ugly itself.* Only because it was using pure Efforts. combining Efforts: *Uranium 235*

STEVEN: Which show was this?

GEORGE: These were improvisations based upon Littlewood's *Uranium 235* in which she did just that. I wasn't in that show, but I knew from the tales the actors told me what they had tried to achieve—and did achieve—to the astonishment of the public when it was first performed. And they were young actors who were moving beautifully, and their reputation was made at that point in England... and then forgotten about again after years, you know.

STEVEN: And that will happen.

GEORGE: Yes, absolutely...

So, those are the qualities of "Wring": *Indirect, heavy,* and *slow.* Work from the Centre but imagine you're wringing out clothes, as your mothers and grandmothers used to do. I guess great-grandmothers now. (*Laughing*) Before the washing machine, they would wring out the clothes to get all the water out. So it isn't just the hand and arms that are wringing, but the *insides* are wringing and that pushes outwardly to the limbs. It's a good visual image for most people on "Wring."

STEVEN: Yeah, that's a strong one to work with.

The Threepenny Opera at Humber Theatre (2005) directed by Maja Ardal—As Macheath *(Colin Edwards)* and Mrs. Peachum *(Alisha Stranges)* face off, they appear to be 'wringing.' Other actors—Back row (l-r): Caitlin Morris-Cornfield, Tyce Phangsoa, Silvia Wannam/ Front row (left): Christian Feliciano; (right) David-William Martel / *photo by Andrew Oxenham*

the glide

GEORGE: "Glide" is nice to talk about now, because it's *light, direct,* and *slow.* But it's the *essence* of slow, that's why we leave this towards the end. It's not slow in its rate of speed necessarily; it can be, but it doesn't depend upon it. As in... look up into the sky and see a seagull gliding by, maybe going a hell of a rate of speed, but the *impression* of slowness: That's what we're trying to capture with the "Glide." You won't hear the feet of the actor when they succeed at this; they will seem to be walking on air, above the ground, and that's important, because the *sound* is light. There is no stomping about in this one: They can move from one part of the stage to the other and still give the essence of slow... but have gone there very quickly.

STEVEN: I remember you always had us work in rhythm sandals or Chinese slippers.

GEORGE: Yes, yes, many of my students at college prefer bare feet, which is OK with me as long as the stage was clean, so there could be no accidents. But I prefer dance slippers of a kind. I bought mine at Eaton's; they weren't the expensive kind you buy at dance shops, we had to avoid that as well (*Steven laughs*)... just for the money.

STEVEN: Yup.

GEORGE: The footgear is so important, it is. It creates, or does not create, the sound that you want. And in this case *we don't want to hear a person move.*

One character that was indeed a "Glide" was the Wife in *The Mechanic.* She always had people coming in and half of them, you know, were her lovers. And she would take over the room with her "Glide," organize everybody, but do so in such an easy, complete way. (*Steven laughs*) This was what we needed for this character.

And now we come to the last Effort, "Slash," which is *heavy, indirect* and *fast.* And I suppose because of all those qualities, we leave it to the end. the slash

STEVEN: You always teach "Slash" last?

GEORGE: Yeah, I do. To put this combination together is quite difficult. It's the one Effort where I encourage the actors, if they can, to leave the floor... and still be in control of their body. So I often use the imagery of the bullwhip: You've become the handle of that whip, so that you pull it forward, take it up into the air, and snap it. Normally you would do that just with your arm, but now you're transferring that energy to the Centre. You snap from the Centre and land in balance again; and since it's indirect, you will probably land one foot at a time. We want it as indirect as possible. You see actors first attempting it, and jumping into the air and

Ten Lost Years (1974-75 tour)—Richard Payne appears to be doing a 'Slash' as (l-r) Grant Roll, François-Regis Klanfer, Peter Millard and Ross Skene look on or get out of the way. / *photographer unknown*

turning right around facing the other direction, but that's missed the point: Their body has remained stiff, direct. The body has got to snap in the air.

STEVEN: That's a tricky one.

GEORGE: I see, on the street, many people walk with a "Slash" and I analyze them. They're heavy, and indirect, and they're "slashing" their way through life.

STEVEN: You wouldn't use the "Slash" for a non-aggressive character?

GEORGE: I wouldn't define people in that way. I'm trying to think why.... Maybe it's too simplistic. Lots of people can "slash" who aren't aggressive. If you want a popular example, I would call Kramer a "Slash."

STEVEN: Oh, in *Seinfeld*, yeah.

GEORGE: When he moves, which is a delight—(*Steven laughs*) I'm not usually praising 'the box' but that particular work is clever. And when he begins to fall anywhere, it's very indirect and all over the place; yet I know that he knows where everything is as he's falling, he's in control.

But to get back to the real world again. The heavy indirect move on the street is a *dominant* Effort, not the full *pure* Effort. But for the actor, he has to learn the pure Effort in order to control the body, and the fun of this Effort is that you're in the air and it's controlled; it isn't anarchy. Also, the indirectness can allow you to change the rate of speed, as in a bullwhip: You start slow... you come up... it gathers momentum... until you *snap*! Which is very fast, so it completes the indirectness you are searching for.

STEVEN: What would be a character in which you used the "Wring" extensively?

exercise: Richard III gets dressed

GEORGE: Oh dear... Richard III, of course. A lot of actors will choose Richard III for their audition piece, and I think simply because I got bored with these recitations that I was having to watch, I would give the actor a job of work: "Now do that whole speech as the humpback is putting on his pants, putting on his boots." And it *does* turn out to be a bit of a "Wring."

STEVEN: Aha.

GEORGE: And as a handicap, I know—I even knew before this time—that getting dressed is one of the bastard things you have to do. I remember in hospital we used to say "Oh my God, this is the worst time of the day!" The struggle to get dressed when you've got a handicap. And you have no choice: You go through it every morning. You learn to be clever about it.

STEVEN: Mmhmmn.

GEORGE: But it's exciting for an actor to break up a speech by changing the Given Circumstances. Uh Richard's a man who doesn't stand there in the middle of the stage just emoting: He's got things to do, he's a practical man, he's a very actively alive man. And to give him such a challenge as getting dressed uhh with the deformity that he supposedly had, that's a lot of fun for the actor. And also, they stop thinking about the tone of their voice, or about Laurence Olivier, and start searching it out... which in itself is a good step. (*Laughs*)

STEVEN: Any time we have a concrete physical task, it seems to help.

GEORGE: Of course, yes, yes.

Analysis & Improvisation using the Efforts

training with the Efforts over time

GEORGE: We do these Efforts every morning. In the first month, I will be the one calling the tune. I will call "Thrust" and everybody will "thrust." Now, instead of stopping, I will say "Press." So they move from direct, fast, heavy movement to a direct, *slow*, heavy movement. So it only means changing the rate of speed in order to achieve "Press."

And then Efforts all of a sudden become more fun, because they don't know what's coming up next. And I'm calling them out aloud and also going around criticizing, to make people more direct, or lighter when they're still heavy.

Now we've done this for several months, every morning, no less than three quarters of an hour. I remember tiring out Donald Meyers and others 'cause I kept them going until lunch break. And they came to me and said "George … enough already!" (*Both laugh*)

STEVEN: I've done that too.

GEORGE: And they were very good, and I suppose I kept them going because they *were* good. When we go on training every day for three years, there would be a point when I wouldn't be calling anything.

improvising in the Efforts: rice paddy

I would take these actors into the wonderful world of improvisation, using the Efforts—and *pure* Efforts only—and sound when they wanted to make it—but *pure* sound. I'd give them the Given Circumstances, only an outline, and the actor would supply the detail. I can recall throwing to the actors that they are in a rice paddy, in an Asian country, planting rice; and some chose to "wring," as they bent down into the water, and then "thrust" the rice into the ground, and stretch their back to relieve the pain in another Effort. So, although that was a very solitary work-action, the actors are responding to each other in terms of the Efforts.

STEVEN: Without spoken text.

GEORGE: With no spoken text at all, but sound, possibly.

STEVEN: Why would you avoid verbal improvisation?

why avoid verbal improvisation?

GEORGE: It's too demanding. People would have to think about grammar, and they'd be frightened to make a fool of themselves. When the actors work in pure Efforts, they don't have the same hang-up as when they work naturalistically. In other words, you put an actor on the stage and you ask him to ... to deal with the Vietnam War, and he's got to think about it. Then the language comes into it and stops him from working, because his responsibility isn't writing.

The words come late. *The physical existence in the Circumstances is the first need.* Even if you were to grunt—which we wouldn't allow on stage in the end result, but in an improvisation any sound is allowed—it frees the actor up to move, to *do*, to take a challenge. It starts with movement.

It is *achievable*, that's what's important—achievable in a manner that doesn't leave you with egg on your face. Not that it's wrong to make a fool of yourself in your work, sometimes that's the only way to learn. But we don't do that purposefully, and directors who do that are wrong—very wrong.

STEVEN: Make fools of actors.

GEORGE: They lose the trust of the actors and they can't gain that back. *An honesty between the director and the cast is essential*, and a belief from the actor that he is not going to be required to shame himself on stage.

That's why we have writers about, you know. And in my world I want to see the *writers* understanding the use of the Efforts.

Efforts and the writer

STEVEN: How many writers have you worked with who have actually participated in the physical work?

GEORGE: I can only think of one: Jack Winter![1]

STEVEN: He did that work with you?

1. Jack Winter (b.1936) – Canadian dramaturge, playwright and teacher. As Resident Playwright at TWP 1961-67 and 1974-76, he wrote 12 plays, all directed by Luscombe, including *You Can't Get Here From There*, *Summer '76* and *Ten Lost Years* (created in collaboration with Luscombe and Cedric Smith).[45]

GEORGE: Not for long, but he did. And he had a great understanding of the Efforts. He wrote *The Mechanic* on the basis of the Efforts, so that the language suited the character. Grappler's language was "dab, dab, dab," all the time. And the words were chosen to accomplish "Dab." In terms of the Wife's language, she "glided" and her words were chosen accordingly. So, of course, he was watching every rehearsal, and taking from the actors what they were giving him. He was inspired by the actors' work and hopefully sometimes they were inspired by his.

But I went to these conferences—the Gaspé and other places—and I argued that *the writer should be in the theatre*. If we were going to build a theatre for this country, we'd better change the rules a little. That was what I was attempting to do....

STEVEN: Take a little break?

GEORGE: Yeah.

(*After a little break...*)

exercise: analyzing ourselves

GEORGE: So the next step along the way is to analyze ourselves. I would have us all sit in a circle and ask one person in the class—usually the show-off (*Steven laughs*)—to walk in a circle. There would be a lot of giggling and, as they're walking, I would encourage the rest of the class to loudly answer the question "Are they direct or indirect? We're talking from the Centre: Is it direct or indirect? Are they light or heavy?" And then: "Are they fast or slow?" And when the majority of the class believes this person to be, say, direct, fast, and heavy, I say: "What Effort is that?" They would say "Thrust," immediately. "And what's the *opposite* of 'Thrust'?" Indirect, light, and slow...

STEVEN: "Float."

GEORGE: It's "Float." It is useful to say, then, "Look: Go over and make a date with this girl in the corner, but your body only allows you to 'float' as you're going to her." Giving something concrete to do is useful 'cause that's the Objective, but they can only achieve it with the physical body that "floats." So that becomes fun to see an actor change his quality, change himself through the qualities of the Efforts. Talk about characterization! Not meaning that we've talked about where his grandparents came from, none of that 'Memory Recall' business—simply working physically. And all of a sudden they're a different person than they were.

So we go through that whole business until we've analyzed the whole class; and if you missed somebody, they'll say: "I haven't done mine yet. No one analyzed me!" Everybody likes to be analyzed, like they like to have their palm read, you know? (*Steven laughs*) It's only a thing to keep actors on their toes, to see that there is a great variety of characters that can be created physically, by being aware of the dominant Efforts.

STEVEN: So we are not locked into the body habits that we walk around with. As actors we can do other things.

GEORGE: Yes, absolutely and the great trouble there ... is that actors often aren't aware of what their bodies are doing. The audience is aware; they're very clued-in to what an actor looks like physically. Everybody knows the John Wayne[2] look. Everybody knows how to imitate that strange walk ... which he calculated, according to the stories.

It's like, if you're in a foggy situation and you see someone coming up, you say "Oh, that's Fred." How do you know? You can't see his face, he's just a blur. But you first of all recognize how he's walking and the dominant Effort that person is using.

I once had, in my class, a man and wife. They were a little older than the rest of us. We were all young then, it was ... What do they call it, 'salad days'?

STEVEN: "My salad days when I was green ... "

GEORGE: Yes, right, well we were all young then, but this was an older couple *to us*. I had them both up on their feet, one at a time. It turns out that the man was one Effort and the wife was the opposite Effort. Therefore, when they had to both take opposites to their own Efforts, it was the woman taking the *man's* Effort, and the man taking the *woman's* Effort. And there was a howl from the group, when they recognized that physically they had become each other! And just by use of the pure Efforts—very fun, and of course says more than you can *talk* about.

STEVEN: Hmmn.

2. John Wayne (1907-1979) – One of the most popular male actors in American cinematic history. He starred in almost 250 movies during his lifetime (including *Red River*, *The Searchers* and the original *True Grit*) and is known for his portrayal of rugged, conservative masculine roles. (46)

“Polished Stories”: Improvising from the Bible

GEORGE: I take little stories from the Bible, you know, and we don’t do it because I’m running a religious school—far from it! (*Both laugh*) We’re doing it because we are a part of the Judaeo-Christian society.

improvisation: the Story of Adam & Eve

I start off with Adam and Eve. And it’s surprising how many ways that this little story, which you think everybody knows, can be interpreted. Especially if you get enough feminists in the group. It’s a great play for them, as they realize what God has done to them (*laughing*) . . . according to ‘The Good Book.’

But we leave that for the analysis later.

STEVEN: At this stage you don’t want to talk too much.

GEORGE: No, I will just divide the play into three, maybe four Units. I won’t choose the actors’ Objectives for them, but I will remind them of the lesson on Purpose: *You cannot be on stage without a Purpose and the Purpose must be related to the Unit.*

And I will ask what elements we should deal with: “What are the characters?” And of course, they will come up with Adam and Eve. I’ll push them, and someone will say the snake, and I will have to correct that and say it’s the serpent. So that you don’t need to lay down on the floor: All we know from the Given Circumstances is that he’s a serpent capable of movement. And they will of course eventually realize that they’ve left out the tree. And all that happens does so in or around the tree.

So somebody says “Where do I go?” and I try to hint that the tree is the centre of the story: “Why go off to the wings if this is the reason for the story existing?” So, eventually he moves to the centre of the stage. At first he feels kind of foolish—he or she—but I try to encourage them in the beauty of the tree. It's something enticing, something the serpent uses. It has life, and it has a Purpose and, because it is a tree, it is rooted to the ground. So we know that as a Given Circumstance. It can't move in the usual sense, but it can blossom, it can expand and grow; or it can wilt and die. That's when it becomes exciting for the actor. He doesn't need to run across the stage to be exciting: He moves *within*.

But what about all the other things in the garden? You've got a class of twelve, or fifteen, and everybody is in the garden. So, what does the garden hold? It holds all the good, pleasant things. And everybody, we know, has not fed on the tree, because they're not allowed to. So, they're without knowledge—without the ability to blush, as Mark Twain would say. They're butterflies, lions, tigers, parrots—which are great to analyze in terms of the Efforts—not working realistically, but choosing the dominant Effort.

So where does that leave Adam and Eve? Sunbathing? (*Steven laughs*) They can do as they please, the world is free. They are at leisure in a garden without the sweat and toil of work. They have no obligation ... according to the Given Circumstances.

STEVEN: You want to stay within that.

GEORGE: Absolutely, those are your fences. That's what gives you the freedom to explore the possibilities.

So, because I want to get on with the story, I will suggest that the first Unit is "God laying down the Law," with God as the main character. Again, the actor playing God: If he stays in the wings, that's a hell of a place to lay down the law! (*Steven laughs*) If I'm the teacher, I'll take over the class in a position where I can, not just dominate it but ... be in touch with everybody ... in the centre of the group. "Would God do less?"

STEVEN: What are they thinking by hiding in the wings? That they will command by voice alone?

GEORGE: They're scared. They don't want to commit too much.

STEVEN: They haven't committed to God's power yet.

GEORGE: They haven't. They're not convinced that they can hold it down, you know. They have to be encouraged to be bold.

STEVEN: What Efforts, typically, would people use to represent God?

GEORGE (*laughing*): Umm the ladies would be different than the men and ... some will try to take *my* Efforts. They've said: "Well, there's only one God in this class!" (*Both laugh out loud*) Which is very amusing.

But, they make a variety of choices, depending on their view of the character, and their own psychology. So there's a marriage of themselves and the character. According to Stanislavski, *you are never only the character.* You use your body, therefore there is a part of you in the character. And it is your choice of Effort that is part of your interpretation of the character.

STEVEN: What is the primary challenge that you're throwing to the actors?

playing-through the play—just through sound and body

GEORGE: The intelligent telling of the story, I suppose. When they understand the Given Circumstances, they've chosen the Efforts, they're telling the story through the *application* of the Efforts.

The next Units would be the "Temptation" and then "Retribution." That makes it very simple: "Can you play these Units through in a row?" This is what the actor can do, even at this early stage: They can move from Unit to Unit.

For instance, when the Serpent completes his role of tempting Eve, we move into the *end* of the second Unit, when Eve tempts Adam. When both Adam and Eve have eaten of the fruit, God must appear. And if the actor is watching his business, He will appear at that point without the director telling him, and *how* He appears will be exciting. His questions for himself will be: "Why doesn't He go to Eve?" He goes to Adam, not Eve. If He is all-knowing, why doesn't He say: "Hey, what have you been doing, lady?" Instead of that, He goes to Adam. And Adam, in the typical male chauvinistic form: "It's all Eve's fault! (*Laughing*) She tempted me, she made me do it!" (*Steven laughs.*) So it proceeds into the third Unit, even without thinking about it.

That's what I want them to achieve: I want them to see how they can get there without disrupting the logic of the story. They will have had *the experience of playing-through the play*—just through sound and body. There is a wonderful sense of accomplishment when they have done that.

STEVEN: Do you get them cast out of the Garden?

GEORGE: "Retribution," you know: He's turned the Serpent into the snake and he crawls on his belly now, and when God says to Eve "You shall bear in pain" ... that's a terrifying thing.

My mother told me years ago how she went to her doctor when she was pregnant with one of us. She complained about the pain and he assured her that it was natural and right that she should be in pain. "That's right, that's what a woman's job is all about..." It was practically a Biblical quotation. He was an old-fashioned doctor. But he was part of the culture, and we all are.

to see what it is that made us like we are

STEVEN: This doctor said this to your mother 150 years after the 'Enlightenment,' so-called?

GEORGE: Yeah. I suppose that's why, now, I'm saying it's fun to analyze the stories of the Bible: To see what it is that made us like we are.

Also, the *clarity* of the Bible: It's a polished story. Like *Ten Lost Years* was a polished story these women and men were telling. They had told the same story a number of times since the Thirties and each time it got more economical, more to the point, and sometimes more devastating.

A polished story: the Bible & *Ten Lost Years*

I remember, always remember, one story we used at the end of the play. A woman whose son went to the war and was killed, she said... "He was killed with the war." And it sounded like a disease.

STEVEN: Hmmn.

GEORGE: Which it is.

STEVEN: Hmmn.

GEORGE: Now what a choice of words! That grabs you... but if we were *writing* that, we would have said "He died *in* the war."

STEVEN: Yeah.

GEORGE: I couldn't write that, nobody could. It's the people *said* them. Barry[1] got them down right.

That's, I think, what the Bible holds: The story has been carefully honed over the centuries and all the excess is gone; there's no padding anymore.

The other thing about Adam and Eve: All the characters were involved in the first Unit—feeding, washing their young, doing all these domestic things. And God lays down the law, and they all hear it. Now, some may not understand it and be puzzled; others may be frightened by the sound. There are all kinds of reactions that the animals are capable of because they're aware of the Circumstances. So, by the time you get to the third

...the Eden left them.

1. Barry Broadfoot (1926-2003) – Journalist who published a collection of memories from survivors of The Great Depression (1929-1939) – the basis for TWP's production *Ten Lost Years*[(47)]

Unit—"Retribution"—the tree is wilting, there's no more nourishment, the animals have changed. Their Eden isn't the same anymore. That's what I think the meaning of this little story is: While Adam and Eve are kicked out of Eden, there *isn't* an Eden any more. And that's the way it very often turned out in our improvisations …

STEVEN: Aha.

GEORGE: … that the Eden left *them*. And they will forever want Eden back again, but it won't be there. With knowledge, you lose something. With every bit you gain, there is some sacrifice. In this case, they have to work for a living. (*Both laugh*)

So all those lovely things I've discovered in a very small and simple story.

The Three Types of Acting

STEVEN: So here we are, Thursday, June 20th 1996, sitting on the back porch.

GEORGE: Ready to start again. Umm I think it may be worthwhile to begin with the three approaches to acting that Stanislavski would deal with: 'Mechanical Acting,' 'Representational Acting,' and what I've called 'Creative Work.'

mechanical acting

So we start with the obvious, first: Mechanical Acting. This is what has been known in the trade as 'rubber-stamp acting.' You see certain ways of behaving as a character and you reproduce it on the stage. So, you roll your eyes, and give some indication of frustration or surprise: That is a mechanical act, which is repeated night after night, in the same manner, without any thought behind it. We'll call it 'mugging.'

STEVEN: Mmm.

GEORGE: And what is mugging? This is shaping your face into a form that represents tears, or laughter, or horror. Each rehearsal, each night, repeating that physical behaviour. We call it 'Mechanical.' We say that there's not truth in it, no accidental truth, because it *blocks* truth. You have to put a mask on. If you want a mask, make one and put it on, but don't use what God gave you—the face—to make masks of yourself and supposedly convey to the audience the deep and difficult emotional strains that a character is going through. It doesn't work. It's... it's a quick device.

The best example of this work is on TV, of course. Some of our own favourite Canadian actors are guilty of the most atrocious mugging: Second City[1] is a result. They have to do these things in thirty seconds, and they're very clever at it, but it's boring after a while; it is unconvincing and can't sustain your interest. Stanislavski writes of 'Mechanical Acting' in *his* age, the 19th century, and it was all over the stage. We have examples of it—old silent films, I suppose. A lot of actors there had great gestures that represented the most delicate innermost feelings and it doesn't work.

STEVEN: Today.

GEORGE: Today, we laugh at it when seeing the films of yesterday.

STEVEN: But would we have laughed *then*, if we were in one of those 3000-seat European theatres, watching somebody from the 30th or 40th row?

GEORGE: The rows don't make any difference to me. Truth is truth: It doesn't change in the 40th row or the 1st row, there's only truth.

But yes, there is a difference, because we're different people now. The technology of that period was enough to engage people in "Oohs" and "Ahhs" as they saw the train rushing at them. We don't do that anymore. We're not fooled by the cinema—except big explosions that knock us out of our chairs—and I find that only annoying.

STEVEN: (*Laughs*) Yeah.

GEORGE: But acting is still the problem. If it's true, it's true yesterday or it's true today. And if it's false, it's false for all periods. I usually make a game of this with the students and ask them if they can recognize 'Mechanical Acting.' I don't even give them a hint but they'll always come up with television, and these quick, so-called 'laughable' comedians.

LITTLE GIRL (*from inside the house*): Hi!

STEVEN: Is one of the features of 'Mechanical Acting' the fact that it's third or fourth generation *imitation of other performers*?

GEORGE: Absolutely right. Blueprints of something else that they remember. Little kids playing Cowboys and Indians have always been able to be shot and fall to the ground very effectively, in a mechanical manner. Little Madeline here, who you heard a moment ago, she knows how to be coy; she knows now how to get

---

1. The Second City – The original Second City began in Chicago in December 1959. Such masters of 'realistic comedy' as Elaine May and Mike Nichols were involved. (s.b.) The Toronto company was established in 1973 and is known for short comedy skits and improvisations. [48]

around us adults, and what is she? Two years old, maybe three? She is educating herself as to what's needed to live in the world, and one of the easiest ways to do that is mechanical work. I was talking to my daughter about it yesterday: If they're considered a pretty child, the adults will say "Oh, isn't she pretty?" and therefore she will behave *as* 'a pretty child.'

STEVEN: Yeah.

GEORGE: Until she's in her teens and then comes and expects to be an actor, you know, which I'll have to knock out of her.

(*Steven laughs*)

This is what is missing in 'Mechanical Acting': There is *no inner stimulus*, it is something stuck on from the outside. In our 'Creative Work,' we expect the actors to have inner stimulus so that the performance may grow. And that's the trouble with 'Mechanical Acting': There's no expansion in it, it's like plaster, things you put on a cut…

STEVEN: Band-Aids.

GEORGE: Band-Aids. It's stuck on, and it becomes an excuse for the character.

I used to get after Ray Whelan for that, who *loved* props.

STEVEN: Oh yeah?

GEORGE: Before he was building a character, he's put on the little specs and I'd say "Let's do without that, at least the *first* rehearsal."

STEVEN: Olivier[2] used to find the nose first.

GEORGE: Yes, the nose, and you've seen the pipes, haven't you? I worked with an actor who loved pipes—the only actor I know who could talk for twenty minutes with a pipe in his mouth and still be understood. (*Laughs*) It was quite an achievement, but it was his cliché, it was his mechanical act.

props, noses, pipes & putting on the coat

STEVEN: Now, if that's a way *into* a deeper truth for an actor, is it a problem?

GEORGE: Ummm yeah, it seldom is. It more often gets in the way of what is possible to discover.

STEVEN: I heard an interview recently with Anthony Hopkins.. whom I think is one of the most truthful film actors around, with a great range.. and he said that his starting-point is hearing the

2. Sir Laurence Olivier (1907-1989)—Actor and director renowned for his work with the Old Vic company in London and for many films. First Director of the National Theatre of Great Britain from 1962 to 1973. (49)

A promotional composite from 1959 / *photo by Adrian's, Toronto*

voice of the character. When he finds the voice, other things start to happen with him.

GEORGE: Sure. I was in a dressing room where a relative of the boss used to come in—he was an old actor, an Edwardian actor—and he would just mosey into the dressing rooms 'cause he loved the smell—the paint, the grease, all that stuff, which we used by the tons.

STEVEN: When you were in England.

GEORGE: In fit-up.[3] And he talked about 'putting on the coat': How he could put on the coat and put on the character. And I found it legitimate, because it was a way in, if you wish. But it mustn't stop at the coat, at the pipe, at the glasses. That's the problem. Then you're saying: "Oh, here comes the pipe on stage." You know, there's no character but there's a pipe.

STEVEN: Here comes the limp, or the funny accent.

GEORGE: Absolutely, these are mechanical *crutches*, which too often get in the way of delving into the intricate lives of the characters.

3.Fit-up – British colloquiol term for a load-in: moving the set into the theatre. Also used for a travelling company or a temporary stage. [(50)]

STEVEN: I remember seeing—I think it was when we were on tour in Venice—a film of Eleanora Duse[4], the great Italian actress. Her gesture was very grand, she was still connected to the 19th century 'grand manner,' but there was a truthfulness in everything she did.

GEORGE: Mmhuhn.

STEVEN: When you talk about 'Mechanical Acting,' you're not talking about the gesture itself necessarily undercutting truth?

representational acting

GEORGE: No. And you've just given me opportunity to move into 'Representational Acting,' which is probably what Duse was all about; I know Sarah Bernhardt was there. 'Representational Acting' can move us emotionally when it's skillfully done, and when it's based upon truth. You are playing something that has been done a hundred times, but you are doing it based upon *an original process of discovery.*

This was true of Laurence Olivier, who would put his cigarette out at the same bloody place, on the same line, at the same moment. Everything was set. This is very much in tune with commercial theatre of our own day so, when understudies come in, they don't have to call back the director and pay him big money; they just get the stage manager to direct the understudy in his positions. No one must have a surprise on the stage. Also, the director insists on the work being done as he did it originally.

STEVEN: Usually because he is off somewhere else by then.

GEORGE: Yes, but he could come back in three months' time and he wants to see the shutter shut up at the exact moment as before, because he thought he'd done a marvellous piece of directing when he told the actor "*Now*... close the blinds." (*Both laugh*) So it flatters him and it makes automatons of the actors. But *they* are playing 'Representational Acting.'

Another example of 'Representational Acting' is Alastair Sim, who I enjoyed in the movies very much, and still do. But on stage he had this old trick: If he had to laugh or cry, he'd bend over and hide his face and shrug his shoulders up and down. It was a sign he was either laughing or crying, but one couldn't tell without the context, because physically he was just making an up-and-down gesture.

4. Eleanora Duse (1859-1924)—Renowned Italian actress, considered by some to be the only real rival of Sarah Bernhardt.[51]

I suppose that's more 'Mechanical' than 'Representational,' but that's the thing: Sometimes an actor will use a mixture. So, *what's important for us is to understand and analyze what we're doing.*

good points of representational acting—Chinese opera

Let's talk about the good points of 'Representational Acting.' For instance, the Chinese opera[5] is full of 'Representational Acting'—based upon their particular culture and observations of what truth is. It can be very stirring, and I remember seeing the performance for the first time in Warsaw. They had on stage seven or eight people with their ancient instruments; then in the orchestra pit, there was a full symphony orchestra (*Steven laughs*); and on stage, there must have been ... oh, I don't know ... perhaps twenty or thirty actors who all seemed to be gymnasts as well. Of course, I found out later that this training starts at a very early age and the actor is indeed a gymnast. And these fables and stories have been told in the same way for many years. And there is an expectation on the part of the audience: They expect a representation to convey the same thing as it did when they were a child.

These actors, as they get older, they take on different roles until they are ancients and they have tremendous makeup to play the old men. But they still have the agility to move beautifully, they're not sloppy in any way. They don't do the double flips over the swords. (*Steven laughs*) That's left for the young men.

So that was a joy to see, and that is very much 'Representational Acting' taken to the utmost. You understand the gestures of the actors. You understand the colour of their beards. The Monkey King wears a certain costume that never changes. And it *mustn't*: It's identifiable to the audience as what that character is.

sometimes an actor will use a mixture.

To bring it to our own age, we are full of 'Representational Acting' in our theatres. Oh, some of us have a little bit of 'Mechanical Acting' overlaying the 'Representational Acting' and maybe even, on certain nights, without anybody knowing, we have some 'Creative' activity going on (*Steven laughs*) ... and that's good.

STEVEN: These lines aren't that clear.

GEORGE: They are not clear. They're only for the actor himself, to be able to identify what he's looking at. Not only 'I was impressed'

5. Chinese opera—National opera that represents Chinese history and culture through highly stylized performance. There are generally four main categories of roles that are further divided into specific role types. [52]

but... 'What was I impressed *by*? Do I accept that, or not? If I'm bored out of my mind, why?'...

Of course, it's my theory—and Stanislavski's, I believe—that each night is different; therefore, you can't rely on the same reactions. And if you don't get it when you're 'representational acting,' you say: "Oh, that's a lousy house. They're dead." They aren't dead; audiences are made up of a lot of human beings....

And the only time they are really difficult is when bus tours have been organized. They're getting a day off school and you're keeping them in the theatre; they're being punished, so they punish the actors on stage. And they keep doing it because it's money!

actors' nightmares

STEVEN: Obviously the kids shouldn't be there on that occasion.

GEORGE: And those teachers shouldn't be there! They go through the aisles, going 'Shush, shush, shush!' to all the kids and I told them at times: "Quiet! You're the trouble! (*Steven laughs*) Not the kids!" If we can't hold the kids in the audience, we have a problem. We don't need a gendarme to help us; in fact, that works against us, because their displeasure at being coerced by the gendarme, by the teacher—it comes out in their response to the stage. I've had things thrown at me on stage—pennies—in tough neighbourhoods.

STEVEN: I've been driven off the stage by an audience.

GEORGE: It's terrible.

STEVEN: It's a horrifying moment, an actor's nightmare.

GEORGE: Well, I've opened at the Theatre Royal, with Littlewood, doing *Twelfth Night*—unfortunately for us, because we were in tights and bloomers and wigs. I played Sebastian and I had this coiffure with bangs in the Elizabethan style. And we followed an artist called "Jane"—a strip artist, a comic in England at that time.

STEVEN: She was the previous show?

GEORGE: She was the previous show, and the audience came in to see "Jane" and here we were giving them Shakespeare's *Twelfth Night* (*both laugh*)... which they didn't appreciate. So the pennies began to fly. I remember we had a net that came down; that was the only time we ever used it. But we carried on anyway, with our bloomers and tights and hairdos (*Steven laughs*) and finally managed to drive the audience away. It took us years to build what we thought was an audience, again.

STEVEN: By the time you were doing *Richard II*, you had the audience back?

GEORGE: Yes but then again, they were West Enders, you see. The Cockneys that lived in the lane, you know, seldom ever came.

STEVEN: Really?

GEORGE: But the women who came in to wash and clean up the stage—this is when we were wealthy and could hire people to do it—they came to see their favourite Shakespearean plays. So they were stimulated by the Shakespearean work but so-so about anything else.

STEVEN: Mmhmmn.... In terms of 'Representational Acting' we talked earlier about the best work of Laurence Olivier.

Laurence Olivier

GEORGE: Oh yeah, particularly in movies. You know, I have seen him on stage and, for me, it just wasn't an experience. I have read critics who held the same thing. And they must have been bold to write that in the paper when he was dead.... because you *didn't*! He was an icon, and there was good reason for that, I'm not knocking his work at all. There are wonderful stories of the chances he took diving off bloody rostrums...

STEVEN: His physical injuries during the filming of *Richard III*, catching an arrow in the leg...

GEORGE: A great achiever, no doubt about it. So you see for a while a man who's dominantly 'representing' his work and then,

Olivier as Richard III (from his film version). Note the nose. / *photographer unknown*

in a moment, for some strange reason, there'd be life on the stage... which is nice to see.

But let's talk about that 'Creative Work' of Stanislavski.

We prefer to take chances, I suppose, in the 'Creative Work.' We want the experience to be *alive*. People experience it through a personal relationship with the person on stage; and if that's true, we must be as alive as the audience.

creative work

We expect, every time we go out there, it's a *new* experience. It *is* for the audience and should be for the actor. We change because we are moved by the audience, or we're moved by something internal that we have now discovered. To be free to respond to that intuitive work, when it does happen, it's just a joyous occasion.

STEVEN: Stanislavski said: "We prepare in order to improvise."

GEORGE: That's a good line. In fact, that is what improvisation is all about.

STEVEN: I'm going to pause. I think Mona's coming in with some food here.

Mona and George as newlyweds, 1958. / *photo courtesy of Karen Luscombe*

Mona always greeted me warmly at the door and often fed us when George and I were recording. But that's not all she did: Mona Luscombe was one of the key people—along with June Faulkner and George—who looked after 'the business side' and kept TWP alive for so many years. (s.b.)

(Later in the day, after lunch…)

GEORGE: With the 'Creative Work,' we have carefully begun the classes without talking about character. We're building slowly, like putting an onion together, a continuation from the first steps until the final performance. One can't expect anyone to build a character beforehand.

This is particularly true for these goddamned auditions, when actors are forced to give something to the director. They're trying to give *the performance*, and the director says "Oh, that's marvellous, that's exactly what we want!" And you'll have three weeks of rehearsal with simply playing lines to other people but *not growing*. So he's given his performance in audition. I want to see an actor of promise in the audition; I want to be a good guesser at that. To see how he moves, how he responds to my directions and see what he can achieve when a new challenge is put to him.

The 'Creative Work' begins the first day, with the relationship with the other people on stage. We go through the lessons to point out the physical space, and the physical relationship, and then these things are carried forward and applied to the building of the character. The search for truth doesn't eliminate questions like the character's environment, their feelings towards other characters, but there might be less emphasis on who the character's great-grandmother was and who she slept with, you know, because it doesn't necessarily apply. So why bother with it? It's like putting on costumes that you don't need.

STEVEN: It just clutters up the work.

GEORGE: Absolutely. And, again, *looks* like the actor's working, but indeed he's only *padding*.

As a *writer* can do. A writer can pad if he doesn't know his analysis, and will do so given half the chance. As you know with me and scripts, I always have a pencil ready to cut out the padding that didn't trust the actor to do his work.

building environments that encourage creative work

STEVEN: How do you move to an environment where 'Creative Acting' is encouraged and 'Representational' or especially 'Mechanical Acting' is discouraged? What has to happen?

GEORGE: Well, 'Mechanical Acting' is outlawed: Let's try it that way. (*Steven laughs*) 'Representational Acting' is put up with but not encouraged. How do you get there? I have no idea. Except, having understood what's needed, you must build your own theatre. I don't see it any other way. That's why I was happy when a number of you fellas went out and built your own theatre. How the hell are you going to have control over these things without it?

STEVEN: I would say it's harder to do that now than when I started companies, or Ray Whelan started companies.

GEORGE: Yes. That's true because of subsidy.

STEVEN: Yeah, and yet twenty-year-olds, twenty-five-year-olds are starting companies, and some of them are extremely dedicated and rigourous in their own way, so it's still happening.

GEORGE: They mustn't give way to the economic shortcomings, always cutting the cloth too much at the expense of the work. That means, of course, rehearsal time to start with.

STEVEN: Usually the first to go, after training.

GEORGE: Training goes first, then rehearsal time comes next. They do so much of this voluntarily when, with a little more struggle, they could succeed; I think they could.

taking care of the business side

Because nothing was harder than it was in 1959. We had no subsidies. I supported myself through TV work and it was years later before TWP got any help at all. And then it was like two thousand dollars for the year, which was nothing. All that helped us do was go in debt—which we did.

STEVEN: (*Laughs*) The banks like that, for you to be in debt.

GEORGE: They seem to, they seem to encourage it. I was in debt for about five years *on my own signature*—which I didn't know about because the business manager at that time didn't tell me what she was doing. So any time we ran short on payroll, she just borrowed more money, and the bank was delighted—I mean, up went the indebtedness, until it had reached nearly six thousand dollars *on my name*. I didn't have *six* dollars.... So you had to watch things, which I did after that and became an ogre, you know, because I was watching it all the time.

STEVEN: It's one of the ways in which you have to protect the work.

GEORGE: Yes, indeed it is, and June Faulkner was a great help in that: When she came in and found that debt, we got the debt paid off so it was no longer a *personal* debt. When we did go into debt after that we managed to involve other people, usually the Canada Council or the Ontario Arts Council, who then felt an obligation. And that's quite right, that they should have an obligation.

Hume Cronyn as Shylock

STEVEN: As we talked about 'Representational Acting' and 'Creative Work,' I was reminded of a great performance by Hume Cronyn as Shylock in *The Merchant of Venice* at the Stratford Festival. The work was very clear, simple. He was speaking truthfully, he was in the Circumstances, he was relating to the other characters. I kept wanting Shylock to come back, the scenes he was in were so good! And I was told that his performance had been more or less exactly that since the first read-through.

GEORGE: Yes.

STEVEN: How do you account for an actor that can work that way?

GEORGE: Well, he's obviously working well. Again, I think that actors who are watching him are not watching that closely. Things change internally, if he's working well, and the smallest changes are caught by the audience. It's flattering to his technique and training and experience that he could do that. And because he *seems* to be doing everything the same doesn't mean that he's emotionally living everything the same.

STEVEN: Aha.

GEORGE: But the outward physical show can be fairly close; in fact, it usually is. We don't change for the sake of change, to say "I must freshen this up, so I'll go over here tonight." We'd be contradicting our own Analysis and it could upset, not only that actor but everybody else on stage, and eventually destroy the meaning of the play. So, from what you say, I believe that indeed was a good performance and contained all those things of preparation, sincerity of thoughts and truth. It came from a new place—not a *completely* new place, but a stimulating centre each night.

a stimulating centre

STEVEN: 'Stimulating centre': Can you talk some more about that?

GEORGE: Well, he's being moved by his *emotional* centre and I think of that as the Centre—not just the brains. The slight inflection is not changing because of the vocal box; it's being affected by how he has taken a *hit* in the Centre, in the solar plexus. And if the hit was stronger on this night than it was on other nights, the voice will reflect it. You're fortunate to witness such a performance.

You told me another story about him[6] when he was being interviewed: "Does it all come together in one night?"... "Seldom ever"

6. Hume Cronyn (1911-2003)—Canadian actor, producer and writer. He began his career on Broadway, later making an entry into film as star in two of Alfred Hitchcock's films. Also performed in *Cleopatra* and *batteries not included* and onstage as Polonius to Richard Burton's Hamlet.[53]

is *the truth*. Because you're balancing so many things on stage and everything has changed from the night before.

STEVEN: Including the audience.

GEORGE: And, while they're included, you can't live on their expectations, or your expectations of their behaviour. Which means, you don't play for the laughs... as you'll be 'caught out' more often.

you're balancing so many things.

STEVEN: But you have to be sensitive to what they are giving you or not giving you. They're another player in the live performance.

GEORGE: They are the other player, *following* what you're doing: They are taking the move from you, so you can't let them lead the play—which you'll do if you let them laugh out until there's nothing left in the laugh. Then they've taken the timing away from the artist and that's deadly; so as you hear where the laugh has peaked, you must move in and be heard, which goes back to the diaphragm work etc. etc...

It's hard work, it really is. After a few years of being away from it, I couldn't bring myself to be on stage again.

STEVEN: It was too scary?

GEORGE: Too scary and the work was too hard for me. I wasn't even in good shape to be on stage. Which you have to be, you're an athlete.

STEVEN: When I did Molière's *Don Juan* outdoors in Ottawa, it was... Well, I was feeling my age and—instead of being continually on stage—had acted maybe once a year, and I wasn't in training. I really had to work. Just to maintain memory.

fitness

GEORGE: Sure, but so many other things are in play. The physical fitness is most important with the actor. On one occasion we took with us an actor, I kept giving him notes every night: "What's going on? You're missing this, you're missing that..." Finally it came to light that he was very high on drugs, on the stage.

STEVEN: Alcohol will do the same thing.

GEORGE: Sure it will. It slows you up.

STEVEN: And it's very hard to keep a sense of alertness and remain true to the rhythm of the play, it's very easy to destroy that.

GEORGE: And you think you *are*, that's the other deceitful thing about it. No, no, you can't afford any of that.

The Magic "If"

exercise: job of work

GEORGE: The next lesson I would take the actors onto something I call "Job of Work." You need a big floor, with lots of room, and they move about, separately, choosing their own little work area. I suggest to them that they are doing a 'job of work.' Around their home, their apartment, so it's something they're familiar with. Usually it's ironing, or washing the dishes, or sweeping the floor.

STEVEN: You try to keep to a fairly simple activity.

GEORGE: Yes, nothing terribly involved: They're going to have to *mime* the tools they'll use—the ironing board, the iron, the wall they'll plug it into etc. Sometimes it's useful for them to reach into the cupboard to get the tools to start work.

Whatever they choose to do I accept... as long as I can see it. And I'm watching all these people scrubbing the dishes or the floor, painting fences, and it's all full of life. Everybody finds it easy to concentrate on the objects they're using. We have done a little mime work by now, so they know enough to *see well* what they're handling, and *they don't have to see everything at once*: They only have to see what they're touching. As they need the table, there it is—but not before they need it!

STEVEN: Yes.

GEORGE: So there's great energy on the floor all around 'cause everybody's doing things, but gradually, as the last dish is washed, they feel silly washing more dishes or starting all over again—which they wouldn't really do.... 'So what now?' They slow down gradually, first one, then another, and I patiently hold still for all this. They look at me and say in their eyes 'Shall I go on?' And I won't give them an answer.

STEVEN: Why?

GEORGE: Because I'm not going to solve their problem for them. The problem that we're dealing with eventually is "The Magic 'If'" so I just let them go until they are bored to death with it. And there will be somebody who finishes ironing shirts, so they'll find something else to iron; they'll keep going and going and look at me—'Should I stop now?'—but still I don't say anything. I let *them* make the decision and when everybody has finally stopped, we all sit down together and I congratulate them on what they've done. I have *seen* the dishes and the cupboards, and as long as I can do that, that's good: They've handled those things well, what they did was true. It didn't *last*, but it was true...

I say: "Why did you and I get bored?"

"Well, I've done it," they'll tell you, "it's done." Well, the *stage* is not 'done'; it's never done if the imagination is still alert.

"You took all those clothes, hung them up in the closet. Why did you do that if you finished the work?"

"Oh, well, I didn't know what else to do" is the answer, usually.

STEVEN: That was when they thought things were finished?

GEORGE: Yes, and then they extended it because I didn't stop them, but eventually they seem to run out of things to do. That, of course, is mistaking the *object* for the *work*. They thought the job was only to iron the shirt. It's not: *The job is the job of Imagination.*

the job is the job of imagination.

STEVEN: Mmhmmn.

GEORGE: Because, with the proper Given Circumstances, you may never get that shirt ironed! If I sent Charlie Chaplin up there, he wouldn't even get the ironing board (*Steven laughs*) in place. He'd be all day trying to get it together. That's the difference. Why did you laugh? Why do we all laugh? Why do my students laugh, when I make such suggestions? It's because *he exploits the Given Circumstances with 'If'* and he can go on until you are tired—but *he's* not (*Steven laughs*) because he's always got a new challenge; he supplies it for himself.

In a play, you're given the Circumstances, the lines, all that: *You* must supply the 'If' to bring it alive. Stanislavski would call it "The Magic 'If'."

So I'd ask the person, for instance, making the birdhouse: "Give me an 'If'." Because it's an intellectual exercise, you think about it before you start, so I say: "Well, the *job* is building the birdhouse, but *what if...*" and I expect him or her to complete the sentence. "*What if* she couldn't find the nails? *What if* she only had three minutes to complete this birdhouse? *What if* she had to have the room cleaned up, and the birdhouse painted, before her mother got home?"... So you can go on and on, continually playing with the Given Circumstances.

fantasy

Suppose then you dealt into fantasy with the 'If': "What if the paint wouldn't stick? What if I can't see it because it's invisible?" Well, certainly that's still workable. The only thing is, you can't contradict the Given Circumstance which you've added: If somebody else comes in and starts to paint, *they* can't be able to see it either. So they must be knowledgeable of your Given Circumstances. Or if they *can* see it, there's something wrong with your eyes. Which, then, is still holding on to the fantasy.

Fantasy is interesting—especially in these days of Walt Disney's terrible films. He contradicts his fantasies all the time. He doesn't sustain the premise he begins with. I only cringe when I see *The Hunchback of Notre Dame* coming out. The look of the man is like a little kid with—as somebody said—a 'bad hair day.' (*Steven laughs*) So, you know, the whole thing is lost—especially on children who want to be horrified by that man, and *should* be. *Then* you have sympathy for him. But if he's a nice cute little guy, what's the point in having sympathy with him later? The story means nothing. Victor Hugo is turning in his grave...

When I convince my actors to deal in fantasy, and they walk through a wall that was there already, they must include that within the Given Circumstances; and if somebody else comes in and *can't* go through the wall, that's quite a surprise to the first actor.

STEVEN: It's got to be accounted for.

GEORGE: Yes! Exactly. That's why actors have got to see what the other person is creating, because they are moving in on his or her Circumstances. They must retain them or they'll be in terrible trouble.

the difficulty of teaching the magic *if*

STEVEN: In working with "The Magic 'If'" with students, you find it one of the most difficult concepts to get across. Why?

GEORGE: I don't know why. It's only "Let's pretend!" But that's difficult: To convince yourself completely to pretend. You're not going to give up that sense of self in order to pretend. Our imagination has been curtailed in our school systems. I went through public school and came out of it a dunce. I spent eight years having the imagination knocked out of me. I think that's one of the difficulties of teaching "The Magic 'If'"—that we don't believe in *magic* any more, and we can't *allow* ourselves to believe in magic without the possibility of being made a fool of.

That's why Stanislavski calls it "The *Magic* 'If'." He also talks about trust: "I didn't say you *were* a snail, I said '*What if* you became a snail?' So you can trust that I'm not lying to you. You're a human being, you stand on two feet, you can talk; but *what if* you were a snail?" Then you have to imagine it.

STEVEN: "The Magic 'If'" is the opposite of that notion of "living the role."

GEORGE: Ohhh yes.

STEVEN: Yeah as much as it frees the imagination, it also frees, I think, the mind and soul of the actor. Say you're playing a 'monster' or... Edmund in *King Lear*: You don't have to go through that yourself. You can apply "*What if*." *What if*... I were in these circumstances?'

the magic *if* vs. memory recall

GEORGE: Oh such a good point, Steven, because the 'Method' school of acting—

STEVEN: The Strasberg version.[1]

GEORGE: Yes. They concentrated for years on Memory Recall, to the point of absurdity. They wanted you to try and think about your father's death, and have real tears pouring down your face. If you do that enough times, you'd be in a psychiatric ward. I had actors come to me who had been exposed to that kind of training who were shattered. They weren't any use until we unwrapped all that.

That was a misreading of that chapter because Stanislavski talked about memory taking shape and changing: The first time, it's one thing; the next time, it's something else. It becomes easier to handle; it becomes more artful, an artistic interpretation of what was originally a horrifying experience. Because you can't put the horrifying experience on stage; we don't want to go through it again, thank you very much. You can't have a rape scene and

1. Lee Strasberg (1901-1982)—Influential American actor, director and teacher. Director of the Actors Studio in New York, one of the most prestigious acting schools in the U.S. Eventually called the 'Strasberg Method,' 'Method Acting' requires an actor to re-live past emotional experiences in order to bring a character to life. (54) "Memory Recall' is sometimes translated as "Affective" or "Emotion(al) Memory." [(s.b.)]

actually rape someone on the stage; you can't have a murder scene and really kill someone; nor can you light a real fire in a fireplace. All these things are verboten. What you *do* need is "The Magic 'If'."

Charlie Chaplin and the magic *if*

Getting back to Chaplin again, I often give the example of somebody who has a 'job of work' that requires changing a light bulb in the ceiling and therefore will get a ladder out and go up and start changing the bulb. I will say "My God, if you gave that to Chaplin, he wouldn't even get the ladder out!" (*Steven laughs*) You know, he wouldn't get it fixed right, and he would slip his leg through a rung as he went up. To ask him to carry up a bulb and change it is a horrendous task. In fact, I used it in one of our plays, called *Faces*—the challenge of changing a light bulb. The actor was able to exploit it to its fullest extent—which was hilarious in this case—but it was *true*.

That's what happens with "The Magic 'If'." It allows you to do the thing—not for its result, not for "This will make them laugh or cry." You tackle it because you're answering the question of 'What if?' and answering it honestly. *I don't concern myself with results*: It may be humourous, it may not, it doesn't matter.

STEVEN: You're dealing with each problem as it comes up.

GEORGE: Yes. They should be able to go on that stage and hold it for thirty minutes and never bore us—and they can do that by the 'If'! More and more 'Ifs' keep tumbling in their mind and they respond, hopefully, to fix the problem. Or don't fix it, depending on their own ability and their wit. So it's a very important lesson and the first step in finding the actors you want.

STEVEN: I found it very enlightening, for students, to show them a short solo film that Chaplin did called *One A.M.* Basically, he's in one set for about twenty minutes and all he does is deal with the problems he sets for himself.

GEORGE: Mmhmmn.

STEVEN: He leaves a taxi, he enters the porch, he is too drunk, he has forgotten his key, he climbs in the window so then, fine, he's inside the house.... But no, he *forgets* that he's inside the house, goes back out on the porch, opens the door with the key, then comes in again. And one problem after the other he finds: Suddenly uhh the stuffed bear—it's part of the décor of his house—it's suddenly *alive* to him. (*Both chuckle*) He's totally frightened.

Charlie Chaplin with fellow actors in *One A.M.* (1916) / *photographer unknown*

GEORGE: He's completed one 'If' and he goes on to another 'If' and another. He's got all the props in the world to play with, and if you've seen the out-takes[2] of his—they're marvellous to see—so you see him going over the same thing again and cutting this and that... but still improvising on his feet all the time. He filmed everything—which is good for us 'cause we see it all. But he's using—without knowing the actual book at the time—he's using all the techniques of Stanislavski's, using them on his feet. All that Stanislavski has done is *analyze the work*. He's given us a way in, because if we're not geniuses like Charlie Chaplin—and there are very few of those fellas—we need a way of working that will bring us to the truth, and not fall into the traps of clichés.

STEVEN: In the Thirties he was quoted in an interview saying that he was using "The Magic 'If'" for all his creative work.

GEORGE: He did so *instinctively* long before anybody had put a word to it. It's so obvious, too, in his out-takes: You see the process. He gets angry at some of the other actors, and shows them what he expects of them—because he was great at that, always showing people what to do. Something I try to avoid, but for him it was OK. (*Steven laughs*) ... But what a teacher—brilliant!

2. *Unknown Chaplin*, a two-part series produced by Kevin Brownlow for Thames Television in 1983.[55]

the magic *if* at TWP: *Arturo Ui* & *Mr Pickwick*

STEVEN: What about times where you've seen "The Magic 'If'" *work*?

GEORGE: Oh yes, I'm thinking about *Arturo Ui*—marvellous use of 'If's! Remember that famous thing with Dullfeet, who was murdered? The fellow shot him while he was shaking hands so that he couldn't reach for his gun. Everybody was plants in the flower shop and Barry Flatman got up on.. what? A case. We had warehouse cases as a part of our set and he was a man-eating plant…

STEVEN: Ha.

GEORGE: … which was in keeping with the threat to Dullfeet's life, and anybody else, so if you got close to Barry, you were indeed in danger of being eaten. (*George laughs*) He did all kinds of things with his features, with his position and his tongue, most convincingly, 'cause it was like a fly-trap.

STEVEN: Did he ever actually eat any of the other characters?

GEORGE: No, he just reached for them (*Both chuckle*) and they were aware of his presence…. But that was the 'If.' The whole play was covered in it, all our work was.

STEVEN: You were gonna tell me an anecdote about *Pickwick*…

GEORGE: Oh yes! Oh, we had a wonderful challenge of doing all the marvellous things that happen to Pickwick. He doesn't travel more than a couple of kilometres from London (*both laugh*) but

Mr Pickwick (1981-82). Actors (l-r): Fiona McMurran, François-Regis Klanfer, Michael Marshall & William Colgate / *photo by Craig Parkinson*

what happens to him in that travelling is *wonderful*, and he's always the butt of it all.

But in this case the Unit had to do with a cricket game between a local team and a much better team. I didn't know how to play, but one of the actors did; Michael Marshall was very expert at cricket. And he had to tell us the rules—which were *hilarious* to us novices. But we played the rules, very carefully, and when it came to improvising the game, everybody took their time at bat and uh the premise was that they would have a problem with the ball, in some way. That it would either hit them and—not to do with just they were bad players—some terrible thing would happen to them each time. We spent all afternoon on this wonderful problem with the actors, who didn't wanna leave it 'cause (*Steven laughs*) they were having so much fun inventing, with the "Magic 'If,'" ways of being defeated by the ball. And we had no ball, but it was *seen to go*. And if somebody up in the audience caught it, we accepted it. It went off swimmingly, all afternoon, with people getting maimed with the ball. (*Steven laughs*) And I always recall Don Meyers[3] coming up early on and taking his stance and then the actor who was bowling threw the ball and Don gave a *terrible* cry... and stood stoically still. Because you don't give way at cricket: You behave yourself. We knew the attitude of the cricketers.

STEVEN: Hmmn.

GEORGE: And then he limped off, carefully protecting his foot, as he had been hit by the ball (*both laugh*) and the actors waited until he'd gone and then they picked up the ball—again, the *invisible* ball. Then a couple of other actors would come up, and then *Don* would turn up again, with his foot wrapped up in a bandage which he found backstage. And once again the ball would be thrown at him, and this time there'd be a freezing attitude on the part of Don who had received the ball on his arm. (*Laughs*) He went off with a sore arm, came back with it done up in a sling and eventually, by the end of the afternoon (*both are laughing*)... he was like a mummy coming out on the stage, he'd been hit so many places: Bandages on the head, bandages—He was well wrapped-up! And not a smirk... as if this game was the most meaningful thing ever played.

3. Donald Meyers—Actor in many TWP shows, noted for his comic performances in *The Mechanic* and *Before Compiègne* as well as for an outstanding 'Caliban' in *The Tempest* with John Neville at National Arts Centre. (s.b.) [56]

And they even managed to *end* the improvisation. It was Ray Whelan and Ray was playing the old lady, the grandmother, among other parts. The ball came at him and he took a vicious swing... with every part of his body... and the pose ended with the cricket bat in the air, his arms stretched out above him, and stayed perfectly still.... So where did the ball go? And everybody looked at each other, all over the field. And there was no hint from Ray... except this terrible swing.

STEVEN: What happened?

GEORGE: Well, they had to figure it out. I said nothing, and they all looked at him. They waited awhile, and he hadn't changed position. And they slowly, together, from around the stage, moved in on him until they got right up close and then they, all together, hoisted him up above their heads and took him off the field. He'd thrown his back out, obviously, and couldn't move. And he *didn't* move. (*Both laugh*) And they took him off in that faith. It was magnificent.

We kept that in, of course. That's how the cricket game ended. I said nothing but sat there roaring my head off. We went on all afternoon! And I was so flabbergasted and on opening night, Whittaker[4], the critic, just loved the show and was telling me so in the back room. I say: "Well one day, Herb, I'll tell you about our cricket game. I'll tell you all about it." I didn't want to tell him *then* because he hadn't written his article yet; it would seem like 'feeding' him—which is very naughty and I wouldn't do.

collaboration with the actors

So the examples in our work are all over the place. That's what made our plays successful so often 'cause it was the actors improvising with "The Magic 'If'" and creating new things I'd never thought of before.

STEVEN: A lot of directors don't realize that, when they're prescriptive with actors, they really rob themselves of all that the actors can give to the work.

GEORGE: Absolutely. And they have a mistaken idea in our capitalist society that they must be the genius; there's only room for one genius at a time. And that's bullshit. My joy was, so often, like

4. Herbert Whittaker (1910-2006)—Distinguished Canadian theatre critic. Originally from Montreal, he began as a stage designer, then moved to directing. Later, Whittaker took up posts with the *Montreal Gazette* and *The Globe and Mail* as theatre, dance and film critic. Whittaker was a prime mover in creating Theatre Museum Canada and the first national chairman of Canadian Theatre Critics Association. Member of the Order of Canada. [57]

Chicago '70, sitting there watching the imagination of twelve talented people go to work.

STEVEN: But I think there always is that creative tension in making a show... between on the one hand a kind of control which rightly or wrongly the director wants to have—if only the responsibility to getting the story out clearly.

GEORGE: Sure.

STEVEN: On the other hand, we want this *preparation* so that we can watch an *improvisational act* take place before our eyes. I think directors tend to fall within two camps, right? Either the 'control freaks' or the uh the 'improvisationalists.' But *Chicago '70* was a situation where creative spontaneity was honoured, but you as director also harnessed that and focussed it....

GEORGE: Sure, yeah, yeah.

STEVEN: ... so that we had, in spite of the pains that all of us went through in that process, something that was exhilarating. And that made a collective statement. But it also had a good form.

GEORGE: Yeah.

STEVEN: Yeah?

GEORGE: That's right. But the director mustn't be frightened of *taking time* to allow the actors to discover *their* truth.

cleverness contradicting the through-line in *Arturo Ui*

Actors can do bad work and you recognize it, if you're trained as a director, immediately. In *Arturo Ui* our actors were so imaginative that Don Meyers played Goebbels with a club foot, limping across the stage, and managed to get Len[5]—the awful Brownshirt—and himself together at one point so that Goebbels managed to step on his hand... all planned ahead of time. *(Both chuckle)*

STEVEN: And Len was playing along with it.

GEORGE: Playing along with it and screaming like hell, unbeknownst to Goebbels. (*Both laugh*) Now that was a funny piece of work which I cut immediately.

STEVEN: Because it was too clever?

GEORGE: It was clever by half, but also was *not spontaneous*: You had nowhere to go. It was stuck on and it corrupted the Unit, because all I could see was those two guys hamming it up. I laughed with everybody else, then I cut it! (*Laughs*)

5. Len Doncheff—Actor who performed in many TWP productions over the years, including *Before Compiègne, Faces, Les Canadiens* and *Richard Thirdtime*. Film credits include *One Night Stand, Strange Brew* and *The Life and Hard Times of Guy Terrifico.* [58]

STEVEN: And did they hate you?

GEORGE: They hated me. (*Both laugh*) But they were contradicting the Through-line. We mustn't take any detours that aren't welcome—even if they're as amusing as that.

Let me give you an example when it did work. It was *Les Canadiens*. Astrid[6] had built us an audience, it was brilliant. She put dummies all over the set—which was supposed to be the Montreal stadium—always looked like it had people in attendance. The dummies were life-size and looked fairly real, with amusing faces. In fact, she made one look like Rick Salutin[7]. Rick never knew. (*Both laugh*)

cleverness supporting the through-line in *Les Canadiens*

STEVEN: Did she make one that looked like you?

GEORGE: I don't know; she might have, she was very clever.

We're in the Forum, in the Fifties when they played the national anthem, and the spark of Separatism was coming forward in a new Quebec. This was all part of the play, using the metaphor of hockey for the politics of the time.

Well, at this moment Len was part of the audience, and the anthem went on. Like a good WASP, he stood to attention and he looked over and the dummy wasn't standing. (*Steven chuckles*) So, after a few curses, he told him to stand up—which he wouldn't—so eventually he attacked the dummy... and both went over the seats (*Steven laughs*) and all you saw were legs up in the air: Len and the dummy were having a furious fight over the national anthem. And *that* was a *good* 'If.'

STEVEN: That's what the scene is about.

GEORGE: Yes, and the next day we would come to the same part, and they had their fight, and this time Len *lost*: The dummy won and came back and sat. (*Laughs*)

STEVEN: Oh, really?

6. Astrid Janson (b. 1947)—Award-winning scenographer for theatre, dance, television and opera. Janson began as a professional costume designer for Toronto Dance Theatre, Global Village and Theatre Compact. Her work with TWP (1974-82) produced many famous set designs and established her as an insightful and collaborative designer. Janson has won eight Dora Mavor Moore awards and is a member of the Associated Designers of Canada. [(59)]

7. Rick Salutin (b. 1942)—Prominent Canadian novelist, playwright, columnist for *The Globe and Mail* and *Toronto Star* and author of *Les Canadiens* (with an assist from Ken Dryden), *1837: The Farmers' Revolt* (with Theatre Passe Muraille), *The False Messiah* and *Nathan Cohen: A Revue*. [(60)]

Les Canadiens (1977). As the players do a pile-up, Astrid's dummy 'audience' observes from the stands. / *photographer unknown*

GEORGE: Len stayed out with his feet up in the air—hilarious! This is wit of extraordinary kind, and all in keeping with the Through-Line and with the Given Circumstances of course.

STEVEN: It seems to me that some directors are afraid of the actors' creativity. Why do you think this is?

exploiting actors in the correct sense

GEORGE: Oh, I think it's lack of knowledge and understanding. They don't want to seem like a fool in front of their actors. Directors sometimes, I think, feel an obligation to be *the* creativity in the show and therefore don't want anyone doing anything of their own. These are all wrong reasons and are based on our society which rewards the 'brilliant' people.

That's why you had critics who misunderstood our work continually. They would talk very often about how brilliant the director is and I remember most things praised were created by the actors. We were creating the atmosphere for the best work of the actor. I was exploiting their talents... which hadn't been exploited before.

STEVEN: Mmhmmn.

GEORGE: This is true in *Ain't Lookin'*[8] where I had an all-black cast. These were all actors who had never been on my stage before, and on very few other stages except to play servants and to be shuffled about as the director saw fit—very often the only one in the cast

8. *Ain't Lookin'*—TWP production (1980 & 84) based on the book *Chappie and Me* by John Craig. It dealt with issues of racism by portraying baseball players touring in one of the 'Negro League' circuits in the 1930s. [61] As of Summer 2012, Robin Breon and Joe Sealy have developed a musical adaptation of this TWP classic.[s.b.]

who was black. I was teaching them to work within the short rehearsal period, and also creating a play at the same time. I have been doing this for years so that I knew how to approach it. And they were ecstatic for the opportunities I gave them and some of them went overboard and were giving me all kinds of things I didn't need. I'd remind them of the Given Circumstances of the ball team and the bus that they were travelling in, and they'd come back to their senses 'cause they knew and understood that. They were talented bright people, who had never been exploited *in the correct sense* before.

And I think that's what you've got to do, and that's what a lot of directors don't know. They don't know Analysis. You see so often plays in which everybody is playing their own play. And this is a lack of knowledge on the part of the director to bring his people together.

STEVEN: Do you think it has anything to do with the fact that many directors haven't acted?

GEORGE: Well, it's tempting to say that, but they can have the spirit without having been on the stage. They don't have to have gone through the process that I did as long as they understand their Analysis. All that being on the stage does is help you be a *better* director. I think it's true of Shakespeare, who must have had a hand in directing as well as writing. The fact that Ibsen was a stage manager for a long time...

STEVEN: I didn't know that.

GEORGE: ... didn't hurt him when he came to writing plays. They're all *in the theatre*. You don't have to be an actor, but you *are* a theatre *worker*—lighting, designing, costuming, anything. They're all adjuncts of the main purpose.

Text Analysis

GEORGE: Friday afternoon.
STEVEN: June 21st 1996.
GEORGE: I'm sitting in my newly-acquired scooter.
STEVEN: Another change of circumstance.
GEORGE: Absolutely.
STEVEN: And you've been able to get around in the neighbourhood.
GEORGE: So nice to get out and be independent. At the moment, I can't make it down as far as St. Clair, walking, it's too far—about ten yards or so, but then I... really need a rest. They told me at the hospital I'd always be wheelchair-dependent, because of the heart. I don't mind that as long as I can, you know, cover ground.
STEVEN: You got this scooter to replace the wheelchair.
GEORGE: Well, it's not dependable any more: Every month or so I send it in to be repaired and that's over $200 a kick. So I put that money towards the purchase of a new scooter and they gave me a decent price on it because I was a customer. (*Laughs*) An unwilling customer. (*Steven chuckles*)

exercise: analyzing the text

So today... Ummm the first step is to read the play thoroughly. The Circumstances are the text, and no one's about to rewrite the text—except in great difficulties when the director is sure of himself and knows the Analysis of the play and can correct the writer.

STEVEN: You read the script once or twice to get a broad view of the basic Given Circumstances. Then what do you do? Do you try to find, immediately, the Through-Line for the whole play?
GEORGE: No, no, can't be done, the Through-Line is hidden. We've read the play through and now we're going to divide the script up into Units.

how big is a unit?

How big is a Unit? It's as much as you can handle comfortably in Analysis. Like the story of the pie: If somebody hands you a pie out of the oven and says to eat it, and you have to eat it all at once, you choke on it. Same way with the script: If you see all this play in front of you, you start worrying that it's too big for you and you could freeze up, actually, at the challenge.

So, we cut it into *pieces that are manageable* and give each piece a *name.* And the naming of it is very important, so I don't name it myself: I'll encourage *the actors* to choose the right name for the Unit.

STEVEN: How do you determine that—what the right name is?

naming the unit

GEORGE: By its excitement. All of a sudden all eyes light up and say 'Yeah, *that's* right!' And up to that point you get a lot of dull observations which may be correct but they don't make you want to *do* anything. So, very important to spend the time on naming the Unit according to what it contains. In fact that's the first question I ask the actors: *"What can the unit not do without?"*

STEVEN: I remember that question.

GEORGE: In order to find out the *centre* of that Unit. It also perhaps determines how large that Unit is. If you have a play the size of *Hamlet*, you don't want to cut it up into threads. [*Steven chuckles*] It will be too much work. You won't find Objectives that are different from one Unit to the next.

The test is to put it onto the stage: You may find out that you've either misnamed the Unit or you've made it too small, or too big, in which case the Unit deserves a greater breakdown.

STEVEN: What do you do if, on their feet, the actors feel... 'Wrong Objective!'?

GEORGE: Then we correct them... as long as they don't contradict the Given Circumstances or the name of the Unit. If that has to change, *everybody* has to agree upon it, because that is what makes the play *one*—that we are all in the same Unit together. (*George laughs*)

unit changes and objective changes

STEVEN: How do you decide when one Unit ends and another begins?

GEORGE: Change of Objective.

STEVEN: For the character who primarily drives the Unit? Or for everyone?

GEORGE: Good point. You never know quite *which* until you're up on your feet. 'Cause you think one is pushing and then you realize, in the playing of it, someone else has pushed you into the second Unit. Then, of course, *all Objectives change because the Unit has changed*; you don't leave anybody in the first Unit.

That may *seem* unnecessary. In *Time of Your Life,* for instance, there's an actor who sits at the table all through the play at the restaurant—

STEVEN: William Saroyan?

GEORGE: Yes—and I remember the actor who had no lines but just sat behind this table—carved his initials into the table top, even actually did so while the play was going on. Later on I thought to myself: 'I'm disturbed at that' ... because he was *taking himself out of the Unit.*

Of course there was no Analysis in that company. This man could seemingly get away with it, just doing his own thing at the table. But there were possibly contributions he didn't make because he didn't move with the Units as they changed; his Objectives didn't change.

STEVEN: He didn't understand his character's connection to the whole piece.

GEORGE: No, and his character *wasn't* connected to the whole piece. The injudicious found that interesting and amusing, but looking back at it years later, not at all. ...

(*Recorder stops. Pause. Goes back on*)

STEVEN: OK after a change of batteries we'll try again ...

GEORGE: And you had a question.

STEVEN: Yes, what was it?

GEORGE: You've probably forgotten by now. (*Laughs*)

STEVEN: Oh, the question was: Where the name of the Unit changes, does the Objective for *every* character change?

GEORGE: I believe so—even if it's a subtle change—because the name of the Unit has changed, and *to ignore that is to leave your character to stagnate without being involved in the overall play.* So even if they have no words, their Objective changes as the play moves from Unit to Unit.

It's important, the *name* you give to the Unit 'cause now—without having mentioned it to anyone—your choice of title is in effect *interpreting* the work. This is why a director like myself, while I encourage everybody to be involved in naming the Unit, I'm very careful that I get the name pleases me as an interpreter.

analysis & interpretation: *When We Dead Awaken*

For instance, being a Marxist, I don't want a religious connotation to affect the interpretation of the play. I'll give you an example. We analysed over a long difficult period *When We Dead Awaken*, Ibsen's last play, which is full of religious metaphors—the whole thing is a religious metaphor. I felt it had suffered from self-indulgence, but I always think that about religious figures. (*Steven laughs*) There was in the class, playing a lead role, a young man who had just found Catholicism. And it's like a Communist who just found Communism, you know: They are more Communist than the Communist. I had no intention allowing the religious nature of the play to dominate the work so we had a real tussle, the two of us, but I knew very well that if I didn't solve this problem in Analysis, it wouldn't be the play I thought it should be when we got to rehearsal because his influence was strong. When he'd start to go astray, I'd remind him what the Unit was named and what we had already thrashed out in Analysis; and that he must be playing that Unit because we agreed upon it.

And so Analysis is very useful for a director [*chuckles*] ... if he's got the kind of Analysis he intends on that play.

STEVEN: On the one hand, you want the involvement of the whole cast in naming it, so that we have a common centre to work from.

GEORGE: Yes.

STEVEN: On the other hand, you want to nudge it, or veer it, in the direction of the interpretation.

GEORGE: Or push it. (*Laughs*)

STEVEN: Push it. (*Laughs*)

GEORGE: Yes. I'm no apologist for that. I choose a play because it has moved me in some manner and there's some things I want to achieve with that play and I'm not going to allow another interpretation to destroy that.

STEVEN: If the religious content is very strong, are you not being unfaithful to the writer if you disregard it?

GEORGE: No, I didn't say disregard it but put it in its proper place. It had a place within the play in the metaphor of climbing up the mountain. So no, it's the *emphasis* that's important. The emphasis that I chose was the one I strove for. Now, I couldn't have kept it if I couldn't have convinced the gentleman who was playing the lead role that it was valid... which I managed to do.

STEVEN: Have you ever encountered a situation where a cast talked you out of an interpretation, or you came to see it differently?

GEORGE: Yes. I can't remember what play it was, but it surprised me. In rehearsal I thought it was going one way and it turned out to be quite different. And I was delighted: It was more exciting than what I had imagined. I remember sitting back and saying... "My God, is this the play we started with?" And I was quite humbled in what had turned out.

STEVEN: So even though you enter with your own interpretation, you *are in the process*; you are receptive to input from actors.

GEORGE: Absolutely, because you have something to change *from*.

STEVEN: It's so clear when work goes off-track that the Analysis has been off, or there just hasn't been enough time spent on it.

GEORGE: Yeah that's right...

exercise: choosing objectives

Having divided the play up into Units, I would do the whole play through—all the Units—before I did anything else—because the next step is very important too: Choosing Objectives *within* a Unit.

STEVEN: For each character?

GEORGE: For each character. And I don't allow them to choose the same Objective; that's not possible.

Two people, you and I, are working together at this moment at a project, but we have different Objectives, in attempting to ask the questions and answer the questions. We seem to be doing the same thing but indeed we're *not*.. in the sense of the Objectives which are different for us both.. but we're in *the same Unit*.

STEVEN: Yes. (*Laughs*)

GEORGE: Otherwise, we couldn't work.

So the Objective now, instead of a noun, is worded with a *verb*. I like the term "I must." What is the correct verb for this Objective? 'I must *be*'? The 'be' verb is inactive and therefore of no use to us. It must be an *active* verb that pushes the actor into the next Unit. So that's.. "I must".. and then the verb.. "I must *awaken*."

STEVEN: That gives you something to do.

GEORGE: Yes. And again, from the name of the Unit—which is a *noun*—you find your Objective. And we say the *main* Objective 'cause it's not the only Objective; in a Unit, you'll have many objectives. But all the others will be related: You won't contradict the main Objective. It's all very well to choose an Objective, but the *playing* it—holding on like a bulldog to that Objective as long as the Unit hasn't changed—is a *task*, and is very rewarding. But you must not let it go.

There are good Objectives and bad Objectives. There are those Objectives that are just not thrilling, not moving; they don't push you ahead. There's a whole list in the Stanislavski book of what *an Objective* should contain, and one is that it *must push you ahead* and not let you stagnate. With the actors in the early days I will make judgements, all the time, whether it's a good or bad Objective: Whether it's exciting to play; whether it interests the actor, or is he just filling in the words for the sake of giving an answer? You've got to have an *active* Objective, one that moves you onto the stage: You *want* to play it. It may be a *true* Objective but it's not exciting: "I must murder my mother." (*Steven chuckles*) But ... "I must *dispose* of my mother" may be more exciting. It depends on the actor 'cause it's his Objective, not mine; he plays it, not me the director. I can help choose the name of the Unit, but when it comes to Objectives it's up to him or her.

STEVEN: And you keep pointing it out when it's not active.

GEORGE: When I'm not satisfied. When *I* don't want to play it, look it that way. 'Cause I'm an actor and I say: "That doesn't make me want to get up and work (*both laugh*) ... but this one does."

STEVEN: That's the key thing about Objectives.

GEORGE: And you know it in the group 'cause everybody will be laughing and roaring, getting excited with the right Objective. When it's a dull one, everyone sits there 'dulling' through.... (*Steven laughs*) while that choice is being made.

Another thing that happens—this is rare, but more so with amateur actors—if the director is not satisfied with the Objective the actor has chosen, eventually he must give that actor an Objective. And that's *disaster.* You haven't got an actor in there then; you've got an automaton—someone who's taken *from you* the name of his or her Objective. In my company you'd never get that happening 'cause the actors would be too ashamed to have the director choose an Objective for them.

Actors should have *wits*. They should be well-read. They should have the vocabulary. Those are other things that test whether or not you are going to have an actor in your company.

But I've seen actors who, on the surface, seemed dull and who *blossom* because they're *encouraged*. They're encouraged by the name of the Unit; they're encouraged, having read the whole play; they're encouraged by the work of others and . . . they become better. And sometimes you get the *wildest* suggestions out of those very people, who have been *hiding* all the time. That's one of the joys of theatre: This is a place of education. *I got my entire education in the theatre.*

encouragement & education

STEVEN: Oh me too, yeah. (*Laughs*) We get to explore so many different realms of life . . .

GEORGE: Exactly.

STEVEN: Ourselves and other people and society, history, art.

GEORGE: If you learn the Analysis of a play, it's useful all through life. We'd analyze things that weren't plays. That's fun. We took Dostoyevski's work. We started on the prologue and we found out that it contained the entire novel. All the elements were in the prologue.

And that, of course, reminds me of *Hamlet*. How could you write a thriller better than starting out with "Who goes there?" You know, the perfect line. Shakespeare understood Stanislavski completely. (*Steven laughs*) Never having, you know (*laughs*) met him because it's four hundred years too soon or something, but anyways . . . you can analyze *Hamlet*, it's easy.

STEVEN: There's such a focus on action throughout Shakespeare's writing.

GEORGE: Yes indeed, the Units just tumble by, even as you're analyzing.

STEVEN: I think *time* is one of the big issues here. I know that with myself—and I've seen other directors toss out or skim over the Analysis work because we have three weeks to put a show on stage.

analysis, time-pressures & opening night

GEORGE: Yes, it's too difficult.

STEVEN: Now I recall having something like eight weeks on *Mr Bones*. I think we had a couple of months on *Chicago '70*. We had a little less on *The Tempest*, I think we only had five; but that was a short rehearsal for us, wasn't it? Five weeks *now* is a *long* rehearsal.

The Tempest (1969) – Caliban (*Mel Dixon*) receives an unwelcome visit from Prospero (*Steven Bush)* and Miranda (*Diane Grant*). Highly transformable set design by Nancy (Jowsey) Lewis / *photographer unknown*

GEORGE: We already had a script, didn't we? (*Both laugh*)

I used to remember six-week rehearsals, as a standard, but sometimes we took eight.

Further to that point you raised: *To do the analysis, you're actually saving time.* If you're afraid 'cause we only have so many weeks and you think sitting about in a circle analyzing a play is not doing anything... but you're doing a great deal, and it's time saved when you get up on your feet.

I've given you an example of *not* taking the time—*Ain't Lookin'*. I wanted to move actors and do all my directing and all that nonsense. So it wasn't until we came to *re-rehearsing* the play, for the touring production, that I sat down—with the encouragement of one of my old actors—and analyzed the play... which gave us a greater depth. It gave us more detail, it gave us a sharper play—and sharper work for the actors. We had a better rehearsal period, even though we have taken that time—a week—to analyze.

STEVEN: One of the actors nudged you to do it.

GEORGE: He wouldn't give up, said "George I think we should do it." It was Ross Skene[1], kept pushing.

1. Ross Skene (b. 1952)—Actor and musician in many TWP productions including *Richard Thirdtime*, *Ten Lost Years* and *Summer '76*. From 1972 to 1985, Ross probably clocked more working hours with George than any other performer. George's teaching/directing assistant and music coordinator on *Ain't Lookin'* and *The Wobbly*. Ross continues teaching privately and, by exercising his public voice as a political community activist, received an Ontario Provincial Award in 2008. (s.b.) (62)

STEVEN: Who had worked with you several seasons before.

GEORGE: Indeed, and saw the benefits of it. And also, we were dealing with new actors who hadn't been through this. That's what scared me, because I had to *explain* the process before we could do it. (*Laughs*) I was scared to death.

STEVEN: Were you always surprised by opening night?

GEORGE: Always.

STEVEN: 'Ah, here it is!' (*Both laugh*)

GEORGE: I always finish things in time but I didn't want to be hampered by the thought that I haven't enough time.. because if you do that, then you start taking shortcuts and destroy the work.

STEVEN: And you start panicking.

GEORGE: Yeah, and it's the wrong thing in the theatre. Some plays I worked for ages on the first Act. I remember Ray Whelan coming to me: "Good God, George, you're only on the first Act. (*Both laugh*) You know, we open in a week's time!"

STEVEN: "Will we ever get to the end?!"

GEORGE: Yeah, and my point was that we didn't know the play until we had correctly analyzed that first Act and got it on its feet and were working with it. When we knew it, the rest went fast.

STEVEN: What about the ending?

GEORGE: What about it?

STEVEN: Well... I recently saw *The Master Builder* down at the Royal Alex. You can't really comprehend that play, at least the Through-Line for Solness and Hilda, unless you know the ending. The whole play turns—which potentially turns your interpretation—in just those last few moments of the play.

GEORGE: Sure, you don't ignore it. We spent a long time on the first Act until we got it to my satisfaction and very little time was spent on the rest of the play 'cause the problems were all in the first Act. We solved those and solved the rest.

Everybody gets worried, everybody looks at the calendar... and I didn't keep a calendar, I didn't. And it's dangerous stuff, but that's life; life has to be dangerous.

STEVEN: It is.

GEORGE: That's the excitement of the theatre: The outcome is never known, especially in new work, and to watch new work being played for the first time anywhere in existence is really quite a high.

STEVEN: How do you deal with, say, a stage manager or administrator who might be watching the calendar a little more closely than you are?

GEORGE: Well, in my theatre as you know, we had a very enlightened administrator, in the form of June Faulkner, and she trusted me to get there. She knew I knew that it was coming up somewhere. (*Laughs*) And you *do*, way in the back of your head you do, but you're still ready to try things and, if they're not right, change them.

STEVEN: Even if the show has opened?

GEORGE: Oh yes, on occasion, sure, sure.

STEVEN: One of the things I see that is so, so disheartening is the fear that can seize a cast as opening night approaches—the fear that friends, family, critics, agents are gonna be out there judging them. Beautiful work that's been done in rehearsal suddenly is pulled back to a more conservative position.

GEORGE: Or it goes *forward*: All they're playing for is the critic in the front. Of course, Stanislavski deals with that in the chapter on Concentration of Attention. And the Analysis helps you because it gives you things to do *intellectually* as well as emotionally and you can be thinking about that rather than who's in the third seat in the fourth row.

exercise: the main objective of the unit

STEVEN: Once you've named the Units, where do you go?

GEORGE: Well, you find the Objective of each actor. You write all these things down on a big blackboard. You draw a big circle and divide the circle up into sections—call them 'Units'—and when we write all the Objectives of all the characters on the blackboard, the main Objective of the Unit will make itself known.

Then we get to our feet and everybody is playing their own Objectives and you see a *pattern* emerge as the first Unit moves into the second Unit, moves into the third Unit etc. throughout the play until you come to the end.

the through-line

And that's what we call a *Through-Line*. But it's very like life: Life has a Through-Line to it, and even if you're not conscious of it, it still is present.

STEVEN: Mmhmmn.

GEORGE: In order to explain that, I have got on the floor with a piece of chalk and divided my own life up into Units. And even though I haven't finished living it yet, I projected the possibilities of it, right or wrong, and then give each uh section a different name and an Objective.

exercise: the through-line of a life

STEVEN: I never saw you do that one.

GEORGE: Yeah I've done it and it's very funny. It sounds a bit self-indulgent, and maybe it is, but it's a quick way of showing everybody that things make sense according to life and nature. It's especially, in my own case, true in school, where I was a quite a dummy, and then choose Objectives like 'trying to get out of school.' (*Steven laughs*) Yet all these add up to a life in the theatre—the time that I was a commercial artist and a painter and ... all the many, many other things that have occurred. By the time you've reached middle-age, you can see all this's pulling together uhhh as it did, thankfully. You may, you know, end up in a hospital with a mental condition—if you break that Through-Line—not be able to carry on. I don't explain that 'cause that's going too deep ... and unnecessary really.

But the next step, I'll pick a student that, I'm guessing, is pretty exciting or everybody would like to hear about, and say: "Right, we're gonna analyze your day, from the moment you got up until you arrived in class this morning." And that can be a great deal of fun—long as your young person can sustain it and is honest—and they always are. (*Both laugh*) They're dragging themselves out of bed; they've got a hangover from last night; and all sorts of things happen, in this day. And get it on the blackboard, analyze it, have a lot of fun with it, and ... and it *works*.

exercise: the through-line of a day

STEVEN: And that you see as a model for a Through-Line of Action in a play.

GEORGE: I take simple things. My favourite is to take nursery rhymes, because they're so volatile and were written with a sense of revolution in them. "Jack and Jill went up the hill" is not about two nice little people (*Steven chuckles*), you know: It's about a lady in the court of Henry VIII and her lover who stepped out of line and were executed. 'One fell down and the other came tumbling after' ... as they lost their heads. It was based on that, or so it's believed. Because the only way the people could pass the news was by making up little stories.

analyzing nursery rhymes

STEVEN: A code.

GEORGE: Yes, a code, and it's our job to break it. You can treat it as two little children and analyze that way, but it's not as fun for me. And if I'm directing it's got to be fun for me.

STEVEN: Yeah, yeah. (*George laughs*) Otherwise, why do it? It's too much hard work.

GEORGE: Absolutely.... Nursery rhymes—simple, eh? They're not simple at all. The Analysis, again, is a great way to go 'cause it's based upon Nature.

STEVEN: You're talking the way Stanislavski might—about how our work as theatre-makers has to be in line with the rules of Nature.

GEORGE: Yes indeed, we are actors who are reacting *as people*. We have to understand what makes us tick and this is one way of doing it. I always say it's not the only way, but it's the best way I know of, and why ignore it? Nothing better has come along and it proves itself when you can analyze Molière and Shakespeare and Ibsen with his technique and it *works*.

analyzing *Les Canadiens*

When I took *Les Canadiens* apart... And Rick wanted the play done in my theatre 'cause he knew I could put a set of developed actors together to make it work; he wanted me there as a producer and paying the bills but didn't want me to direct. I took his advice and interviewed a number of people he suggested, and then some of my own, to see if they would tackle it. When I couldn't find anybody—and he couldn't find anybody—I said: "Alright, if it's going into my theatre, let's get on with it; but I want to talk to you on our own." And I went through an Analysis of the script with him, which took three days.

STEVEN: You talked through the whole play together?

GEORGE: Yeah, because there were scenes in that play I knew shouldn't be there, from the point of view of the Through-Line. They just took off in the wrong way, although they were interesting in themselves—and he loved them of course. I spent the three days trying to prove to him why the end of the play was wrong. It dealt all of a sudden with kids on the street playing Russia and Canada—'cause it was Canada against Russia in those days—and after having written a play that was quite powerful, he reverted to the children in the street. And I tried to prove, by the Through-Line, that this was wrong.

Also, he had the play moving from outside to inside and I said:

"No, the entire play must be played in the Forum, without going outside." He didn't believe we could until he saw it.

STEVEN: What did that achieve?

GEORGE: Continuity.

STEVEN: Unity of place.

GEORGE: Yes. And the Forum was such a powerful metaphor that was silly to lose.

STEVEN: And you found all the scenes could play there?

GEORGE: Well, I *made* them play. When they walked up the Montréal Mountain, I just had them walk up to the top of the Forum, which is quite steep. And the dialogue worked fine, in a very sensible way. When they were supposed to be outside buying tickets to see the game, I created those Given Circumstances *within* the Forum. And the interviews with the hockey players I put into the Forum—which one could assume had dressing rooms. When they all had to learn French, I brought the French teacher into the Forum and she had a hell of a time getting across the ice (*Steven laughs*) ... to the joy of all the players. Although there was no ice there, it was beautifully painted by Astrid, so that it looked like deep ice. And that worked.

In terms of the Through-Line, the play needed cutting.

STEVEN: Did you come to a consensus on that?

GEORGE: Well, I thought we did, I was sure we did, but writers who want their work produced are willing to say lots of things before the production, unfortunately. I mean, it's hard for them: They don't want to argue too much, I suppose, with the director who owns and runs the theatre. (*Steven chuckles*) They fear they'll lose it.

STEVEN: Yup.

GEORGE: So I rehearsed it all and, for his benefit, I rehearsed that last scene ... to the anger of the actors. (*Laughs*)

STEVEN: The actors didn't believe in the scene either?

GEORGE: No, they didn't believe in it. And anyway, up until the last day I kept trying it different ways, trying very hard to make it work, but in my heart I knew that it wasn't going to and when it came to the last rehearsal, I cut it. Rick was very upset and I didn't find that amusing, I found it difficult, and we talked in the office and—

STEVEN: The tape is rolling by the way.

GEORGE: Yeah.

STEVEN: I assume this doesn't … This is OK with you?

GEORGE: Sure.

STEVEN: Yeah?

GEORGE: Oh yeah, I've told this story many times. (*Steven chuckles*) I went over it again, why I was cutting it, 'cause it contradicted the Through-Line and he agreed … finally. I only realized at that point that he hadn't really agreed with our Analysis when we were talking before; otherwise, this problem wouldn't have come up the way it did. But he did agree, and I did make a few more cuts and I explained *them*.

you don't have self-pity on the stage.

One thing was self-pity. Which he mentioned years later in one of his columns in the paper. So nice. … You don't have self-pity on the stage. It's an anathema.

STEVEN: Why?

GEORGE: It's self-indulgent, it's seeking sympathy on a personal level which is unacceptable to an audience.

STEVEN: You mean, for a *character* to express a moment of self-pity?

GEORGE: Yes.

STEVEN: How do you deal with all those many moments in Chekhov, for example, where the characters—

GEORGE: It's funny—

STEVEN:—seem to be in a *world* of self-pity——

GEORGE:—it's funny, it's not serious.

STEVEN:—depending again, interpretively, on how the director and actors play it.

GEORGE: I wouldn't interpret it in the naturalistic manner that so many people do. It is a foolishness on the part of Uncle Vanya and his foolishness makes him a clown. I know that because I saw it directed by Littlewood. In fact there's a lot there to take advantage of. …

Anyway, I must dig up Rick's remarks, because years later he recognized the value of cutting the self-pity out of the play. In any case, we went on with the play to be a wonderful success; it could have run for a year, but didn't.

a bumper-year at TWP

STEVEN: Because of previous bookings that kept you from running longer?

GEORGE: Yeah, we had a bumper-year that year …

STEVEN: That's such a problem.

GEORGE: . . . and I had committed myself to Pam and *The Club*[2]—which took off marvellously—and then along came Lindsay Kemp[3] and everything worked for us. Which is odd, isn't it, in a year?

STEVEN: To have a season that actually makes money. (*Laughs*)

GEORGE: Yeah, yeah and we did too.

STEVEN: With socially conscious theatre.

GEORGE: Exactly, yeah. It was *timing* too, it was right for it. And the play was a *good* play, *Les Canadiens*. It was valuable. . . .

STEVEN: Ahhh what Stanislavski called "Table Work". . . . .

GEORGE: It is intellectual work. No one is required to emote but only to think well, to use their wits, and contribute. Everybody must contribute.

STEVEN: Why is it important for actors to learn to do Analysis on their own?

actors doing analysis on their own

GEORGE: Well, they'll meet directors who don't do it and they have to do the best they can—as actors always have to do in any kind of circumstances which aren't pleasant. And they have the advantage if they've analyzed their work. I did it on *Long Day's Journey into Night*, which is a play I don't care for—Talk about self-pity!

STEVEN: Great piece of writing in some respects, though.

GEORGE: In some respects, but its overall look is very *down*. Oh, self-indulgent work! He was wonderful when he was a young man writing plays about the sea, which I played in. But I played this play at The Crest, where there was no Analysis done and I did my own.

STEVEN: You played Edmund?

GEORGE: I played the O'Neill part, the young man with tuberculosis. It certainly helped me to get through the work—to analyze—although it wasn't until we got into performing it that I was able to encourage other actors to join me. We would talk about the Units and when we had named them, I would explain what was necessary to choose the Objectives. It was worthwhile talk, because

---

2. Pam Brighton directed *The Club* by Eve Merriam which played at TWP December 1st 1977 to February 14th 1978. *Les Canadiens* played from October 20th to November 19th 1977.(63)

3. The Lindsay Kemp Company presented *Flowers* adapted from Jean Genet (March 28th—April 14th 1978) and *Salome* by Oscar Wilde (April 19th—May 7th). *Flowers* was held over from May 12th to June 10th.(64)

they were bright actors. Jimmy Douglas played the older brother. I think we had better performances as we went on.

STEVEN: O'Neill scripts respond well to Stanislavski analysis.

GEORGE: Yes I think they do.

The Crest Theatre production of *Long Day's Journey into Night* (1960) directed by Leon Major. Actors (l—r): David Hooks, Gwen Ffrangcon Davies & George Luscombe / *photo by Robert C. Ragsdale*

An 'Alice in Wonderland' unit from *Chicago '70* (1970). Actors (l-r): Carol (Carrington) McGrath, François-Regis Klanfer & Ray Whelan / *photo by Zodiac Photographers, New York City*

The Through-Line, Epic Theatre and "Using the Actors as the Scene"

GEORGE: You remember when we chose to do *Chicago '70*. We had so much material, some we didn't use. Remember 'The Wall'? Didn't find its place, didn't have the dynamics that *Alice in Wonderland* did, which you brought in.

STEVEN: It was a good improvisation but it just didn't fit in that show.

what the work requires

GEORGE: Anything that would push us into another direction wouldn't be suitable.

STEVEN: Well, the Through-Line accepted some things and rejected others as we came to understand the material better. But in a collage, episodic structure that we had, the Through-Line is not always so easy to see as it is, perhaps, in a Chekhov play where it's laid out for you to begin with.

GEORGE: Yes, it's laid out for you. *If you can find it* (*laughs*) and if you are aware of what you are looking for, in that there *is* a Through-Line.... As there is in Shakespeare, as there is in Chekhov, and as there was in a new work that we improvised because we were aware of the *necessity* of the Through-Line. *It's like a tree that pulls us all together.* And you have to know *why* it is you're throwing this out, or keeping the other.

STEVEN: It is so easy to fall in love with things we've created and not always so easy, in new work, to make the separation between what the work *requires* and what was just a joy for us to make.

GEORGE: That was so true in *Ten Lost Years*, where I could spend an afternoon improvising a particular thing that I thought was very flattering... and throw it out by the end of the day. That's what kept the play moving so tight, was the ability to not accept everything just because you did it.

how you use your time

STEVEN: One of the pressures, now, on new collaborative work is just the *time* to work things up... and time to throw them out if they're not serving the project.

GEORGE: It's how you use your time. People are always complaining about the lack of time and yet I've seen time wasted terribly. The coffee and doughnuts become far more important than the play. Flapping about, with things that really didn't matter. And to me, that is time wasted.

STEVEN: Although sometimes the 'flapping about' has to happen before you actually land and do something.

GEORGE: I guess that's true... except that there seems to be no Through-Line, no shape that is clear, in what they are doing all this *for*.

an example of losing the through-line

An example of that is, I suppose, this English company which I just saw recently. They were full of energy, and much to be admired compared to what we see going on at the present time. It had a—

STEVEN: —a woman's name.

GEORGE: A woman's name.

STEVEN: As the title.

GEORGE: As the title, yeah. And it was her story[1]. And I said: "Why did you bother with the story?" I didn't think it was that important, politically or socially.

It was an interesting piece. They had given credit to the company for building it, and that was fine. One of the things I liked very much was building a barn by simply picking up the boards. The actors, who were holding the boards upright, were mooing and making the animal sounds that were necessary. (*Steven laughs*) And I thought it was delightful.

But, you could see that barn being prepared... rather than it coming organically out of the flow of the play. And you'd see that repeated over and over again until it became a show of 'Oh, isn't this clever? '... rather than being moved emotionally by the story itself or the telling of it.

1.*The Three Lives of Lucie Cabrol.* Adapted by Simon McBurney and Mark Wheatley from John Berger's short story and performed in Toronto (1996) by Théâtre de Complicité.[(65)]

STEVEN: Aha.

GEORGE: The next event was anticipated, physically, by moving the props about.

I might have got surprised by what turned out, but I knew 'Oh, we are going into something new now!' Rather than it flowing naturally and easily out of the physical apparatus that was a part of the play....

The opposite example was Peter Faulkner's box in *Ten Lost Years*. It was an orange crate that was in the middle of the stage—part of the furniture of the house that was ending up on the street. And when somebody had bought this, bought that, nobody had bought the little orange crate. I wouldn't let them move it until it moved naturally, according to the next moment of the play. And what happened of course was a rich man came along who needed his shoes shined; and Peter sat down on his little orange crate and shined the man's shoes. So, it was *there*, we didn't have to go and look for another orange crate for him to put his foot on. We didn't take the orange crate away because that would have been false—just clearing the stage for the next scene. That's what I'm getting at, you see.

Peter Faulkner's orange crate

STEVEN: Mmhmmn.

GEORGE: This other production, there was always somebody clearing the stage for the next scene. (*Laughs*) And I find that organically *wrong* in terms of improvisation. It should flow easily.

STEVEN: I didn't see the show, but it sounds like it was a choice to not have transitions.

GEORGE: No, absolutely. And I could see them, the actors, congratulating themselves: 'How smoothly this went!' and 'How nicely this next effect happened!' But we were very conscious of the *effect* rather than the *play*. And we would even try to guess what the next one was going to be when they were getting ready for it. So we had, in a sense, *left the flow*.

STEVEN: Well, it brings me to one of the questions I've wanted to ask you: You talk about the influence on your work of Littlewood, Laban and Stanislavski, and I know there is some influence of Brecht, but you haven't talked about it very much. And this is how some people, I think, read Brecht: To interrupt the flow with an obvious set change... something that *breaks* the narrative flow.

go with the flow? or interrupt it?

GEORGE: A misunderstanding of "Alienation."[2] They've picked up the wrong end of the stick completely. It's not to interrupt anything. It does sometimes jar, but in terms of the work that has preceded.

STEVEN: It always has to do with what precedes and follows.

GEORGE: Of course. Life flows, life changes. Even our discussion here has flowed from our discussion before we put the tape recorder on. Out of our own concerns and worries. So no matter how far out in 'left field' it seems to be, it is a natural development of that which has gone before. And that's what Brecht is about. He just has wonderful taste in his choices of what he decides you should be concerned with. But it doesn't alter the flow of the work.

epic theatre: *Mother Courage* with Littlewood

I know this from experience of working in *Mother Courage*—the first production ever done in the West—with Littlewood. She played Mother Courage—much to her dislike because she hadn't wanted to play in it, but Brecht insisted: There was telephone calls going over the wires, very hot and heavy. But he trusted her and he knew what kind of performance he would get. And from one who was in it, it was quite incredible. What was great about it was the experience of playing in Epic Theatre[3] at that time. Theatre that *mattered* as well.

I've seen lots of interpretations of Brecht since coming home and I understand now Brecht's concern. (*Steven laughs*) Because people didn't have the background to understand the *toughness* of the play. I saw a production of *Threepenny Opera* at Stratford. It was a disaster. Oh, everybody thought it was lovely because it was 'pretty' and it was 'joyous' and all those nice things, but it missed the point entirely. It's about murder and—

STEVEN: I don't think of those qualities with Epic Theatre—beauty for its own sake. In fact, when I saw the Berliner Ensemble over there before the Wall came down, they weren't at all attached to conventional physical beauty, in the way the men and women were dressed. There wasn't that kind of 'glamour' in their work.

---

2. Alienation—One common translation of Bertolt Brecht's "*Verfremdungseffekt*"—also called the the "A effect" or "estrangement." "Alienation" aims to remind the audience of the artificiality of the theatre with techniques such as direct address to the audience, 'disruptive' use of songs or signs, and anti-illusionist staging and lighting.[(66)]

3. Epic Theatre—Theatre that employs the *Verfremdungseffekt* and grew from the belief that theatre's purpose is to present ideas for the audience's judgement we well as to entertain. The audience should always be aware that they are watching a play, and not an imitation of reality.[(67)]

The Theatre Workshop production of *Mother Courage and Her Children* (1955), showing Joan Littlewood as Mother Courage and George as The Recruiting Sergeant / *Photo by John Spinner. Courtesy of Theatre Royal Stratford East Archives Collection.*

GEORGE: They weren't trying to prettify anything to please a bourgeois audience, which is what we do.

STEVEN: I was asking why you never did more Brecht besides *Arturo Ui.*

GEORGE: Yeah, I went to the source and I thought Büchner[4] was the source. And instead of doing Brecht—which at that time, the 60's, was seen everywhere—I thought I'd introduce them to Büchner, who was the inspiration of Brecht. And when I came across *Woyzeck* I was really excited by it.

Brecht & Büchner

Ours was the first production of *Woyzeck*[5] in North America, as far as I know. Somebody did all the research on it years later and wanted copies of my programme because, evidently, we were the first.

STEVEN: Really?

GEORGE: Yeah. And I used *Woyzeck* many times with the students. I would talk of the Given Circumstances of the end of the play where he drowns. That's when he has murdered his mistress and he decides to hide the knife. The actor would throw the knife into

4. Georg Büchner (1813-1837)—German dramatist and writer whose most prominent work, *Woyzeck*, was the first German literary work to have a working-class man as the main character. [66]

5. *The Death of Woyzeck* (1965)—The title of TWP's version, adapted by Jack Winter and directed by George [67]

The Death of Woyzeck (1965). Actors: Edward H. Sanders as Woyzeck (foreground). Back row (l-r): Victoria Mitchell, Edward Kelly & Gwen Thomas / *photo by Tess Boudreau*

improvisation: *The Death of Woyzeck* using the Efforts

the lake. Which immediately meant *all the other actors became the lake*... and as if the knife had landed close to an actor, he would move in what we call "Float"—but in a very quick way as if the ripples were going out across the lake. And in that moment you knew everybody, no matter how they were dressed, were playing the water.

STEVEN: Ha.

GEORGE: And they were responding to the behaviour of Woyzeck, who was the centre of the Unit. He would go into the lake and try to retrieve the knife and throw it further. And, so doing, would lose balance and be taken up by the water. And so, for the first time, he too would 'float,' as the water had floated. And the actors who were floating with him would float his hat off his head, and his jacket off his back... and these things floated about the room with the actors. And all you could concentrate on was the jacket... until everybody stopped floating... became the people again. Woyzeck had disappeared because he had drowned. He was no longer Woyzeck: He had taken up the physical behaviour of the other actors. And we got a sense that he had *gone*... without going. He didn't rush off to the wings but... you were right Centre Stage... and you were no longer seen.

STEVEN: And you didn't bring in other special effects.

GEORGE: That's right, other than lighting. And that's a good example of *using the actors as the scene* and very naturally, out of the demands of the play, becoming the water. It was always successful, even with actors who were very new to the work, and they loved doing it 'cause it was so exciting. And in a moment they could all stand and take a bow (*laughs*)—*as the actor*, not as the scene. But to get them used to the idea of changing so quickly, that's the magic of the theatre: Doing it right in front of you.

STEVEN: But not the kind of 'preparation' that you talked about earlier, with *Lucie Cabrol*?

GEORGE: Exactly. Nobody rushed off to bring in blankets to create the sea—as you would do in a Chinese theatre, which is very lovely, but none of that was necessary. *Less and less is necessary... if the actor knows how to move.*

It's the same thing that happened with *The Mac Paps*. That's how the play began ahh with a table, chairs, all heavy furniture. But that's all—just the hard-backed chairs and table that you would find in a hall prepared for people to speak. And a few speeches were made about having come together for the purpose of raising money for the International Brigade. And those fellas who had volunteered their time and lives, to go and fight for democracy in Spain. And as the speech was being made by R.H. Thomson, very beautifully improvised, then he would mention Spain: "And at this moment in Spain there is already some boy out there preparing to fight!" And in that moment the furniture would go—the actors would lift the furniture because they themselves were on board a boat that was uhh being torpedoed, the boat was going down. And the furniture was all over the stage, being lifted by the actors who were now 'floating' and 'slashing.'

using the actors as the scene—*The Mac Paps*

STEVEN: Creating the explosion on the sea without any naturalistic tools.

GEORGE: The furniture *was* the boat... which was now floating all over the place. And the lights changed... and in the next moment they were soldiers fighting in Spain. And within a *moment* this had happened.

Class and Economics

GEORGE: So much time is taken on the costume, the look—which is all right—but equal time should be spent on *the meaning of the work*. Which we too often ignore.

we don't have the working-class in the theatre.

I think we ignore because we don't have the working-class in the theatre. We don't have people of worldly experience. You see, one of my complaints to Jack Winter was: "For Christ's sake, Jack, will you go out and get a job?" (*Steven laughs*) His whole experience was university. It was just typical of Canadian theatre. And I wanted him to go drive trucks so his concerns would be changed.

STEVEN: Went to see *Arcadia*[1] at the Canadian Stage's big theatre, the Bluma Appel. And one of the things that struck me—the production aside, which had many good things about it... the *set* looked like the *theatre*. There was no alienation of the playing-space from the walls of the auditorium. It all looked really nicely decorated, very upper-middle-class 'aristocratic' style. And about three-quarters of the audience was dressed to suit the decor.

matching décor

GEORGE: Yes, yes. (Laughs) And you know, the existence of TWP hasn't made a goddamned bit of difference. (*Laughs*) I hate to say it.

STEVEN: I think you don't really believe that.

GEORGE: *Individually* it has made a difference, but *we didn't change the nature of theatre*. No no, we are economically dominated. The economics cannot be underestimated.

STEVEN: We have our two major theatres in Ontario basically serving the tourist industry.

GEORGE: And they won't be allowed to fail. There's too much money invested. The boards of directors are business representatives.

---

1. *Arcadia* by Tom Stoppard, performed at CanStage in the 1996-1997 season.[(s.b.)]

Even when you get unionists on the board, they don't bring in their concerns of labour—I know this personally—and therefore change the direction of the support for the theatre. They come in and are so delighted at being, like Bob Rae[2], in the company of business, that they *become* business. This is what was wrong with Bob Rae and this is what I've seen happen with the unions that I worked with at one time and got money from. You know, in order to survive as a theatre.

boards, business & unions: the economics cannot be underestimated.

When we produced *The Working Man* by Len Peterson, we went to a dinner and we had to convince the other unionists, supposedly, of the value of them all coming and supporting *The Working Man*. And you know where the dinner was held? At the Westbury Hotel which was at the time the chic-est hotel going, with the chef who was absolutely the talk of the town and with a waiter behind every person at the table. And the table was so huge I couldn't talk to the person across the table, so you ended up talking with the person *next* to you. But behind us was a lackey, who was there to serve us. (*Steven laughs*) This was a union meeting… or so it pretended to be. Archer, delightful man, he was the head of…

dinner at the Westbury

STEVEN: David Archer?[3]

GEORGE: Yes, head of the OFL at that time, and his other occupation was a board member of the St. Lawrence Centre. "Well," I said, "how can you be both? How can you join us at TWP and be at the St. Lawrence Centre? We're opposed."

STEVEN: I think, to his credit, however good or bad the productions were, Leon Major[4] tried to politicize that bourgeois space.

GEORGE: Oh absolutely.

STEVEN: Through Brecht's plays, and other plays that had some serious content in them.

GEORGE: Yes, but *the house was a bourgeois house*; and the audience was… like the audience, years later, of *On Golden Pond*… looking back sweetly at life.

---

2. Bob Rae (b.1948)—NDP premier of Ontario from 1990 to 1995. In 2012 a Liberal MP from Toronto and interim leader of the federal Liberal Party. (68)

3. David Archer—President of the Ontario Federation of Labour, 1958-1976.(69)

4. Leon Major (b. 1933)—Distinguished director and producer of theatre and operas. From 1969 to 1980 he was Artistic and General Director of Toronto Arts Productions, the founding company of St. Lawrence Centre for the Arts. (70)

I remember John Sewell had just lost the election to Eggleton, for Mayor of Toronto and—

STEVEN: Bad day for Toronto.

GEORGE: It was indeed. And I was in the house—I guess it must have been opening night—and at intermission we came out and uhh I saw John Sewell and he smiled at me, 'cause we had a nodding acquaintance, and immediately was saying how much he enjoyed the play. And I said: "What ridiculous nonsense this is, John! These are the people that threw you out of office! (*Steven laughs*) And you're admiring this?" ...

You see, it was that bullshit about getting old-aged, and the nostalgia trip. And the lovely performances of the individual actors *were* fine, nothing wrong with that, but we're talking about the *philosophy* of the work. I would have rather seen something about the bag-ladies, you know, dying uhhh in the streets of Toronto, which was happening at the time.

STEVEN: And happening now.

GEORGE: And happening now. Oh (*laughs*) .... exhausted.

Concentration of Attention

STEVEN: What a beautiful day.

GEORGE: What a place to go to sleep in, isn't it? Good Lord…

STEVEN: Yeah, yeah.

GEORGE: Lovely garden… Ahhh…

STEVEN: Thursday July 11th.

GEORGE: Ah yes… yes… Thursday the 11th—one day before the 12th eh? What a shambles. What can you do about that?

STEVEN: The 12th of July?

GEORGE: Must we blame it on the Irish? (*Steven laughs*) Good God. Delightful people, you know. I've got drunk with so many of them in London, and they were so great when we were over there the last time.… But what a tragedy, what a terrible terrible tragedy.

the troubles in Ireland

STEVEN: The 12th is not a major day in Canada now, but I guess it still is in Belfast.

GEORGE: It had been. The Orange Day Parade in Ontario was a very big thing in the 30's and the 20's. Ah, terrible attitudes, the whole thing's pig-headed; it stops you from joking about it at all, it's so tragic. I had one very good play passed on to me from Mary Durkan[1]. It was about the guard and his prisoner and ahh the Irish was very legitimate, the accent, the swing of the script; it was so good. One of those I regretted not having tried to get done. It was dealing head-on with "The Troubles": When a guard makes a prisoner a prisoner, the prisoner, in turn, makes a prisoner of the guard. Too bad I can't remember the name.

1.Mary Durkan—Actor, Director and Artistic Director of the Bloomsday Festival—an annual event in Toronto which, on June 16th 2010, celebrated its 25th anniversary. Mary informed me that the play she brought to George's attention is *A Rat in the Skull* by Ron Hutchinson.[(s.b.) (71)]

STEVEN: Theatrical script?

GEORGE: Oh yeah.

STEVEN: It didn't stay at the level of naturalistic conversation?

GEORGE: I'm afraid it did. (*Laughs*)

STEVEN: But you would have done something with that.

GEORGE: I would have tried, because of the subject matter. It's so important, that's why I'm buzzing around about it now, you know. We must tackle these things. It's like when Behan[2] was asked to do a play, by Joan Littlewood, relating to the hostage situation which was happening at that time uhhh in Eastern countries or something and he said: "I don't know a damn thing about that, you know, but I'll talk about Ireland." And the result was *The Hostage*. But he took the same problems and examined them in the milieu that he knew. And was very successful, as you know.

STEVEN: Were you involved in that first production?

GEORGE: No I wasn't. Joan sent me the script, I had just left her. And she asked me what I thought of it: I don't think I ever wrote back, I was just so flabbergasted, it was so good. But again, that was a very straight narrative play that she turned into a great theatre-piece.... And you talk about Ireland, you talk about all of us.

STEVEN: England's oldest colony. And that seems to be the hardest to let go of.

GEORGE: In *Richard II* he says: "Oh I'm off to Ireland!" He's got so many problems at home and he says 'To hell with it, I'll go to Ireland and bash them around!' (*Steven giggles*) Which he did. And they wore it around their neck ever since. No way out. It's a good title: *No Way Out*. They can't see a way out.

Major[3] uses it for political purposes at the moment. Major thinks he's got something to gain by it, by "the Troubles." 'Send more troops over!' Which they've done. "More troops over, more troops!" Same as Richard II. There's no way out, there's no learning.

STEVEN: There's too much invested huh?

GEORGE: Yeah, including people.

STEVEN: (*exhaling*) Yeah....

GEORGE: It was a long time before I realized that the landlords kicked the poor people from Scotland to get them off the land

2. Brendan Behan (1923-64)—Irish poet, novelist and playwright; one-time member of the Irish Republican Army (IRA).[72]

3. John Major—Prime Minister of the United Kingdom, 1990-1997.[73]

where they could raise sheep—which were more valuable than the Scottish peasants—so they sent them off to Ireland and they created Belfast and the good jobs go to the Protestants..... Ohhh God. We're rambling on, aren't we, Steven? Good way to start the morning—"The Troubles!" (*Steven chuckles*)

Well, I should try to get a start—I'm avoiding it, you see—to get started with a most difficult problem: *Concentration of Attention.*

concentration of attention

So we begin at the beginning, as Alice said, and come to the end, we hope, before the day is dawned. (*Steven laughs*)

I have everybody in a circle again, and we sit down this time and talk a little bit about people who can hold your attention on stage and others who don't seem to be able to. Some people, *at moments*, will have a grip on you and your concentration will be complete. You won't be worried about the fan turning in the auditorium, you won't..

STEVEN:.. be looking at your watch.

GEORGE: Yeah exactly: "How long till the pub opens?" All of a sudden you're gripped, and what *is* that? We must be able to analyze it. And we invent exercises to improve our own ability to concentrate. And it's not good enough for directors to say "I want you to concentrate here." Well Christ, we know that! But how do you *do* that? Stanislavski makes the observation of Salvini[4], I think it is, Italian actor/singer. He talks of him, a small man standing on stage who closes his fists and in that moment captures everybody, *holds* them. They don't take a breath until he lets them go again, when he opens his fists.

STEVEN: Aha.

GEORGE: Of course, I didn't witness that (*laughs*) but I'll take his word for it. What is that power?

Well, Stanislavski would start with a spotlight. I tried that once because I had a theatre, had a lighting man; we arranged it all ahead of time, placed the spots in the right place.

exercise: circles of attention

STEVEN: Between the three different sizes—the small, medium and large circles?

GEORGE: Yes, exactly. The concentration of attention changes with your circles. And of course it's spectacular when you use lights,

4 .Tommaso Salvini (1830-1915)—Renowned Italian actor, most well known for his portrayal of Othello. He had extensive voice training but ultimately pursued a career in theatre.[74]

but I have never used them since because the control must eventually come from the actor and it's his decision where his outer limits are.

STEVEN: Mmhmmn.

GEORGE: Now they are sitting down in the circle and there's space between them. I'd say that "you are the centre of your own concentration ahhh but that's not to be mesmerized!" Some people would think 'Oh I must look like I'm concentrating': The eyebrows go together and stern looks come upon the face and some people act up a little, and you'd expect them to be told-off because they're not doing it right. Nonsense! Nonsense! There's no right or wrong in that way.

"You are the centre of your own concentration; therefore, take a healthy interest in all that surrounds you ... *but within a particular size.*" And sometimes I've used the image of a hula-hoop: 'You are the middle of that hoop and you mustn't allow your concentration to go beyond the defining area of a hoop' ... which takes in the elbows and the knees, and often people will cross their legs, so they've got their feet involved in it as well.

STEVEN: Mmhmmn.

GEORGE: And I say: "Now you've got an area of concentration and you've defined it." And now I say: "Give *me* your full attention!" As quickly as that, because it must be understood that Concentration of Attention is as quick as a (*George claps his hands*) slap on a hand; you don't need preparation for it. That's why the people who screw up their eyebrows go all wrong, you see: They're trying to *prepare* to be concentrating.

So they've given me their Concentration of Attention. Then I will start the questions: "What did you notice in that area that you hadn't noticed before?" Simple question, and people will be confused by it, as usual. You will sometimes get people right off the bat saying "Oh, I've noticed that my pants are torn at the knees; I've noticed that I'm very scruffy this morning; I've noticed the floor is not as clean as I thought it should be." (*Steven laughs*) On occasion you will get somebody in a student class: "I didn't notice anything." ... "What?!"

STEVEN: Where were they? (*Both laugh*)

GEORGE: Exactly. "'Didn't notice anything ... ' Well, we best go back and look again." Coaxing: Try to *coax* all the time, that it's fun to notice that which you hadn't noticed before because you're too busy with the world. You come into class and there's a whole *noise* of people, all sorts of things happening around you, but you don't notice *particulars*... and you take that time out to notice particulars.

Then we play a little joke: "What colour tie are you wearing?" "Oh, I don't know." "What colour's your shirt?" And their eye focus is on me and they mustn't look back, I won't let them. And I say: "Well, how come you didn't notice these things?" So we keep going back to this smaller area until they've come to understand it. They feel their back become sore, or they're shifting their bottom as they're sitting.

STEVEN: They become more aware of these things.

GEORGE: Yes, all of a sudden these things become noticeable... to a large extent because there's nothing else to notice. You say: "Won't you get tired in that small area?" Surprising how they don't; there's more and more things to discover in that smallest area.

STEVEN: Now, typically, how much time would you spend in a small circle?

GEORGE: I think it'd be 20 minutes. And everybody must answer the question "What did you notice *now* that you didn't notice the last time?" We do that twice, and three times, because it's beginning to dawn on them *there's so much more to see*. So you've got twelve people to fifteen people, it's gonna take you quite a while to go right around the room.

"Well now let's *expand* that area of concentration to take in whatever you think is the first three and a half feet in diameter from your centre out. That includes the back, the front, the sides, all of it."

STEVEN: So it's a bit bigger than the hula-hoop.

GEORGE: Oh yes, now we are at the *medium-size* Circle of Attention. It usually includes the knees or the legs of their neighbour, and some will get quite excited by that. Then you know you've got good people. And others will try to keep away from the other person.

STEVEN: Is that fear of invading other peoples' space?

GEORGE: Yes, holding back to the old comfortable one, and afraid of not knowing what to do if they did include somebody else, because that 'somebody else' may not behave the way they think they should behave. Because now you're risking something: You're out including other people. And they can do as they please, can't they? (*Both chuckle*) They can include *you*, for instance.

And again we'd get the most amusing descriptions of the other person's trousers and "Why is that other person's arm so funny-looking and bent [*Steven chuckles*] when they're supposed to be concentrating? Why are they doing this?" So the questions are as much a part of the lesson as the direction from the director.

Then it's obvious, from there we go to a *larger* circle. I usually move to six foot so there is no question that other people are involved. And then ... do people stay frozen in their sitting position? Or do they begin to explore the space that has now allowed them to include the other person? But then to still hold on to the six-foot area is difficult to do.

STEVEN: Because there's that much more to take in.

GEORGE: Yes, where is the line drawn? It has to be drawn in your mind. There usually isn't a great deal of movement, but we're *beginning to see the group*.. and then I'll say: "Right! Back to where *you* are the centre of your concentration." So *we're always coming back*, it's like strengthening a muscle, to bring it back to the size that you want it. 'Now I can handle the smallest size; now I can handle the medium size; now I know what the large size is; then the whole room—Oh my God, the whole room? Where does that end?'

STEVEN: So you work with *four* areas?

GEORGE: We're not finished yet.

STEVEN: Oh, OK!

GEORGE: Suppose we make ahhh Judith here the centre of her own concentration, but everybody else's concentration is on Judith. All of a sudden all this power, twelve to fifteen people, is concentrating on one young girl. And she's managing because she is the centre of her own concentration; she has nothing to do with them, nothing at all ... *unless* they get into her area of concentration. And that's fun, when they finally do. She'll see a hand come into her area (*both laugh*) which she often will revolt against, or tell off, or throw out ... or just accept.

Then they give their attention to me and again we'll ask

questions: "What did you notice about Judith's hair? What did you notice she was wearing?" And the details, which are lovely and embarrass Judith no end (*Steven laughs*)—what she didn't do or did do with her hair that morning—but all in very good fun because *now we're looking at people like we haven't looked before,* because we're absolutely curious. And so we can hold our interest on this other person for a very long time, having built all the steps carefully.

STEVEN: What does Judith do to keep from being overwhelmed by all this attention?

GEORGE: She concentrates on her own self, where she is the centre of her own concentration.

STEVEN: So she stays in the hula-hoop.

GEORGE: She stays. She has no responsibility for what they're doing.

Now you can then choose someone else—and they all want to be chosen eventually, you know. And then you do two or three at once.

exercise: exploring other points of attention

And then I did something I learned from *Woyzeck*: I had them concentrate on the space under the stage, which Woyzeck must do. He concentrates below the earth...

STEVEN: Hamlet has to do that too.

GEORGE: ... and he hears voices underneath him so that you have to listen *below* the stage.

And then we'd play with *time* as well, we'd say: "This morning you came into the theatre. Cast yourself, in your imagination, out to those doors; let that be your area of concentration and only that." And then interesting things happen: People would become sometimes relaxed, or rigid. Their body takes on the attitude of that morning, when they remember it again.

STEVEN: Back to the frame of mind with which they've entered the door.

exercise: walking about in the centre of your own concentration

GEORGE: Yes, yes.... And then finally I encourage them to *stand* and keep that centre where they're the centre of their own attention, still—the smallest circle. But now... *you can take it with you.*

Then I would ask them questions like... "What does it feel like to walk about in the centre of your own concentration? What circumstances does it remind you of?" It always reminds me of Union Station, you know, where you're waiting for the train to come in

concentration and awareness: solitude in public

and everybody's individual—maybe looking at their watch, looking at their baggage. Then you hear the train from a distance and everybody in the station is concentrating on the train. There's no *individual* concentration anymore.

STEVEN: What do you do if an actor becomes too self-absorbed in the small circle and tunes out the rest of the room?

GEORGE: If that's what his area of concentration is, he's right. There's Concentration and Awareness. *Concentration of Attention is different from Awareness.*

I ask the actors to give me an example of *Solitude in Public.* It usually comes down to somebody sitting in a streetcar reading a book and they're completely in Tahiti with Gauguin and yet he's able to get up and get off at the right stop. How does he know he's at the stop if he's in Tahiti? (*Steven chuckles*) He's *aware* of the streetcar, he's aware of the people shoving him, moving in on his area, but he's *holding his concentration* in Tahiti. Which is different from mesmerization. *We don't mesmerize ourselves*, we're aware of what's going on.

John Barrymore and the cat

STEVEN: All these points of concentration are *chosen.*

GEORGE: Yeah, yes, we make the choice.

I remember the story of John Barrymore.[5] Somebody was watching him give his 1000th performance of Hamlet, and on this particular night he was going into "To be or not to be" and, whether he's brilliant or not, everybody's just listening to the *great voice,* as it was.... And a cat crosses the stage... and just at that moment when you shouldn't have a cat. (*Steven laughs*) Being a good actor he uh reaches down and picks up the cat and addresses the rest of the speech to the cat.

STEVEN: Ah!

GEORGE: And brought the whole thing alive! Instead of fighting it, he'd *used* it, gave it his complete concentration and *awakened* the speech like it hadn't been before.

I've used that in rehearsal on many occasions by changing the actor's area of concentration and surprising him with it.

Having now practiced Concentration of Attention, I would give them an improvisation that was designed to test their powers

5. John Barrymore (1882-1942)—American film and stage actor. One of the superstars of his generation, he was well-known for his portrayal of Richard III and gave 101 performances of Hamlet on Broadway before taking the role to London in 1925.[(75)]

John Barrymore as Hamlet in 1922 / *photographer unknown*

improvisation: the oasis

of concentration. So I choose four people, I think, and the rest of the class would sit aside and I'd describe a road on a hot summer's day. You had three travellers on this hot dusty road—and I'd say where the road was, from one end of the stage to the other—and in the centre would be an oasis, a stream possibly, a cool place where they could take a breather. And the three travellers would take a rest there. They would still be in the centre of their own concentration, but they would have something in common—the road that they had travelled on, and the oasis. Then the fourth person would enter, also a traveller on this road, and he would remain concentrated on his own centre of attention while all the others would give their complete concentration to that fourth person …

STEVEN: Aha.

GEORGE: … and would not abate until the fourth person had—for their own reason—rested, stood and carried on down the road. Once that happened, the three people returned to their own centre of attention and, gradually, they too would get up and leave.

Nothing is said. That's one of the advantages of describing that it's a hot day and you're tired. (*Laughs*) "There will be no running around, please." If they're good, all of a sudden your imagination starts jumping up and down. Who is this fourth person? Why is he deserving of this attention? Why are they concentrating on him and nothing else? Why haven't they seen each other, but only him? And it has all sorts of mysticism involved in it ...

STEVEN: Mmhmmnn.

GEORGE:.. which is always fun—especially when it's a hot day and near the water. So that they've told a little story without being conscious of it. And I've seen people become *beautiful* in this little exercise—students particularly who are rather awkward themselves, not knowing what to do when they first come into class—they're absolutely looking beautiful. 'Cause other people look at them and see them in a different way; they are interesting enough for that person to concentrate on. Although, Steven, we've *said* nothing to that person—not "You should think they are the Messiah just returned!" None of that at all, but they've done it themselves.

STEVEN: Just by giving attention.

GEORGE: By using the tool of Concentration of Attention, nothing else. No background, no "Who is your mother?" Just using the tool that Stanislavski set out. And using it *correctly*. That's why I'm always saying that some people have read the book[6] cursorily, quickly, but haven't really *used* the book—because *it's a book of doing*, not of talking. It's a book where you take the exercise and use it.

Imagine you have twelve to fifteen people and you break them up into different groups: All the different things that are going to happen on that short walk on that road. Just a joy. And also those who don't succeed reveal themselves to each other.

STEVEN: But do you find that, in watching other people *succeed* in the exercise, light bulbs will go on for *them*?

GEORGE: Absolutely, the smiles come over their faces, the giggles, and they want to tell you how they interpreted that scene. It's like poetry. It has its own meaning for the person who's witnessing it.

STEVEN: So that we can invent our own story.

GEORGE: Yes, it's wide open. Wide open.... We used to say in Canada: "There's no theatre if we don't have the scripts."

6. George is surely referring here to the *first* part of Stanislavski's major book on Acting, translated by Elizabeth Reynolds Hapgood as *An Actor Prepares*. Jean Benedetti has, more recently, edited and translated *An Actor Prepares* and *Building a Character* and brought them back together in one volume, as Stanislavski intended, under the title *An Actor's Work: A Student's Diary* and many key terms are translated differently—eg., "Throughaction"(J.B.) instead of "Through line of action."[(E.R.H.) (s.b.) (76)]

Nonsense, nonsense! We just needed *Imagination* and this is what Stanislavski is about.

When we've lost our Concentration of Attention, we don't have to know the *reason*; we only have to know that it's lost and that you have the tools to get it back.

There are so many things in the world to disturb us and in rehearsal we bring the world in with us, and that first little while it's hard to get the mind where it should be.

STEVEN: Just getting into the room is one of the major challenges.

GEORGE: Absolutely, absolutely. Again, that's why I've blown my top in rehearsals when people bring food into the theatre. That's when I resent the carelessness of people—to bring things into the theatre that don't belong in there! ....

Lovely bird having his bath.

STEVEN: In the birdbath, down there.....

GEORGE: Yeah ... that..... Ahhh I think that's Concentration of Attention for today.

STEVEN: OK.

Imagination

imagination that needs no help

GEORGE: There's that kind of imagination which is possessed by some lucky people, that everything they see they can turn into most amusing happenings in the retelling of it and have us all laughing. There was a particular fellow and him and I were on 'digs duty' late at night.

STEVEN: Where were you?

GEORGE: We were all in the back of a truck and two of us would jump out and see if there were any 'digs' at this place—rooms for the twelve actors. And Jack and I went, and we're just young kids then, but it was in southern Ontario and we'd go to these homes and we'd ask: "Do you know of any places we could put up a dozen people for the night?"

On this one occasion this woman came to the door, little woman she was, and she didn't have any room herself but she knew of a place that was big enough probably to take care of us all. And she pointed up where we had to go and, immediately as she did that, her shoulder would hurt like mad. Of course, she had rheumatism.

STEVEN: Ah.

GEORGE: And she wouldn't be able to tell us what it was and... (*Laughs*) every time she lifted her arm up to point the way, it would hurt again. And I felt, you know, very disturbed at this. And we finally got enough information out of her that we went back to the truck.

And that evening Jack started on about this old lady—Jack Merigold[1] was his name—and every time she put her hand up, the

1. Jack Merigold—Director, actor and stage manager. Partner to Ben and Sylvia Lennick in Belmont Productions and in Theatre in the Home. Company Manager for TWP following the departure of June Faulkner in 1978. (77)

arthritis hit in the arm: "Ohhhhhh!" He had us all in stitches. He had taken this little truth and made it so enormous that it was very funny... and it was still true.

STEVEN: In the moment when you were with her it was painful.

GEORGE: It was painful, it wasn't funny at all. I felt we should get away from the door, you know, to give her a chance to recover. (*Steven chuckles*) But his *interpretation* was the result of a great imagination. He already has it, he's equipped.

STEVEN: He didn't have to train to get that.

GEORGE: Nothing at all. That is the kind that takes whatever is there and builds on it—a kind of imagination an actor wishes he had.

imagination that needs prompting

Most of us are more like the *second* kind of imagination—the imagination that needs prompting. We can take off once we're given a little lift. And this is where most of the students find themselves.

no imagination at all

The *third*, which is *really* a problem, is that which has no imagination at all. No matter how much you prod, the person can't take off. To that kind of a person I usually say: "Better you take up accountancy. You're gonna make it very difficult for yourself if you don't have imagination that responds to suggestions."

exercise: passive object in nature

Having determined the three kinds of imagination, I'll ask everybody to accept themselves as a passive object in nature... and that could be a log, a mushroom, anything that cannot itself move... and the reason for that is you don't want an exercise in which people are going to run around. This is a sit-down, quiet, imaginative exercise.

So... when they have an understanding of what they are, then I will start asking questions: Where? What? When?

STEVEN: Each actor one by one?

GEORGE: One by one. And it soon becomes obvious everybody enjoys it, because they're trying to guess what object the person has chosen to be. I'll start off with things like "What are you capable of seeing about you? What can you hear?" Some will choose to be in a different epoch. They will choose 'tree' and they will know all that has happened in that tree. And I say: "Have things always been the same for you?" "Oh no, no, no, it was quite different a long time ago." And they must try to answer in the language of that tree—which is difficult. I say: "What do you hate?" "I hate this terrifying sound that's coming at me." "Is it a threat to your existence?" See, I too have to be careful about *how* I ask. "Yes, I'm sure I'm not going to be here once it's passed." And I say: "What makes you say that?" "Well, I've seen others be eliminated by such a thing." And of course it was the lawnmower and the person was a piece of grass. They've imagined the fear, the horror of being removed, and yet they could tell you: "Well, it's OK, I'll grow again." (*All laugh*)[2]

On one occasion we had an amateur group of actors and we had an 'elderly lady' with us. She was probably mid-life, I suppose, but I was a young kid in those days: Everybody over 30 was ancient, you know.

This lady was very pleasant to everybody, so she would make the tea and bring cookies—which we didn't ask for, but they would be there, it was her little contribution, made the classes very pleasant ... and she was portraying herself as 'a very nice little old lady' ... who is middle-aged.

Then when I tried this exercise on them, all of a sudden her whole body was changing: It was becoming taut, it was becoming prickly, it was becoming nasty. This was so unlike her and, as she was telling the story, it finally became clear she was a *prickly rose bush.* (*Both chuckle*) And she was taking it out on the dogs and the people that came near her. She wasn't 'a nice little old lady' at all! (*All laugh*)

And that's when people get a taste of how fun it is, and how easy it is, to be prodded with your imagination; and then your improvisations become much fuller *and the world doesn't seem as difficult anymore.*

It's like my good friend Barry Flatman in *Arturo Ui* creating a man-eating flower: Anybody coming near him was in danger of being eaten! (*All laugh*)

the body itself changes in their answers.

I ask questions about *the senses*, because I don't want them to tell me what they are. So I'll say: "From where you are, can you see about you? Can you smell anything? Do you think that you've been there long?" If you've been there a long time: "Well, it's because others have come and gone who were very similar to myself," they would say. So there is a questioning, continually, based upon the senses.

2. Gary, a neighbour, is now listening in. (a.m/s.b.)

And then ... the *body! The body itself changes* in their answers. They will sometimes be freer than they've ever been before; sometimes they will breathe differently. A whole series of physical behaviours prompted by the imagination. That was the point I wanted to make, Steven: We're leading to the *right life* of your imagination.

STEVEN: What's the difference between the right life and the wrong life?

the right life of the imagination

GEORGE: The right life produces *physical action.* I remember one actor imagined he was coming down a hill skiing and he had taken on the form of a skier—as a result of trying to explain to me what he was up to—and he could feel the wind in his cheeks and his hair. That's the other thing: *You can't know ahead of time,* when you're building the character, *where the imagination will take you.* It's gotta be free to go there, and you are physically different than you were when you started.... And that's the *right* life of the imagination.

STEVEN: Yeah.

GEORGE: Enough said.

STEVEN: We'll talk again tomorrow.

George on tour, 1950s / *photo courtesy of Karen Luscombe*

Improvisation

(Lively birds, very present throughout)

STEVEN: So here we are on the *in*glorious 12th of July.
GEORGE: Oh, my God, yes. It's a day to talk of violence, isn't it?
STEVEN: Yeah, marching in Belfast.

improvisation: institutionalized violence

GEORGE: Yes, well, one of my improvisations I like to call "Institutionalized Violence." And immediately people think of terrible things and yet there's violence of an amusing kind—if you think the dentist's office is amusing, and certainly it's institutionalized: He's permitted to create his violence in his office.

STEVEN: I was just there this morning.

GEORGE: Well, there you are. You know (*Steven laughs*) what horror that is.

"*What if…?*" If the day is right for the convict to be put to death. He'd be in his cell and a couple of guards would have to come and get him. They'd probably be accompanied by a priest and the warden, and they'll take him for a walk down a corridor to the place of hanging or electrocution. That's it—his last walk and into the death chamber and somebody kills him. And I've always thought that that has enough horror to stimulate the most dulcet of imaginations. Just the trip alone, the long last walk…

These politicians who can so glibly say "Oh yes, bring the death penalty back." Well who's pulling the switch? What do you do to a man that pulls the switch and causes the death of another? Even if he's wearing a uniform—and they always are! Joan Littlewood dealt with it in *The Quare Fellow*[1]. And it's a terrible ordeal they

1. *The Quare Fellow* by Brendan Behan, which deals with condemned prisoners awaiting execution, premiered at the Theatre Workshop in 1956.[(78)]

go through and they try to wrap it up in institutionalized behaviour: Long walks, long discussions, the right way to tie the knot—there's a whole ritual that goes with it all. The other prisoners in the jail, they know their time is coming, so it's full of horror.

STEVEN: All sanctioned by the state.

GEORGE: All sanctioned by the state, yes.

So having talked a little bit about that, I let them go to it, and they'll sit down with paper and pencil in groups, usually of about four to six. And they choose themselves what parts they will play and then they will break the play up into three Units. If they wish, they can go for four.

analysis before improvisation

I'm looking at one now that we broke up years ago. The first Unit was "Secure the Prisoner." That's what they chose to call it. And uh that does oblige everybody to accomplish that before they can move onto the next Unit.

Then, the second Unit becomes "The Long Walk." You ask again: "What can a Unit not do without?" And you say: "Well, the priest may be there, but it is 'The Walk' that is so awful." In the *first* Unit, there may or may not be difficulties, but "Secure the Prisoner" does contain that element of struggle. So if there's an attempt of escape at the last moment, that will have to be foiled somehow, in order to move into the second Unit.

Ahhh then the play has a third Unit and it is "The Death." I suppose you could go into last-minute reprieve, the governor's voice—but *it's up to them*, the actors who are creating the play. And if we want to face the terrible nature of being put to death by the state, then they will complete that third Unit as "Death."

And each actor will choose his Objective. The prison guards will choose such things as, for "Secure the Prisoner"… "I must take hold the prisoner myself." The other guard may say something similar, but *not the same*: It will be a different Objective because they are different people. But they have one thing in common: They're both in the same Unit and playing under the name of that Unit.

Then the prisoner has his own Objective:… "wish to put on a brave front," "I must look good."… But he may not *at all* in the Circumstances as he plays them.

It's like the mistake so many young actors make when they are playing the part of a man inebriated. They usually 'play drunk.'

Well, you don't 'play drunk': You try to walk that white line as surely as you can; you do your very best to give the appearance of being sober.

STEVEN: Yes.

GEORGE: And it could be the same here. He may not *achieve* escape in the first Unit, but he may *try*. And the Given Circumstances won't *allow* him to escape. 'Cause the name of the Unit is "Secure the Prisoner."

Oh, we didn't say anything about the priest. He may be welcoming, he may be unwelcoming, depending upon the behaviour of the prisoner. He may be a damn nuisance to the warden. From the warden's point of view, the priest may have his work to do, sure enough, but he mustn't waste time. Mustn't go too far. Mustn't get in the way of the guards. There are all kinds of interesting Objectives coming from the *name* of the Unit.

And in "The Long Walk," of course, it may be up to the priest just to read The Good Book and to mumble his words through (*laughs*) as he makes his way down the corridor. And his Objective will be, I suppose… "that the job be done well."

I can just imagine them all congratulating themselves: "Well that was well done!" (*George laughs*) As people do at funerals, you know: "Oh, well, wasn't that a lovely funeral?" We congratulate ourselves, sometimes, when we carry out the institutional demands.

STEVEN: Which is one way of not dealing with what's really happening.

GEORGE: Absolutely: We don't play the *real* part. And don't wish to. There is something inherently evil about the destruction of a human being. No matter what nice things you say about it.

Sitting back and watching these improvisations, they're always a surprise. You allow people to bring all that they can to the improvisation. *You don't tell them what to do because they are obligated to the first Unit: "Secure the Prisoner."* Someone takes the initiative because their Objective pushes them to do so: All of a sudden there's the prison guard, with nothing to say, but he rushes over and grabs the fellow from the back and chains him up. And the priest is already reading the last rites over his head.

STEVEN: And so they are moving into the second Unit.

GEORGE: So they are moving already to the door, which the warden is happy about 'cause he can get on with it. And so people have, by *playing their Objectives*, determined what the *main* Objective is for that Unit.

STEVEN: Do you remember when you first developed this particular improvisation?

GEORGE: Uhhh I'd always been intrigued by that possibility of somebody being put to death. And it's OK, according to our society, that this be done.

STEVEN: Well there has been significant opposition to it in Canada.

GEORGE: In fact we don't have it at the moment.

STEVEN: Yeah, not since the Sixties.

GEORGE: That's right. The Reform Party[2] is anxious that we bring it back. You can bring back the death penalty and it will supposedly solve your problems.

STEVEN: It is like the example you gave yesterday of Richard II: Things were falling apart in England? Invade Ireland. (*Chuckles*)

GEORGE: Absolutely, absolutely.

STEVEN: What's the purpose of this improvisation?

the purposes of this improvisation

GEORGE: I don't know how to put it in one word. Like turning over the stone and seeing the evil that crawls out. We realize all the different parts the people are playing . . . to do something that terribly evil. We don't have to be religious to understand that: Just to be an artist is to know how obscene that is—an obscenity! . . .

And *an actor gets his knowledge not just intellectually, but emotionally.* And on his feet! And of course he's trying to find the truth of this moment. I won't let him scream his head off, you know, and throw his arms about for no reason, or *for effect only.*

Stanislavski talks about a man attempting to kill himself. And to take the gun out of his desk, hold it to his temple and blow his brains out. It's not just a question of 'Is the gun loaded?' There is an awful lot to go through before you face that question about you pulling the trigger. And to step into the abyss . . . . It takes so much emotional involvement to find the truth of these moments.

And *that's* what we're doing while we're doing this improvisation. We're choosing something that is particularly difficult, but something that deserves examination.

---

2. The Reform Party (1987-2000)—When the Progressive Conservative Party still existed, Reform was farther to the Right on the political spectrum.[79]

We have so many guns on the street and young people are killing each other. We've come through a war where genocide was part of a state programme. It came down in our own age, with Bosnia. The killing is so easy. An actor must take the steps of a society's violent behaviour and understand it, or try to. I don't have any answers.... As is obvious.

STEVEN: Did you ever use this improvisation in building a show?

GEORGE: Well, its first purpose is to train actors. Put them in something that's challenging.

STEVEN: High stakes.

GEORGE: Yes. Yes, indeed: A good way of putting it.

It has its obvious social value. The moment they start to analyze this small improvisation, they're questioning: "What *about* the death penalty?" They can't just brush it aside anymore.

use of extreme situations in building shows

You remember My Lai[3], when we introduced it into *Chicago '70*. We improvised our way around there a number of times. We have Bobby Seale[4] being gagged in the court, but we mix that with Vietnamese people being killed by the soldiers in My Lai. So it became—it *meant*—both things.

Poster for *Chicago '70 / courtesy of the designer Theo Dimson*

3. During the American War in Vietnam, there was a massacre of 500 civilians by U.S. soldiers at My Lai on March 16th 1968.(80)

4. Bobby Seale (b. 1936)—Civil rights activist, co-founder of the Black Panther Party and one of the defendants in the so-called 'Chicago Conspiracy Trial.' Later ran for Mayor of Oakland, California, losing the election with the second-highest number of votes.(81)

As I think, Steven, there's dozens of times in which we've made use of such extreme situations. I remember improvising Auschwitz over and over again. And we never used it, we threw out the improvisations.

STEVEN: And it will inform the rest of the work—even if it isn't there, per se, as a scene.

GEORGE: Absolutely. It's part of that experience.

improvisation: the burning of Joan of Arc

I have another exercise which I developed lately, because I like the story so much. And it's the story of Joan of Arc, when she's going to be burned at the stake. And it's not just the French who are doing it but the English in the background who are insisting the French do away with this martyr.

STEVEN: Or witch.

GEORGE: Or witch. And that she must *admit* to being a witch, or we can't burn her. And we break it up into three Units and here we have a whole town to play with and it's a great deal of fun. But they, all the town, must move from Unit to Unit.

STEVEN: And you typically use a three-Unit structure here?

improvisation misunderstood

GEORGE: If you go beyond three, very often you may fail 'cause there are so many things to do when you're still not using dialogue.

I've seen some wonderful moments when Joan has gone up in flames and, using the Efforts to do so, at the last minute *disappears*... 'cause the body is no longer there... but a heap of rubble among the twigs and ashes that were left. And then you get somebody come and clean the rubble away. Because it's a market square and business must go on.

And when the actors are working correctly, they make these little discoveries. If you were depending on one person to give you all this information, you wouldn't succeed. That's what improvisation is about: Finding the truth that is not obvious to you, always.

People have misunderstood improvisation so badly. I abhor these things that appear on the stage, and on CBC at present, where they *presume* to improvise on a word from the audience. And the objective there is "to be funny"—*not* to improvise. Their work is an abomination.

I had them in my theatre for a short time because I thought they were discovering something else. When I saw a bit of it, I kicked them out and told them to find some other place to work. It just was so unpleasant, and what they left behind was unpleasant. People leave behind something, always, in the theatre: The atmosphere of uncaring, the 'do anything' attitude, undisciplined.... All these things are like old ghosts: You have to clear them out of the theatre.

STEVEN: We've probably given far too little importance to the way a performance space accumulates the energy and practice of everybody who has worked there.

GEORGE: Absolutely, absolutely. If you recall, I was such a fusspot with my 'No coffee, no food, no hamburgers... no fucking McDonald's (*Steven laughs*) in the theatre!'

improvising towards a scripted play: Schweik's emergency

STEVEN: Could you give us examples of improvisation on a scripted play?

GEORGE: *The Good Soldier Schweik* was full of it. It was difficult to keep up with the actors. The train, for instance: I would lay that out, as to who was doing what and where, and how many people and what we should be achieving—eventually the train stopping, and Schweik being marched off to prison for having violated the railway code, therefore missing part of the war. (*Both laugh*) And you have to wonder if that wasn't what it was all about in the first place....

And even those who were just passengers all had Objectives related to that Unit. "Emergency," I think we called it—"Schweik's Emergency."

And I'll always remember Ray as Schweik. They're going to the Front and he's sitting there next to his generals and he becomes curious about the little emergency cord and starts asking questions about it: "How much do you get if you pull the cord?" (*Steven laughs*) "Ten dollars." "Oh, well, you'd get a lot more people pulling it if you raised the price, you know." (*Steven laughs*) His logic is always wonderfully backwards.

Then he pulls the cord of course and the train comes to a screeching stop. All pandemonium breaks out and the actors all ad-libbed this work. It made everyone roar with laughter when rehearsal was over. They loved it. Jack Boschulte convinced me—by that time I was writing the script—he said: "Leave it open, George." He wanted to improvise it every night. (*Laughs*) And I did it as a treat for them. That's the kind of actors they were.

STEVEN: That was the first show I saw at TWP. I guess it was your first production of *Schweik*.

GEORGE: Yes, the first one; it was the best one.

STEVEN: That's why I wanted to work at your theatre.

GEORGE: Yes, of course, good.

We went through the whole Second Act that way, by laying out the Given Circumstances, and then playing it.

How successful the dogs were! Marvellous! And Nancy was very very good with her costuming, which kind of fluffed all over the place. So everybody could be a dog—Schweik's dog. He goes into the business of stealing dogs, and that's how he's making his living, with his good friend Yannick, who's really the culprit . . . and looks like a dog. Those dogs were so beautiful! Everybody outdid each other: They wanted to be the best dogs! (*Steven laughs*) And Keith Dalton, bless him, he really captured the whole thing 'cause he was a blond fuzzy fellow and he would *do such things*! When Schweik was in the kitchen trying to cure his rheumatism, the dog would curl up in a way—it was so funny!—and get his tummy scratched, you know. You couldn't hold them back. Nor would you want to!

those dogs were so beautiful!

But it all started with this, Steven—this little improvisation about the man being executed. See, the challenges are so great in that simple exercise in which there are no words required. Therefore *the emotions* are very much in play. And with the skill of using the Efforts, you know how to move and you're not *afraid* to move.

STEVEN: With experienced actors, did you keep them to the three-Unit structure?

GEORGE: No. We'd take off as far as they could handle. But all these experienced actors came through the same training. It wasn't until the third year that we had such gorgeous work being done.

The Power of an Ensemble

the six TWP companies: gains & losses

STEVEN: My son is reminding me lately of the challenge that Cito Gaston has with the Blue Jays this year[1]. They had this amazing team two years ago and now he has to rebuild it with a lot of young players. You went through a similar process with the TWP company three or four times.

GEORGE: Oh, I counted *six* that I would identify as companies.

STEVEN: Six.

GEORGE: Yeah.

STEVEN: What did you gain and what did you lose each time you ended one company and started another?

GEORGE: Yes that's a good question 'cause you *do*, you hate what you lose. You *do gain* 'cause the doors are open again for young fellows and young girls to come in. And it's most difficult—but not impossible!—to bring other people in and be successful at it. Very often you'll lose them, because the *other* actors are talking *shorthand*: We know the work so well that you're talking *through your hands* and you're leaving somebody behind. Which is a great shame. These are losses which you are aware of....

We toured *Letters from the Earth*, which was very successful, a wonderful improvised play brought to life from Mark Twain's *Letters from the Earth*.

We got to Ottawa and all things changed. The circumstances were not good: We had to abide by IATSE[2] rulings, which meant that my men couldn't be at the board. I had these actors who took work in the commercial world, in TV land, for other

1. 1996[(s.b.)]

2. IATSE—"International Alliance of Theatrical Stage Employees" is a labour union which represents technicians, artisans and craft persons in the entertainment industry. [(82)]

theatres... and when they returned to me, I had a terrible time with some of them.

commercial work vs. creative work: *Letters from the Earth*

STEVEN: Did they feel they were coming to new interpretations of the material?

GEORGE: Partly. I think also ego: Performing in a new city, in front of new people. I gave notes every night. They were playing for the laugh; they were distorting their own work; they were *mugging* of all things! Personally I had a very, very hard time. It was soul-destroying.

STEVEN: Why did commercial theatre and television work against what you were trying to achieve? I think I know the answer, but... *mugging*?

GEORGE: You go into other theatres and you 'get jumped' because of *what you do*—not because of your potential. And you go to a TV situation, you're expected to perform for the director *while* you're getting the job there. And you do that same thing over again ten times and it turns out to be mugging because there's *no depth to it.* It's a whole series of *mugging behaviour patterns*, which are then dished-off to the public as a performance. And I, of course, object strenuously to that—and particularly so when I see good actors doing it. That breaks my heart. And I get furious—as they all can tell you.

Aint't Lookin' (2nd production 1984). Performers (l-r): Patricia VanStone, Ross Skane (on drums), Bill Martins (on keyboards), Doug Johnston, Sandi Ross, Bruce Nelson, Johnie Chase, Gene Mack / *photographer David Chiasson*

what makes a team or ensemble?

See, the analogy of your son, about the baseball team, is very good. Gaston has got to build that team again, and there's things *he* doesn't build: There's the playing together of the team. We say: "Now they are trained, right?" They can throw the ball well, they can bat—whatever it is—.350 ... " But they are not a team.

STEVEN: Not a team yet.

GEORGE: Until they're *anticipating* each other. Actors are no different in that sense. When I was in the Littlewood company, part of an ensemble there for about four or five years, we knew what was going to happen to each of us, on that stage. There was no fear. Uhh there were plenty of reasons to be frightened (*both laugh*) but there was no fear in doing something that made sense, you see, 'cause we knew each other so well and we'd look into each other's eyes and the story was told in that moment.

the actors moving the choice of plays

I figured that I was lucky when I got three years out of a group of actors. And they defined—when it was really good—they *defined* the work... as much as *do* the work. They wouldn't put up with me giving them any *ordinary* thing to do. And I remember this happening in your company. That you demanded more of the theatre and you were *right* to do so. You demanded more of the director, you demanded more of the plays. We were brave enough to throw out plays when we had planned them, to choose another one.

STEVEN: That's almost unthinkable now.

GEORGE: Unthinkable, absolutely. And even when we had subscription seasons, we'd throw the subscription out and we'd say "To hell with it!" ... and play something else. As the time *determined* it. Because it was too important not to miss *this time*. Very often the play wouldn't have meant anything a year and a half later, but at that moment it was being played it meant *everything*. This was true of *Che Guevara*, this was true of *Chicago '70*.

STEVEN: The Chile play[3], *You Can't Get Here From There*—that was very much of its time.

GEORGE: Very much of its time.

But I even felt the same with *Ain't Lookin'*: All of a sudden I just said "That's right, that's right *now*, I must find it *now*." I had a job finding the book 'cause it was hard to get hold of.

3. *You Can't Get Here From There* by Jack Winter (1974) portrayed the aftermath of the U.S.-backed coup against the elected government of Chile on September 11th 1973 when the Canadian embassy in Santiago refused to provide safe haven for pro-democracy Chileans fleeing for their lives.[(s.b./j.w.) (83)]

You Can't Get Here From There (1974). Michael Marshall and Milo Ringham as the Canadian ambassador and his wife / *photo by Robert van der Hilst*

STEVEN: It was out of print?

GEORGE: No, just a Canadian book, so who cared about it? I happened to hear Don Harron[4] interview the author, John Craig, on radio. I finally wrote Don and he sent me a copy. But he was an ordinary guy who *did* play baseball. He was kind of crude, y'know? He was amusing and a lovely man. Became big friends with me. But he wasn't 'in the swim' of what's important; he would never know who Robertson Davies was. He was talking about sports and nobody cared a damn—except *me*, who saw it as a real opportunity to show the exploitation of the black person in our society, through the athletes.

I can't emphasize enough uhhh *the actors moving the choice of plays*. You have to have a very good team for this to happen. And a knowledgeable group of people who are in tune with your own desires—politically, socially.

STEVEN: One of my favourite shows at TWP was *Summer '76*[5]. It was one in which your way of working with the actors, your sense of theatricality, the design, the script and the issues, and the skill level of the performers working in the vocabulary was at a very high level. *Summer '76*

GEORGE: Yeah, I couldn't agree with you more.

4. Don Harron (b. 1924)—Distinguished Canadian actor, comedian, journalist, director and author. His diverse credits include acting on *The Red Green Show*, directing the 1956 TV film version of *Anne of Green Gables*, and working as a host for CBC and CTV. In his 'Charlie Farquahrson' persona he performed throughout Canada for decades and authored several books.[(84)]

5. *Summer '76* (also known as *Olympics '76)*, collectively created by Jack Winter and the company, explored the intersection of idealism and corruption throughout the history of the modern Olympic Games. Performed in 1975 and 1976.[(s.b./j.w.) (85)]

STEVEN: You had very experienced people in that cast.

GEORGE: Yes, we did. I was always disappointed in the reaction to that.

STEVEN: Why was it so cool?

GEORGE: I can only think of it in terms of politics. Because, as you said, the skill was incredible, and their inventiveness! Because we had to invent every year of these Olympics—which could have been a real drag—and *was* if you saw Leni Riefenstahl's film[6]. (*Chuckles*) But we had to invent new things every time. Like the weightlifting—which became two actors on the end of the weights fighting the fellow who was trying to lift them.

So, why wasn't it well-received? Because we had the nerve, the temerity, to criticize the Olympics which were taking place in Canada *that year.* We reminded everybody of the killing of the athletes[7]. It was horrible. We portrayed all this on stage and... not only was it reasonable for that to happen in the Olympics but, going back to the Greeks, it had *always* happened. These things were vicious in the beginning and we said they're vicious now. And the fact that they were taking drugs in our own day is only an extension of that viciousness. And they all tried, if you remember, tried to claim that there were no politics in the Olympics during that year.

STEVEN: Hmm.

GEORGE: Everybody knows better now, you couldn't make such claims. But in those years they were claiming "There's no politics at all!" But it was *all* politics. And I think the critics who didn't like it wanted to support the Olympics. We satirized it. And even Astrid managed it with her wonderful design.

STEVEN: Oh it was a great design.

GEORGE: And the plastic-looking colours that were used were so phony. Nobody observed that. You see, I mean, the designers get lost, don't they? People won't see what they can't see, God knows.

Nor did it improve when we took it on tour to London. The reaction there wasn't much better. They loved *Ten Lost Years* 'cause, again, they could appreciate the nostalgia.

---

6. *Olympiad* (1938) which was filmed at the 1936 Olympics in Berlin. The film is a glorification of human physical achievement. Riefenstahl is a famous and controversial figure—an early female film director and also a maker of propaganda films under the Nazi Party.[86]

7. During the 1972 Games in Munich, eight Palestinians kidnapped and murdered eleven Israeli athletes from the Olympic village. The incident sparked international outrage and provoked the most severe military strikes from the Israeli government since the 1967 war.[87]

STEVEN: They could put it far enough away.

GEORGE: Yes indeed.

STEVEN: So, was it just because of the *experience* of the company that that show's artistically so strong?

GEORGE: It was certainly that; they had been together quite a while. Also, they were musicians in their own right. There was hardly anybody who wasn't familiar with an instrument—which I've always tried to encourage. So we had *sound on stage*, not recorded music. When we wanted the sirens to scream in the Second World War, Grant Roll used his trombone. He had to learn to do that because he didn't play the trombone.

understanding what the play is up to

So, they know what's needed. They understand the play's intention. Twelve brains on the stage is still better than one.

STEVEN: Working together with a common purpose.

GEORGE: It is *understanding what the play is up to*! Without saying, they know what the Through-Line is.

Well, Steven....

Summer '76 (1975-76). Actors (l-r, front): Richard Payne, Ross Skene & Grant Roll; (l-r, back): Peter Millard & Diane Douglass / *photographer unknown*

The Theatre of Politics and Politics *in* the Theatre

(*Before the tape started rolling, George and Steven were discussing connections between activism in the 1930s and 40s and the recent 'Days of Action'*[1] *in Toronto.*)

STEVEN: You saw signs of hope.

GEORGE: Oh absolutely, absolutely. As a young fella, I opened up on the stage singing and my songs, you know, would have been old Joe Hill songs, "The Preacher and the Slave." Whereas, *none* of that on the stage at *this* thing. Billy Bragg was there, it was all rock music and it was rock music adapted to the times. The protest was the same, it was great, I loved it. And I loved the sense of immediacy and presence; it was a very optimistic day. There we were, thousands of us, all protesting against one son-of-a-bitch. He certainly did one thing: He brought us all together. One positive act. (*Both laugh*)

STEVEN: It's Friday November 8th, near one o'clock, and George and I are sitting in George's living room.

Days of Action, media biases and the Jean-Louis Roux controversy

GEORGE: You've reminded me of the Days of Action and of what we're doing here—talking about acting. *How important it is that the artist be militant!* Not just, as some would like to think, 'objective'... or just going along with what has already been produced in the past, but important in our day *to make a statement as artists*—in our selection of material, in what we play. Because we are

1. Days of Action—Beginning on Dec 11th 1995, the Ontario Federation of Labour and the Ontario Coalition Against Poverty led a series of eleven *city*-wide strikes and protests in an attempt to rally *province*-wide support against Mike Harris' "common sense revolution." His "workfare" policy required welfare recipients to work in order to receive welfare and was strongly opposed by social activists. Labour sought to protect workers' rights from what they saw as the Harris government's corporate-based political/economic agenda.(88)

fighting a *wave* of intolerance from the media. That is, every day on the goddamned TV, the mildest interpretation of events is always *slanted*. And of course it's slanted on a Right-wing perspective. Even when, it seems to me, they don't mean to.

STEVEN: It's more like force of habit, huh?

GEORGE: Yes indeed it is, they don't even have to be *cajoled*. They know what's expected of them—to be this, what *they* think is 'middle of the road,' but indeed is very Right-wing. The apologies for Jean-Louis Roux[2] and his behaviour, just recently.

STEVEN: Over having worn the swastika in 1942.

GEORGE: And having joined in the bashing of Jewish shops. And *excused* that he was only 19. Aw, sod that! (*Steven laughs*) You know, we create revolutions at 19! We are the leaders at 19. We move our society. I, for one, was on picket lines at 16. And this would be in 1942. So you know your mind. Within a couple of years I was drafted, I got my notice. I didn't have to go 'cause the war was over—but I mean, this idea that you are young and therefore excusable is not acceptable to my mind.

And it's not that you can't change: Everything changes, and you *must* change as you grow older, but I see *no condemnation of his viewpoint at that time.*

And in the job that he was holding, Lieutenant-Governor, he represents the government and the people. And I don't see any *contradiction* of his view: It was just high-jinx of a young boy wearing a goddamn swastika.

STEVEN: In 1942.

GEORGE: To hell with that! In 1942, when we already knew! The Red Cross was informing us of the concentration camps.

STEVEN: It wasn't just the propaganda of the Left denouncing Hitler by 1942.

GEORGE: No. And we'd already been through the Spanish Civil War. Not that many people *knew* about it. Except of course in Quebec, where they put up pictures of Franco[3] in every house. I know, Raymond told me.

---

2. Jean-Louis Roux (b.1924)—Renowned actor, director, playwright and, briefly, the Lieutenant-Governor of Quebec. He is also a member of the order of Canada and was appointed director of the Canada Council in 1998.[(89)]

3. Francisco Franco (1892-1975)—Head of State in Spain following his victory (heavily supported by Hitler and Mussolini) in the Spanish Civil War.[(90)]

STEVEN: Raymond Belisle?

GEORGE: Yes indeed, charming fella who was in *Les Canadiens*. It was common for the crucifix on one wall and Franco's portrait on the other. And this was pushed by the Church, of course, and I'm sure that Roux was pushed to the same thing, in the schools.

STEVEN: You were mentioning all the young people on the Days of Action.

GEORGE: Oh, it was inspiring. I couldn't see them because we were so dense a crowd and I was in my scooter. But the politics was firmly in tow by these young people; they understood. Good, good speeches. Very optimistic, isn't it, to be in such a group?

We get so often battered by the media, and there's so little history from a Left-wing point of view. It's easy enough to be swamped by *their* interpretation of the economy but it is important the artist be able to express this sense of injustice that was obviously there on the Days of Action, in the people.

You know that our friend Rich Payne[4] sent me some scripts and he's working very hard obviously to involve the unions and progressive-thinking people in his company. And I think that's tremendously encouraging. I'd love for it to succeed.

workers' theatre

Not many people know that when I first came back from Europe, one of the first things I did was try and build a "Workers' Theatre." I had a lot of friends in the union movement. And when I came back I looked them up. I knew I couldn't get money from them, but I wanted their connections in the union. I wanted to set up a chain of places to play within union halls and develop a company that would play to the workers. Play work that had meaning for them. And that's what I would have called a "Workers' Theatre"—the workers coming to me—and that's how you'd make your money.

STEVEN: Right.

GEORGE: Worked for about 3 or 4 days figuring out how to do that, making a lot of trips and talking to a lot of people and trying to get encouraged. But I... I couldn't get the information that I

4.Richard Payne (1949-2010)—All-around theatre man, visual artist and educator. Acted three seasons with TWP: *The Captain of Köpenick*, *Ten Lost Years*, *Summer '76*. Playwright: *The Yellow House at Arles* (with Dennis Hayes), *The Common Stench Revolution*. Created Downsize Theatre Company for collaboration with labour and other activists. Directed, dramaturged and co-designed *Beating the Bushes* (2003). A late notebook includes plans to create a 'George Luscombe People's Theatre of East York.'(s.b) (91)

needed, or the co-operation that I needed, to tackle all the union halls in the province. It didn't come off.

In the meantime I worked as a commercial actor and finally built TWP. Which was *not* a "Workers' Theatre."

Life on the Line (1981-84), directed by Alec Stockwell. Steven (foreground) with Ben Cleveland-Hayes (on drums) and co-author Allen Booth (on keyboard)
photo by Alex Neumann

But I hadn't seen a hint of it till I saw Rich's ambition in these papers. Maybe the time is coming ripe for it now. I was sorry that we didn't have a group ready with guitars, drums and fiddles and perform for the strikers on that Day of Action. Lots of people did, professional people, very good. But there should have been someone there *from the theatrical community* to put on the stage what people were angry about.

STEVEN: Well I know that Richard has done some shows in Port Elgin—the CAW Labour School—and uh when I was working with Mixed Company[5], we did a bit of that for two or three years.

5. Mixed Company Theatre for Social Responsibility—Co-founded in 1982 by Steven Bush and Simon Malbogat who later served as Artistic Co-Directors with Allen Booth and Nancy Hindmarsh. Simon has been sole Artistic Director since the collective ended in 1988-89 and MCT has continued to use theatre as a tool for social change, working with community, education and the workplace.(s.m./s.b.) (92)

GEORGE: Yes, your play *Life On the Line*[6] was very successful.

STEVEN: And Don Bouzek's Ground Zero Productions[7] shows up at rallies and performs at labour halls. But that work tends to be 'invisible.' Perhaps in Scotland and parts of Europe, it might have a higher profile; here it tends to be 'underground.'

GEORGE: Well, timing is everything. You know, the Right has swung so far to the right in everything—and it has been so devastating to the economy, to the social life of our society—that it's not going to be cured by voting for the Liberals next time. I mean the damage is done. It would be nice to think that artists could take advantage of the feeling that people have. The frustration. That they now are suffering and will continue to suffer.

it's not enough to have good intentions

It's not enough to have the right ideas and good intentions. You have to be well-trained as an artist and therefore your work is applauded by all those who don't believe in your ideology. But they will be caught up in the quality of your work and therefore listen more carefully. Sloppy amateur work won't do. It's got to be done well and then people will be attracted.

STEVEN: Why aren't there more TWPs?

no militant schools of acting

GEORGE: I think because *the very training of actors in this country is bourgeois.* And they're not exposed to the history of their country, or any history. They *will* talk of New York. They will talk of England, we're still a colonial country. But there's no militant *schools* of acting. That's a great shame. (*Laughs*)

So it isn't that the actor doesn't *want* the exposure that he should be getting: It's what's available.

Not everyone is capable of creating a theatre. It takes a peculiar kind to do that. Willing to give up, for a long time, personal acclaim.

STEVEN: You pay a price, if you build a theatre.

GEORGE: You pay a price, certainly. You lose 'the mainstream' for a while. The applause can come later in your life—which doesn't do you a hell of a lot of good—(*Steven laughs*) but that's not a

6. *Life on the Line* by Steven Bush and Allen Booth, produced by Mixed Company Theatre, played in Toronto and toured Ontario and as far west as Edmonton from 1981 to 1984.[(s.b.) (94)]

7. In 1997 Ground Zero Productions, initially based in Peterborough and Toronto Ontario, re-located to Edmonton Alberta. The company uses theatre to effect social change. It produces plays for the labour movement and community organizations committed to social justice. Its creations are often intermedial, and their collaborations are often international.[(95)]

George, c. 1980 / *photographer unknown*

complaint because the joy of living in your own experience, and building a theatre, is so satisfying.

the joy of living in your own experience

STEVEN: So, the joy of the work itself continued to pull you forward.

GEORGE: Well, you remember that sometimes I used to get all dressed up in my 'go to the bank' suit. I had it in my office somewhere, and I'd go down to the corner and argue for our existence again—which I would make a joke of and we'd all laugh about it.

And it was very serious stuff outside the theatre. But it was *outside* the theatre, it wasn't *in* the theatre. So they couldn't harm the theatre, they couldn't. It only came in terms of satire: We made fun of it, the peculiar view of 'putting bums on the chairs.' "How many people have seen it?" Well, for me, it had been fine if *one* person had been moved.

But they were interested in numbers, of course. So we had to justify our existence all the time. Over and over and over again. Until it finally ended up that we couldn't justify it. We couldn't satisfy ... *their policy.* And we went broke. It finally ended up that we got no more support from them 'cause they were fed up with me.

It had to be work that was somehow going to please the audience, I suppose. I never chose work for that reason. *I chose it because I was inspired by it*... or the actors had made me inspired by their choice.

STEVEN: Hmmnn.

GEORGE: There are goals we never met, before I was finished with the theatre. We never had the French, for instance, on the stage with English. Bilingual theatre wasn't a dominant desire of the company. We spoke English and therefore the tradition goes to Shakespeare.

goals we never met
1. bilingual theatre

I always remember going to the Old Vic.[8] Joan talks about it in her book[9]—when she 'sent Luscombe off to the Old Vic' to get rid of my English pretensions. We were both doing *Richard II* at the same time, at Stratford East[10] and the Old Vic—

2. to play against other theatres

STEVEN: That's pretty cheeky.

GEORGE: Yes, we did it purposely. Then we went to see each other's work. It was a hoot, and we learned a great deal, as actors.

STEVEN: That is the sign of some kind of maturity in a culture.

GEORGE: Absolutely, yes. It isn't competition at the lowest level. (*Chuckles*) The Old Vic was doing it down the road, in the West End—the beautiful town where the beautiful people were. And one of the last scenes of *Richard II* is Richard in prison, when he talks to one of the minstrels outside and says "Here I am a king without the freedom of a minstrel!" Very good, very touching, and John Neville[11]—bless his soul, a very nice man—he was playing Richard, and he was draped in wonderful clothes, and lit by lights that created a lovely blue grey impression, quite gorgeous to look at. He stood quietly in the centre, and went through these recitations, and then of course he's murdered, as the play insists.

8. Old Vic—Theatre and Shakespeare repertory company in London, England with a history going back to 1818.[(95)]

9. *Joan's Book: Joan Littlewood's Peculiar History As She Tells It.* Also appears as *The Autobiography of Joan Littlewood.*[(96)]

10. Theatre Royal Stratford East, where Luscombe performed with the Theatre Workshop, opened in 1884.[(97)]

11. John Neville (1925-2011)—English-born actor, producer, director. Neville began his professional career in London at The New Theatre, establishing his reputation as a lead actor mostly through a range of Shakespearean and classic roles. Artistic Director of the Stratford Festival 1985-89. In 1988 he starred in Terry Gilliam's film *The Adventures of Baron Munchausen* and in the 1990s the popular TV series *The X Files* as the 'Well-Manicured Man.'[(99)]

Well in our production, the lights came on and there was a great scream as Harry Corbett tried to free himself from a chain, and he was in burlap clothes that were scratchy and ill-looking. He looked like some dog on the end of the chain, which is exactly what Littlewood wanted. Eventually he was slaughtered by myself and another one who played the murderers and... What in the hell was this all about, an example of *what*?

STEVEN: We were talking about the two interpretations...

GEORGE: Yes, well the one at the Old Vic would've been 'blocked,' of course, very carefully. But *we* wouldn't find our way in such a manner. It was a Marxist interpretation of *Richard II*, which I found very exciting and played many roles in it. We all improvised in terms of the meaning of the central Objective and all the actors understood it.

See, what I wanted to do so often was to play *against* other theatres. I purposely chose work that somebody else had chosen too, in order to make the comparison.

STEVEN: What was an example of that?

GEORGE: *Captain of Köpenick.*[12]

STEVEN: Somebody else was doing *Köpenick*?

GEORGE: Well, Leon Major had scheduled it for his season, so I scheduled it for mine. But as soon as I did that, and it became public, he withdrew his. He missed the whole point.

STEVEN: Oh, that's too bad.

GEORGE: And then we ourselves failed with the production, for some other reasons. But the idea that you should compete is *theatre*. It was something that I was trying to encourage—my ideology against theirs, my non-religious against their highly moral shows. Fight each other on those issues.

STEVEN: And the artistic formal questions too.

GEORGE: Of course, of course and the quality of work would come into it—*(Steven laughs)* which we were very confident in, weren't we? And what a joy for the audience!

The other thing was to set up Workshop Productions right across the country: Halifax Workshop Productions, Newfoundland Workshop Productions, a Vancouver Workshop Productions. And they would have reflected their environment and their attitudes.

---

12. *The Captain of Köpenick* by Carl Zuckmayer is about a cobbler posing as an officer and about the power of uniforms.[(99)]

3. workshop productions right across the country

We were very much a Toronto company, I thought, and we reflected this city; and I think we did it very well for so many years. But it would have been great to have seen other companies built up across the country, reflecting honestly *their* communities. I think of any of Shakespeare's plays—of one done in Toronto and one done in Newfoundland—they'd be so wonderfully different and both valid. It seemed to be enough to keep *one* theatre going. I couldn't branch out in that way.

STEVEN: Yeah. . . .

So why do you think after all the efforts—your 30 years or so, other companies that have grown up influenced by your work—we have still, for the most part, a theatre that isn't very politicized? Why is this? Just because the temper of the times has been so reactionary since the Thatcher/ Reagan/ Mulroney era?

why haven't we had more effect?

GEORGE: There's no sense of revolution in this country. We have shied away, in our past, from revolutionary action. I don't think that's the full answer but I think that's a good one. The very founding of this country is opposite. We had a police force in the shape of the Mounties who could take care of the entire West, no problem: 'Just leave your guns at the border.' There's a feeling of admiration for the government. On the one hand, that can be a good thing—like our Medicare and our belief in organizing from the state down. But there's certainly a lack of . . . of *objection* that must come from the artist.

The only place you get it is in Quebec. Where the artists're part of that whole sense of revolution. Not a bloody one, but a *change*. Our artists do the opposite: We behave ourselves. And part of it's, as I say, brainwashing of the press. And there is a sense we prefer the quiet life to the revolutionary life.

STEVEN: I can think of so many individual examples: Some of Passe Muraille's work; Michael Hollingsworth, VideoCab, the Hummer Sisters; companies in the Prairies, East Coast uhhh the wonderful things that Guillermo Verdecchia has done with *The Noam Chomsky Lectures;*[13] some of the Native writers. . . . But what I continue not to understand is why all this hasn't somehow made a bigger change in the mainstream theatre . . . and also the way the public *looks* at theatre.

13. Co-authored by, and performed with, Daniel Brooks. Premiered in 1990.[(100)]

Why haven't we had more effect?

GEORGE: I don't have the answer! *(Both laugh)* But the fact is we haven't. We don't seem to benefit from each other's experiences, nor even discuss them very much.

STEVEN: Maybe it's an impossible question. I'm troubled by it, you know, *frequently*, so I thought I'd force it on you and see what you came up with. (*Laughs*)

GEORGE: There are so many answers that there is no one conclusive answer to it.

STEVEN: ... Uhhh political problems in the theatre itself, why 'dirty tricks' happen. We've all either experienced or heard stories about back-biting, betrayal, 'palace coups.' Why do we waste so much time and spirit fighting these kinds of battles?

politics in the theatre: boards vs. artists

GEORGE: You'll notice that you don't have 'palace coups' if the theatre is a failure. Nobody wants a failure. When you're successful and there is something to be gained, *then* you're in danger of the board of directors ousting the artist.

STEVEN: Which has happened more than once in English Canada.

GEORGE: Indeed. Seems to be a pattern.

When I was very young and innocent uhhh Jimmy Lovell[14] told me a story about building a theatre which became very successful and—wouldn't you know it?—*he* was kicked out, the founder and artistic director, and the board took over. It lasted about a year and then the whole thing was finished forever. This was in Manchester, England.

STEVEN: He was an actor that you worked with in rep?

GEORGE: That's right. He put me on to Littlewood and changed my career considerably. And then years later I brought him over here to help me and he came and it was great excitement! It was during the first production of *Hey Rube!*

And he told me that story and I thought that was devastating. But I've heard it repeated over and over again so many times and ... wouldn't you know it? Even though I was prepared, it happened to me: I was fired by my own board of directors. And you'd think that I had had enough warning, that I could have held control of the theatre I had built after thirty years ... but no. There was

14. James Lovell—Actor and director. He was the first to help George understand Shakespeare and the Elizabethan Theatre.[(101)]

a prize to be had and that was a theatre worth nearly a million dollars, the property and the building. I won't go into that long story, but *nevertheless it happened.*

And the quick answer is that the *goals* for the artist are different than the goals for the businessmen who are usually on your board. No matter how well meaning they are—and we've had well-meaning boards of directors! The board, if there were to be any, should be there *in support of* what those artists have done. And it never works out that way. They want a bigger, I suppose, influence in what's going on; whereas, in fact, you've spent years training *yourself* how to do this job.

I don't think there's any place for a board of directors with the artist.

We managed 'cause there was no such thing as boards when I began in '59. And therefore they couldn't place one on me until later, way way down the road. I could resist the Council's insistence for a board of directors, and we'd say: "No, we have our advisors and we don't need any more."

It's *a mistrust* of the artist, that's what it is. From the grant-giving bodies. There's an inherent mistrust. It's *a nineteenth-century idea*: That he's a bohemian, likes to live in an attic, he's funny, wears funny clothes and he...

STEVEN: doesn't mind starving.

GEORGE: And he's *better* if he starves. And he's no good at business so we very clever business people have to look after him. But these boards *don't* look after you, they only interfere with you.

STEVEN: I was one of the directors of a small Toronto theatre and I approached the head of the theatre section, one of the arts councils, and asked—this is after several years of operation... "What do we need to do to move from *occasional* 'Project' to *ongoing* 'Operating' funding?" And I expected an answer like... "Well, do better shows" or "Get a stronger artistic team together" or...

GEORGE: Yes. (*Laughs*) How naive you were.

STEVEN: "Find better playwrights or scripts..." But the answer was...

GEORGE: I can see it coming.

STEVEN: "Get yourself a high-powered board of directors." (*Both laugh*)

GEORGE: Absolutely.

STEVEN: You knew the answer.

GEORGE: It's always the same. Businessmen can make money, therefore they are a success. I've seen businessmen fail all over the place, so have you. Leon Major told me this: On bended knee he begged his board to raise money so they could last. They didn't. They twiddled their thumbs. They came to all the parties, with their dress-up suits, and they brought their wives, to show off, and yet did none of the really tough work that you have all these influential people for. I uhhh... Terrible, the problems they cause. You only have to look at Stratford. And that wonderful kafuffle that made the headlines for about a week.

STEVEN: Which particular kafuffle was this? When the four directors were fired by the board?

GEORGE: When the four directors were fired, yes that was it.[15] Yes, but that in itself was a repeat, you know, that nonsense. Many years ago, they had the Toronto Arts Club, or whatever it was called, and they got ambitious and were going to do a season. And they let it be known that they were going to hire Peter Ustinov[16] to be the artistic director.

And I know this from backstage gossip in the dressing rooms. What happened was that this group of wonderful, bright businessmen—the Toronto Arts Board or whatever in hell they called themselves—said: "Dear Mr. Ustinov, please come over and be our artistic director. We'll pay you $40,000 for the season." And in those days that was a great deal of money. And Ustinov, upon receiving this information, leaned back in the dressing room and turned around to three or four actors who were there and said: "Anyone want 40,000 bucks? They can go to Canada and get it." And one of them said: "Yes, I'll take it." And he became their artistic director.

What a way to do business! And that wasn't Ustinov's fault. That was the naiveté of this board of directors who were supposed

15. In 1980 Pam Brighton, Martha Henry, Urjo Kareda and Peter Moss were appointed as a four-person artistic directorate to succeed Robin Phillips. This decision was revoked a few months later, causing national outrage. John Hirsch was then appointed the new artistic director.[(102)]

16. Sir Peter Ustinov (1921-2004)—Actor, producer, playwright, novelist, raconteur and UN ambassador. Often called a "Renaissance man," Ustinov was noted for his versatility and wit. He won numerous awards, including an Oscar, an Emmy and a Grammy, and was made a knight by Queen Elizabeth II in 1990.[(103)]

to be so clever. They were made fools of, and they deserved to be made fools of, by the artist. And that lasted one year before the fella went home.

And to say that you can't build a theatre without them is nonsense. Uhhh give me a couple of people who are being paid to fundraise: What do you need with a board of directors? That's a better solution than to have a group you have to meet with every month to jolly them up to make them feel at home... and they are doing very little. I think it is a poor way in which to organize theatre, but I don't think it is going to change for a while.

STEVEN: I have one related question. We have often seen strong efforts to bring artists together—the struggle for the 'Status of the Artist' legislation, for example. Under-employed communities can *tend* to eat themselves alive; I think that happens a lot in the theatre. When have you seen examples where we have overcome in-fighting?

competition: it's destructive in terms of the work.

GEORGE: I can think of PACT[17] when we belonged to it. There were meetings in which you felt some enthusiasm, when all the theatre managers were of a mind to work together, to improve conditions. But we're all scraping for the same couple of bucks from the same organizations. And that's this thing about *competition: It's destructive in terms of the work.* I remember trying to say at meetings: "Would we stop trying to, all of us, split the pie up? What we need is *a larger pie*!"

STEVEN: Mmhmmn.

GEORGE: When I read through this thesis that Delia[18] wrote, it takes my breath away. 'Cause every other goddamned page is about meetings to help the theatre survive... trying to do all these things *besides* trying to put the shows on. And one would think 'Well, isn't this nice, we can put our shows on and enjoy doing it!' But a great deal of the effort was taken up with these other problems. They never solved themselves. I don't know whether they could.

17. PACT—Professional Association of Canadian Theatres. " PACT is a member-driven organization that serves as the collective voice of professional Canadian theatres. For the betterment of Canadian theatre, PACT provides leadership, national representation and a variety of programs and practical assistance to member companies, enabling members to do their own creative work."(104)

18. Delia D'Ermo authored an MA thesis at McGill University published in 1993 and entitled *George Luscombe's Life and Art 1926-1989.*(105)

Relations with Playwrights

GEORGE: I couldn't find the directors and writers to work with. You know? There were a few. Even those few I usually alienated. Like Rick Salutin. The success I made of *Les Canadiens* should have guaranteed that we work together for another 5 years or so.

STEVEN: You'd think, huh?

GEORGE: The difficulties usually have to do with *interpretation.* From my point of view, it'd be a lack of understanding on the part of the writer of his craft. Like the Through-Line: This Unit is obviously not a part of the Through-Line and I'd throw it out. And sometimes I'd be subtle about it and try to convince the person it should go, but eventually it would go because I had an obligation to put the damn thing on the stage. And in that sense, I'd have the last word. But the last word would often cause me to alienate the affections of the writer. Now the only one that didn't happen to was Mario Fratti. (*Laughs*)

the final word

STEVEN: Was that because he was off in Italy doing something else?

GEORGE: He was in the States. But when I invited him up, he thought it was wonderful we were doing his work. Not that I hadn't changed it: Practically re-wrote the whole text during one summer, in order to make sense of it. And to cut out the obvious religiosity—and that, I thought, was the wrong interpretation. I wanted a revolutionary, not an admiration of Jesus Christ, on the stage. But Fratti didn't mind at all, he thought we had *improved* the work. Or said so.

But that may have been his American experience: Just so delighted to get it mounted!

STEVEN: Yes, sometimes writers can be so desperate that they will put up with anything.

GEORGE: Yeah, but when you're working in Toronto, it's a lot easier for writers. And no reason it shouldn't be. That's good, they get the work produced. Whereas, in the States, you can go a long time without ever getting it on the boards.

STEVEN: My only dealings with an American producer were for a play that Tony Pearce and I wrote and we never let them do it because they insulted us so much by saying "We'll give you a hundred dollars and tickets to the opening." (*Both laugh*) That was the time I was active with the Playwrights Union, so we didn't want to put up with that.

GEORGE: No.

STEVEN: I've always been treated much better by Canadian theatres. But one of the big issues of the Playwrights Union contract was author having the final word.

GEORGE: That's nonsense, from my point of view. And if not, one says the director has the final word. But there has to be some give-and-take.

STEVEN: If you've got a good working relationship, very often those problems can be worked out. But if you don't, how is the writer's work to be protected?

GEORGE: But *should* it be protected, you see? What should and shouldn't be, this has to swatted out between the director and the writer. Especially with new work. You have to see how it develops in the rehearsal process. A script is a script, but a play is not a play *until* it has been produced on the stage.

STEVEN: But things that you *think* should be cut, before rehearsals, *on their feet* they may prove themselves. And the other way around: Things that you thought were strong scenes may collapse.

GEORGE: Yes indeed. You can't know until the process is taking place. And in my process I have a way of analyzing the play, it's not slipshod, you know; it is not just 'Maybe this will work and maybe this won't.' There's a reason for it. And having done that for 30 years, I expect people to respect it. You know, they'll think: 'Maybe this guy knows something.' But often just the opposite is true.

It is an ongoing dilemma, no matter what we say here. Because tomorrow I get together with somebody and it would be the same struggle all over again.

Jack Winter

When I had the writer in the theatre, as I did with Jack Winter, very often the plays were developed as we rehearsed on the stage and he would write *into* it as it was going on. And he would take what the actors had contributed: If it was valid, he would keep it and if it wasn't, he wouldn't. But he would be *led* by their contribution. And uh even then, I would be throwing work out that didn't work, in my opinion.

STEVEN: You and Jack had years of experience together, so you had a way of talking with one another that wouldn't have been the case with Rick or other writers.

GEORGE: No, that's right. Even though with Rick I had worked several times—*Fanshen* and…

STEVEN: *S: Portrait of a Spy*[1].

GEORGE: I wanted him to call it *I Spy. (Both laugh)*

hindsight, time & second productions

You know, with that one, it was after the first preview that we saw then how it should have been produced. It took that long. And him and I both agreed on the physical interpretation which would have changed drastically. Because we lost on it: We lost money, we lost the audience. It took us all that time to realize that what *should* have happened *physically* on the stage was the building of that chess board—which I had introduced—and each piece finally came off, naturally, as the play progressed.

STEVEN: Aha.

GEORGE: And that didn't happen. The director—who I chose—didn't see it. And by the time Rick and I saw it *together*, it was too late. We had no rehearsal time left.

STEVEN: Some situations, of course, you could have put one of your other shows on for a week or two, taking that one back to the rehearsal hall… and brought it back.

GEORGE: And it would have succeeded as a play. But by the time the light dawned, it was too late.

STEVEN: Oh, that thing about hindsight! You remember *From the*

1. *S: Portrait of a Spy*, by Rick Salutin and Ian Adams, Canadian journalist and fiction author. Ran at TWP October 18th—November 11th 1984.(106)

Boyne to Batoche,[2] which you and Jack supported through a very difficult time. That was my first time directing in a couple of years and one of the things that happened was losing control of the physical production.

GEORGE: Yes.

STEVEN: Two months later I re-wrote the play. I re-set everything on a Red River cart. So it would play around that, with multi-purpose items, as if there were some imagined touring theatre…

GEORGE: Oh that sounds really good.

STEVEN: … of the age. It *concentrated* everything. I never found, in the rehearsal, a way of using the space that would focus the story. I found it two or three months later.

GEORGE: 'Focus' is the right word, because it had no focus on its first out. Full of wonderful things with no central focus. You needed a second production. Rick and I used to talk about that—the value of a second production.

STEVEN: Which so few plays in Canada get.

GEORGE: They don't get it, very seldom. *Les Canadiens* was a second production. And *The Wobbly*: In the second production, it was great. But it was *reviewed* in the first production. Didn't get a chance. And that happens so often.

STEVEN: Well thanks, George.

GEORGE: I think that's it.

STEVEN: Try to meet again in the near future. It's November 8th. Sometime in July, we met last…

GEORGE: Oh yeah, long time, long time.

STEVEN: Try not to be… so far in the future.

---

2. *From the Boyne to Batoche* by Steven Bush and Rick McKenna, about the fateful encounter between Canadian historical figures Louis Riel and Thomas Scott, ran at TWP September 16th—October 6th 1974.(s.b) (107)

Last Conversation: "The Search for Truth"

STEVEN: December 11th '96. Sitting in George's livingroom.

GEORGE: One reason that Vakhtangov[1] and others broke away from him was that Stanislavski was *determined* that nothing should alter from that course. And I base my early work with actors on *Actor Prepares* and developing the techniques that Stanislavski gave us.

training begins with Stanislavski

And therefore you would think I was building a Naturalistic theatre. Which I am not. And never did. And it's full of a 'stylized' kind of theatre which is very Brechtian and uhh Chinese-influenced—Chinese opera which I loved so much when I first saw it. And the influence from Commedia dell'Arte. Music Hall from Joan Littlewood. But always based upon the search for truth as understood by Stanislavski.

And this is what people have missed, you see. Because *it is that search for truth that is so valuable*, it has been for me, through all the productions. That your sense of what is true and what is not does not alter because it is a 'flamboyant' production. But you must have, at the basis of it, a sense of *truth*, the actor's ability to *discern* truth, and *that* you get from Stanislavski's work.

STEVEN: Even if you are wearing a Commedia mask or doing circus tricks.

GEORGE: Whatever region you go into, there must be a basis of truth. It cannot only be technique on the outside. I'm trying to say *why it is so important that the training of an actor begins with*

1.Evgeny Vakhtangov (1883-1922)—A director and pupil of Stanislavski, who brought together Stanislavski's naturalistic style with Meyerhold's grotesque style to form what he called "fantastic realism."(108)

Krysia Jarmicka-Read in *Hey Rube!* with Grant Roll in background (1972-73) / *photo by Robert van der Hilst*

Stanislavski. Stanislavski's search for *what it is* when you believe it, or *don't* believe it. When an actor is working well, or when he's kidding us. Whether he is trying to 'get away with it.' And to be able to *judge* that—even as a director—you must have that sense.

STEVEN: Now occasionally we see great acting in film and it often comes from a Stanislavski base, but film and television have frozen acting in the form of Naturalism. Very rarely do we see anything else.

The Visit on film and at TWP

GEORGE: Yes, I'd like to give an example of that. The other night, when I was watching 'the box' again, the old movie, *Visit of an Old Lady*—Dürrenmatt's marvellous play—and this was a version with Anthony Quinn...

STEVEN: and Ingrid Bergman.

GEORGE: Yes. And it was delightful, in a Naturalistic sense.

But Dürrenmatt never meant it to be Naturalism. We played the *play.* We had a woman... Maja,[2] marvellous actress... carrying two

2. Maja Ardal (b.1949)—Actor, director, playwright, teacher. TWP company member for several seasons. former Artistic Director of Young People's Theatre, co-founder of Contrary Company. Employs the Laban Efforts when working with 4th Line Theatre, when directing productions such as *The Threepenny Opera* for Humber Theatre and other schools and when performing her own plays *You Fancy Yourself* and *The Cure for Everything.*[(s.b.) (109)]

Jeff Braunstein & Milo Ringham in *Letters from the Earth* (1973) / *photographer unknown*

puppets on either side of her body. And Suzette Couture was playing a gentleman. See, we were mixing sexes long before uh uh really because of Suzette's insistence on her playing a *man* in the crowd. She did it wonderfully. She educated me in that production.... And we had an Old Lady, she was Diane Grant, she was great! She was all *artificial*... which is what Capitalism was, you see.

STEVEN: Which is what Dürrenmatt intended.

GEORGE: Which is what Dürrenmatt intended. So she wasn't a beautiful lady, you know, having great love scenes—all that shit that Naturalism loves to indulge in for the sake of somebody's idea of what the public wants. Uhh she had a wooden leg. She had part of her body missing; it was a steel plate. She was made up of all these parts and pieces. And then you try to make love to a person like that! Great fun.

Our train was created by all the actors. There was a great trunk in the middle, which Barry Flatman got a hold of, and all the actors were doing different things to make the train come into the station and then leave. Finally Barry dropped this lid down—'Boom! Boom!'... and he brought the train alive in our ears and in our eyes and it was all done in the open on the stage.

And they were marvellous characters, in the village. And not a hundred extras like they do in the bloody movies where everybody is running around falling over each other. *These were actors used to space*, creating crowds out of their use of the stage. It was uh very highly 'stylized' in every way. But it was full of truth and the actors all applied the imaginative work of Stanislavski. . . .

I remember uh taking a few students who had been well trained in movement and we were improvising the lynching of a person. And there were three of them, two fellas and one girl. And they were working in the Efforts and they threw the rope over the limb. There was no rope, there was no limb, it was mimed. And as they threw the rope over and pulled on it, in the Efforts, the person being lynched was drawn up. Again, in the Efforts, she got to the top, and they tied her off, and she was lynched. And she swung in the breeze. Now, she didn't swing normally, she couldn't; her feet were still on the ground. But as she swung, *she changed her Centre*. And the rest of the body hung from the Centre of *the neck*. And it was very, very moving. And it was an extraordinary few moments—one of the moments you'd like to get on tape, right? And uhh we all knew we had had an experience.

violence on stage without naturalism

Nobody was hurt. Nobody was dropped through an actual trap door—as I did in *The Murder of Maria Marten*[3] when I was in fit-up. And nobody was *in danger* of being hurt. And yet the artistry of that moment was heightened . . . just because there was nothing else to worry about.

STEVEN: Hmm.

GEORGE: There was no Naturalism. It was all done with the technique of theatre.

Now the critics would always say: "Well, they're dancing. Somebody choreographed it well." It's nonsense. What we did was learn how an actor should move. And that the theory of Stanislavski's applies mentally, psychologically, *and physically*.

And *that* you don't see in directors' work because they are imitative of movies and television. I haven't seen the directors I know *even caring about* searching for a new way to speak. And I was worried about being dogmatic 'cause I'm sure there are young people who are trying to find new ways to talk.

3. *The Murder of Maria Marten, or The Red Barn* by Brian J. Burton. The story is a sensational tale of murder and deceit based on historical fact. In August of 1828 Maria Marten's lover, William Corder, was arrested and executed for her murder.[110]

STEVEN: You mean 'talk' in...?

GEORGE: 'Talk' in that big sense: New ways to reach the audience with what they have to say. And not satisfied with the limited notions of Realism or Naturalism. And not being *eccentric*—in the sense that this is only for the elite and if you don't appreciate this, don't come to see us, that kind of foolishness. No. Our theatre attempted always to be popular. We never thought it necessary, or even right, to try to explain this to our audiences. They don't want to hear all this.

searching for a new way to speak

STEVEN: They want to see the work.

GEORGE: But what we want to do, in the work, is to reach them on all the three levels—intellectually, psychologically and physically.

STEVEN: Your talk about *The Visit* made me think of a production I saw staged by Robert Lepage in Ottawa. He's one who has broken the stranglehold of Naturalism. One scene where all the people are driving through the country in their—is it yellow?—yellow sedans, new cars they are getting for co-operating with Clara...

The Visit staged by Lepage

GEORGE: Yes...

STEVEN: Uhhh instead of cars, he had people on revolving office chairs, moving across the stage. This was a bureaucracy at work, you know. An office on wheels.

GEORGE: Yes, yes, lovely, great, great.

STEVEN: One of the challenges with students is to get them to *claim their space.*

GEORGE: Well, you have to let people see the *potential* of the theatre space—and themselves in it—and use it all through the training period. It's no good saying "Well, I'll do this with this play" if your actors aren't capable of doing it. Otherwise you'll find yourself telling them all where to move. I always felt that the potential of the actor was not used... in everything that I saw.

let people see the potential of the theatre space.

STEVEN: You're surprised that more people don't aim for the lab, the workshop, the playpen.

GEORGE: Yes. That more artistic directors don't see the fun of having a company of actors that stay together for a few years and all the wonderful experimentation that you can do with them, and they with you, on crazy ideas that might work, and find out that some of them do and some of them don't. But to do that you have to have *a lab situation.* They want to take hold of a season and produce successful plays. But I don't hear of many who are *building a continuous situation of work*.

building a continuous situation of work

When I started TWP I was so insistent that this was not going to be a repeat of Theatre Workshop. I wanted to keep open enough here to see what kind of a theatre Canada should build. And if I was going to have a long-term theatre, I had to have *long-term economic plans*, as well as artistic plans. Therefore, I couldn't do the group theatre as it was in Theatre Workshop: I couldn't expect people to last ten years with me, and give up their natural family life; they would have to be supported financially. So when we became a *professional* company, I paid the actors to stay with me all year and wrote into their contract—a studio contract that hadn't been heard of before then in Canada—I wrote in two weeks holiday. I began that way with the intention that *the theatre was their main occupation*. Any television work was supposed to be 'gravy,' but they didn't have to spend their time knocking on producers' doors. In fact, I tried to convince them that, when you're good enough, the producers will be coming into our theatre and picking you off the stage, and ultimately we'll change the nature of theatre practice in this country.

All that did not happen as I describe it, but some of it did. A little of it did, I think, Steven. What do you think?

STEVEN: Well certainly some of it did. Even Garth Drabinsky[4] admitted that it would have been impossible for him to do his shows without the talent that's been developed by the not-for-profit sector.

GEORGE: Well I'm glad he finally said that.

STEVEN: Yeah, someone reported it to me yesterday.... But uhh one thing that happened, in at least Toronto theatre by the mid-70s, was that a lot of people had become really frightened of collaborative work. Then, the economic situation started to get worse, which meant either fewer productions or less rehearsal time.

GEORGE: I wonder if that business ... uhh how did you put it?

STEVEN: People becoming frightened?

GEORGE: Yes, I wonder if that wasn't enhanced by artists who get swallowed up in technique and figure that 'Well, you're a

4. Garth H. Drabinsky (b. 1949)—Theatre and film producer. Director of Livent which presented such major commercial successes as *The Phantom of the Opera, Kiss of the Spider Woman* and *Showboat*.[(111)]

professional if you know how to handle it *technically.*' It's more like *technology taking over.* I'm thinking again of television and the movies, and that creeps into the theatre. "Oh yes, I can do a rehearsal in three days: Monday I'll do the first act; Tuesday we'll do the second act; Thursday we'll do the third act; and uh Friday, it's a technical day; and Saturday we'll open." I think I'm arguing against this uhh 'being so efficient' kind of attitude. Everything is cut-and-dried in technology. You have to know how the camera operates, you have to know how the lights move.

technology taking over

There's lots of technical things to know in the theatre too, but how many people know how to 'thrust' and how to 'press' and how to 'float'? These are techniques we as actors know. How many understand 'butting your cues,' you know, until there is not a cigarette paper's room for breath?

STEVEN: Unless you want it to be there.

GEORGE: And in the movies you learn *not* to do that because you'd lose your close-up, you see, if you butt your cues. What you do is you hold back a long time, giving the camera a chance to get to you and you 'pad it' a great deal.

STEVEN: In many ways it's an opposite technique.

GEORGE: That technique is okay for the movies, let them keep it. But don't bring it into the theatre! (*Steven laughs*) If we continue in this way, our theatre will only be a pale imitation of the movies.... ... God, that's rambling on.

STEVEN: What would you say is the essence, or the main idea, of your approach to acting? Is it possible to put into a few words?

GEORGE: Uhhh no..... *The search for truth based upon the lessons of Stanislavski*, I'd say, is the beginning. I can't think of anything more than what we've managed to put down of the teaching programme.

the essence of acting

Epilogue: "Protection for the Journey," or "What the Centre is …"

STEVEN: A life in theatre, as a theatre worker, can be full of joys and pleasures and blessings. It also can also be *really hard*. There are a lot of dangers in it uhh I think, to the spirit … the psychological damage that a lot of people sustain in the theatre.

I'm imagining a group of students come to you. They are dedicated, they're passionate about wanting to say something about the world uhhh but they also see resources are being dried-up, on purpose. What do you say to them? What would you offer them by way of protection for the journey, for the life in the theatre?

GEORGE: I'm always optimistic, now, and I see young people getting together, I try to advise them *to build themselves*. Let *them* become the builders. Don't depend on what exists. The infrastructure, if it falls apart, you can't do anything? That is not true. The theatre doesn't depend on that. It's enhanced by good buildings, but it doesn't depend on it. And therefore, *they* are the theatre. The theatre is the actor. Like Lope de Vega said: "Two planks, two actors and an emotion." And that's all you need. And it's true. It's still true. It will *be* true. That's the joy of it and it comes around to what we were saying in the beginning: *What the Centre is … is the actor himself.* And to do a good job.

And to train him to do a good job has been my responsibility … and will become others' responsibility, as they go on.

But that's where it is. It's within the actor himself. Not in the accoutrements. …

STEVEN: Thanks George. Thanks for all this time. ….

GEORGE: Uh, uh if I go down this list …

STEVEN: Should I be taping?
GEORGE: No.
(Tape stops. End of recorded conversations)

George and Mona, circa 1958 / *photo courtesy of Karen Luscombe*

Memorial Tributes to George

Our father

by Urjo Kareda

In 1960 George Luscombe mounted a play called Hey, Rube! *in a 60-seat basement theatre in Parkdale. It ran for only five weeks, but it changed everything*

The building still stands at 47 Fraser Avenue. The basement windows are boarded up now, though broken glass still lies on the ground. The sign says Quality Plating Co. Ltd.; there's a bicycle chained on the sidewalk and glimpses of workers inside. The large building next door is for lease. Smaller buildings across the street have been converted into residential dwellings. A sunny day helps to warm the image of this forgotten urban pocket waiting for the transformation that is moving slowly, loft by redeveloped loft, westward along King Street just to the north, past Liberty. It is difficult to believe that something important happened in the basement of this Parkdale building forty years ago. Here George Luscombe, born and bred in Toronto, launched Workshop Productions, a sixty-seat theatre that altered the city and the way it understands itself.

A double bill of plays ran for a week in December 1959. Another double bill opened six months later. And early the following year, Luscombe introduced *Hey, Rube!*, which was to change everything. It was a signal event, jump-starting the city's alternative-theatre revolution. The Toronto Star's drama critic Nathan Cohen alerted his readers that this play "stands head and shoulders above most drama productions shown in Toronto, or likely to be shown, this season." *Hey, Rube!* ran for five weeks, played to 2,000 people and rewarded its eighteen participating actors and technicians with $37.83 each—their share of the profits. It established Luscombe and the company that later became Toronto Workshop Productions as a trailblazing creative force.

George Luscombe died of heart failure in February, at the age of seventy-two. When I heard the news, I felt personal grief, even though I hadn't ever been more than an acquaintance and had not been in touch with him for years. Moreover, he had not worked in Toronto theatre for a decade, and there had always seemed a dissonance between Luscombe and the Toronto theatres—considerable in number and vigorous in their determined energy—that came after his. The accomplishments of their seasons—the current one ends unofficially with the Dora Mavor Moore Awards on June 21—were in some ways at odds with the principle upon which he built Toronto Workshop Productions. Yet his career served as the paradigm, the theatrical DNA, for what has followed. He went first.

Hey, Rube! was about a company of fiercely proud but bedraggled circus performers, an inescapable metaphor for TWP itself. The source of Luscombe's artistic vision came from Theatre Workshop in East London. He spent three years there in the early fifties learning from its celebrated leftist-radical theatremaker, Joan Littlewood, whose later widely influential productions included *The Hostage* and *Oh, What a Lovely War!* Luscome absorbed the notion of an ensemble that stayed together to collectively produce innovative work with a political thrust.

Luscombe's TWP productions evolved from a succession of ensemble companies, each created with exceptional, daunting rigour. The actor-director Maja Ardal remembers auditioning for the company in 1970, when she was a twenty-one year old well-trained graduate of Glasgow's Royal Scottish Academy of Music and Drama. "I wanted to be a part of where it was all beginning," she recalls. The severe audition process involved forty actors assembled for weeks of workshops in Luscombe's method. They worked full days on improvisational processes based on Stanislavski, movement drawn from Rudolph von Laban ("I developed thighs of steel," Ardal says) and complex collective scenarios. Luscombe sat in front, apparently ready to spring onto the stage at any moment. At the end of each week, he would read out the names of the actors who could come back next Monday. Eventually, perhaps a dozen survivors remained to become company members, with a season's contract (fifty dollars a week before they joined Actors' Equity, ninety dollars after).

"George's point," says Ardal, "was that we, the actors, had to be able to fill the empty space with the energy beyond us. It had to become an instinct, like the back of our hand. An actor had to pursue his work as if life depended on it. And George's politics swirled around it all. He taught me social criticism, to be suspicious and intelligent about political structures. Politically he was what I'd call a flexible artistic socialist. The ideal was to be incredibly democratic, but we were also an army with a pretty intense—dare I say fascist—leader?"

Only three years later, the designer Astrid Janson, just starting her splendid career, approached Luscombe for a job. He never once looked at her design portfolio, but quizzed her instead about her politics. As it happened, she'd been affiliated with SDS (Students for a Democratic Society) at university, and so Luscombe, following his instinct as usual, offered her the position ($120 a week) of resident designer. "He had so much faith," says Janson. "The greatest thing about George was that he started with no preconceived ideas. He would start with the actors, musicians, movement, perhaps some text, and then move outward from that." The stage was sacred to Luscombe. Most companies prepare plays in rehearsal halls, moving into the theatre and onstage only in the final phase of production. Luscombe worked on the stage from Day One. Once, in Janson's absence, he asked where she was and was told that she was working at home. She was immediately summoned and berated: "Design is not done at home. It is done in the theatre. You have to be there, to watch, to see the actors."

Luscombe's abusive verbal attacks on his colleagues were the shadow side of his genius. He often reduced Astrid Janson to tears and then would tell her not to take it so personally. "There's no other way to take it, George" would be her answer. As in so many artistic organisms, the pattern of relationships was an extension of the family, and many in the TWP company would acknowledge Luscombe's domination as the father figure. At his best, he offered the reassurance of the parent who believes that his kids can reach their goals, in the full knowledge of how hard it will be to achieve them. And when the group as a whole accomplished something difficult—a moment, a scene—he would be dancing on air.

Janson feels that Luscombe was aware of the emotional turmoil and confusion he created, but could not stop himself. "He was a good teacher," she says, "and good teachers often have this contradiction. They have so much passion that it makes them demanding and impossible." There is also the reality that an undercurrent of masochism—punishment as reward—is sometimes not very far from the process of creation. As Ardal acknowledges, a quarter-century later: "I loved being scared of him."

Out of such stirrings-up, such tension between openhearted commitment to his artists and a vehement need to control them, George Luscombe and Toronto Workshop Productions created a glorious body of work. It takes no effort at all to summon into memory those productions that defined the company's uniqueness: *Mr. Bones* (1969), an examination of racism in the form of a minstrel show; *Chicago '70* (1970), about the conspiracy trial that was the aftermath of the riots at the 1968 Democratic convention; *Mr. Pickwick* (1971), an adaptation with the joy and energy of Dickens himself; *Ten Lost Years* (1974), an extraordinary evocation of the Depression in Canada; *Les Canadiens* (1976), a provocative fusion of hockey mania and Quebec politics. These and other shows seemed to invent their own style of political drama, one in which sharp questions and ideas shared the arena with fabulous theatricality. Luscombe celebrated human energy, the human body and, most compellingly, the human spirit. The productions looked stunning, but the visual was always integrated with the way his shows danced and stomped and roared. On the best nights, you could feel the ground rocking into new patterns beneath your feet.

"Deep down," says Janson, "George was a born actor. That's what Littlewood groomed him for—not to be a director, but to be her star actor. It's where he got his powerful instinct for engaging an audience." That intuition for an audience's pulse was always connected to the compassion he felt for those who were disenfranchised or marginal. Thus his finest shows were filled with feeling—though never sentiment, something he loathed and feared—as well as fire.

For many years George Luscombe and TWP had a long, strong run. Throughout the early 1960s, they produced two shows a year, toured Ontario and for four summers played in Stratford, in a park beside the Festival Theatre. By mid-decade, he was ready to move from Parkdale to downtown Toronto. The company leased a former car showroom at 12 Alexander Street, renovated it into a 300-seat theatre in a month and opened the doors on New Year's Eve, 1967. The move was a big deal for TWP. Everything was magnified, and the company was forced into an accelerated maturity. The resourceful June Faulkner was hired as general manager, and a subscription series was introduced; to generate a season, TWP was now expected to produce a new show almost every month.

The new pace created new pressures. At times, there was a logjam of TWP hits, so many that it was difficult to know what to do with them. At other times, the work seemed thin, repetitive, predictable, preaching to the converted. Tours to Expo 67, the Venice Biennale and other European locations stretched the energy and resources of a small staff. In 1974, a fire tore through the building the morning of an opening.

At the same time, there was a flourish of new alternative theatre companies, each scrambling for a home, an identity, an audience. Inspired by Luscombe's example, the new theatres also reclaimed and renovated existing spaces: Factory Theatre Lab in its warehouse space above a garage on Dupont Street, Theatre Passe Muraille in its church hall in Trinity Square, Toronto Free Theatre in an old gasworks on Berkeley Street, and Tarragon Theatre in a former cribbage-board factory on Bridgman Avenue. They, as well as the evolving civic theatre at the St. Lawrence Centre, were all wooing an audience excited by the prospect of seeing Canadian plays—stories of one's own community. There were few lasting links between Luscombe and the younger companies, perhaps because they were more specifically committed to emerging playwrights. This was the one species of theatre artist whom he had difficulty accommodating. "The playwright was never a strong presence in George's space," says Ardal. "They were always hovering somewhere in the background. George was so afraid that we would dribble away in words what we could show with our bodies." Even longtime writing colleagues like Jack Winter eventually drifted off.

The move downtown did not produce the new audience that Luscombe had hoped for; a populist in his spirit, he was frustrated to be offering his work to the same people again and again. He hated establishment theatre, whether it was Stratford or the institutionalized "official" civic theatre. When Maja Ardal told him that she was leaving TWP to work at the St. Lawrence Theatre, he said: "Oh, so you've retired from theatre!" Janson had the same experience and, even in later years, would hesitate to tell him she was designing a play by Eugene O'Neill or Tennessee Williams, because he had such disdain for what he saw as their self-indulgence. There were many fallings-out, things that were never mended; Luscombe was never willing to loosen his grip. There had been eviction crises in 1977 and 1981, but TWP got full control of its building at 12 Alexander in 1984, at a time when there was real doubt about the company's future path. Two years later—certainly, in retrospect, too late—Luscombe handed over TWP to a younger director, Robert Rooney, while still keeping himself a presence. Two years after that, they were both dismissed by a new board of directors that had some interest in handing over the now-valuable property to developers. It never happened, but TWP didn't survive, either. The theatre at 12 Alexander fell into disrepair, though it was later reclaimed and renovated one more time—in a manner not much to Luscombe's liking—as the home for the gay and lesbian theatre company Buddies in Bad Times.

George Luscombe seemed to create and play out the scenario that has been replayed, individually and collectively, by virtually all his Toronto theatre successors. There is the struggle for an initial foothold, and the first defining hit. There is the credo that a theatre company needs its own building, needs to be a family. The story continues with the move to bigger quarters and their attendant bigger problems. Successes prove as difficult as some failures: How do you move on? There is the departure of the artists who have been closely connected to the original vision. The question of succession arises next: Who should be chosen? Who should do the choosing? And the final chapter—the brutal dismissal by a board of directors out of sympathy with that founding vision. In the epilogue, a deposed or departed artistic director lives in a kind of exile, his creative powers undiminished but lacking a platform upon which to demonstrate them.

This dramatic pattern of a director's career as well as a company's history—rising action, falling action—is a legacy left for us, lived for us, by George Luscombe. His original impulse to create a theatre that could have a dialogue with its city has now expanded into a community of such theatres: they are now one of Toronto's defining traits. Other things could not be passed on. There is now neither a realistic economic basis nor funding available for Toronto theatres to hire companies of actors on season-long contracts. We are unlikely to see that kind of ensemble again. Nor do we have theatre companies driven by one director's style. (Even the closest approximation, Richard Rose's Necessary Angel Theatre Company, is defined more by the writers that it presents.)

We also no longer have so definitively a political theatre, and that is our loss. Where have we repositioned the kind of compassion that Luscombe's work regularly expressed? Or is it true, as I sometimes fear, that the new and younger audience is one defined most precisely by a reluctance, perhaps even an inability to feel, share pain, empathize? The flow of legacy can travel in indirect channels. I would argue that Luscombe's committed stance on behalf of the underdog survives most vividly in the work of a very different kind of theatre artist—the prolific George F. Walker, whose six-play *Suburban Motel* cycle last season spoke with a feeling for the disinherited that would not have embarrassed Luscombe himself.

In others, the legacy is more direct. George Luscombe said that he lived on Joan Littlewood's shoulders, and generations of artists who worked with him know that they live on his. Astrid Janson has continued to design using the lessons that he taught her: work from the inside out, with the actor at the centre of the world. Maja Ardal, who went to run Young People's Theatre, still follows Luscombe's method. "I left with a suitcase filled with choices," she says. But from George Luscombe, these were surely all one and the same choice: to be an artist, to be independent and responsible, to analyze, to act, to bring something of one's self to the stage.

Urjo Kareda. Arts, *Toronto Life*. Toronto: June 1999
reprinted by the kind permission of Shelagh Hewitt-Kareda

Firebrand director 'made sense of the world' *by Ken Gass*

George Luscombe's visually and socially dynamic productions were a dominant force in Toronto's early alternate-theatre scene.

The explosive growth of new Canadian plays and theatres in the past three decades has done little to shake the towering figure of George Luscombe from his pedestal. Luscombe, who died last week of heart failure at the age of 73, was a director absolutely unique in his vision, passion and social commitment. His visually and musically charged productions dominated the Toronto alternate-theatre scene throughout the 1960s, and he continued directing until the late eighties.

Luscombe grew up in a working-class environment in Toronto's East York during the Depression era, his high-school career undistinguished except for art classes and music. He worked as an actor in England in the fifties, notably with Joan Littlewood and Theatre Workshop, her soon-to-be-famous left-wing Stratford East company. Then Luscombe returned to Toronto and, in 1959, founded what soon became Toronto Workshop Productions, in a 60-seat industrial space on remote Fraser Avenue.

Luscombe's production of *Hey, Rube*—a collective creation developed largely from improvisations about the backstage life of a circus—became a signature piece, and instantly established him as a directorial force to be reckoned with. In 1967, he moved the company to a prime downtown location at 12 Alexander Street, establishing a 300-seat theatre in the midst of a high-rise residential area. He toured his ensemble to New York and European theatre festivals. For a time, he also performed summer seasons at Stratford, though he made no secret of his disdain either for the Shakespearean Festival's imported British style or for the bourgeois conventions in most regional theatres at the time.

Luscombe found theatrical fodder in virtually every social issue of the day. *Chicago '70*, based on the watershed trial of the Chicago 8 (who stormed the 1968 Democratic party convention), hit the stage with resounding success while the issue was still smouldering in the newspapers. *Mr. Bones* dealt with racial issues through black minstrel-show traditions. *You Can't Get Here from There* dramatized the plight of Chilean refugees against the backdrop of Pinochet's CIA-sponsored military coup of 1973.

Time and again, Luscombe proved that strong socialist themes were not incompatible with a highly theatrical style. As Maja Ardal, then an actress in the company, explained, "George not only made sense of theatre; he also made sense of the world."

But his intense, firebrand personality frequently led to clashes with other artists. "Let's throw this in the sentimental bin," he once declared of an emotional scene by John Herbert, author of the off-broadway success, *Fortune and Men's Eyes*. Herbert withdrew his play, *The World of Woyzeck*, and subsequently produced it himself.

TWP's repertoire combined original collective creations, new plays by Canadian and other contemporary writers, and adaptations of classic texts from Aristophanes to Dickens. Two of Luscombe's greatest successes were *Ten Lost Years* (1975)—his and Cedric Smith's adaptation of Barry Broadfoot's best-selling book on the Depression Era in Canada—and *Les Canadiens* (1976), Rick Salutin's imaginative mix of hockey and Quebec politics. The latter led to another classic standoff, when Luscombe made changes to the script without the writer's consent and Salutin threatened to sue for an injunction to prevent the play from opening. Ultimately, the diplomatic skills of TWP's long-term manager, June Faulkner, prevailed; the production garnered rave reviews and later a Chalmers Best New Play Award.

In the early seventies, with the sudden emergence of Theatre Passe Muraille, Toronto Free, the Factory and Tarragon theatres, all espousing new Canadian plays, Luscombe found his position challenged. The new companies delivered a fiercely nationalistic all-Canadian voice; Luscombe's viewpoint remained international. The Factory and Tarragon championed the playwright above all, while TWP focused primarily on Luscombe's directorial vision.

Over the decade, with increasing competition for already dwindling council grants, TWP began to suffer economically. Despite the highly successful "champagne season" of 1976-77—which included *Les Canadiens*, Eve Merriam's *The Club* and the flamboyant Lindsay Kemp company from England—Luscombe was soon forced to scramble just to stay afloat. In the neoconservative 1980s, he came under fire from the critics, as in the 1983 *Globe and Mail* review that said he was "once considered one of the bravest and cleverest directors the country had produced, before he devoted his large talent to the endless iteration of a simple, forties-style, left-wing agitprop theatre."

Though aware of changing sensibilities, Luscombe continued with uncomprimising vision, producing plays such as *The Mac Paps*, based on Canadian volunteers who fought against fascism in Spain, and the *The Wobbly*, an old-style Luscombe show celebrating the short-lived "One Big Union" movement of the Industrial Workers of the World. While Luscombe's dream of a permanently funded ensemble remained elusive, his influence survives in the scores of actors he worked with in the past four decades, including Jackie Burroughs, R.H. Thomson and Victor Garber.

Luscombe justly described himself as a survivor against adversity. After all, TWP had survived a fire in 1974 which gutted the interior of the building, and had narrowly survived several attempts by developers to demolish the theatre to make way for housing projects. The eventual financial collapse of TWP in 1989, and unsuccessful attempts by a new board of directors to give the company a more conservative repertoire, caused rancorous debate in Toronto theatre. The building was bought by the city, and ultimately renovated as a home for Buddies in Bad Times (whose mandate, gay and lesbian theatre, was one major social issue Luscombe had never tackled).

In 1994, Luscombe suffered a massive heart attack that resulted in quintuple bypass surgery, and later the amputation of both legs above the knee. Recovery was painfully slow, but eventually he returned to teaching at the University of Guelph and began planning a possible future production of *King Lear*. The real amputative loss was forced separation from his own theatre and, for us, the realization that he left the stage too soon.

Ken Gass. *The Globe and Mail*. Toronto:
Saturday February 13, 1999
reprinted by the kind permission of Ken Gass

George Luscombe 1926—1999

by Alan Filewod

In his signature play, *Hey Rube!*, George Luscombe crafted the story of a ragtag group of circus folk stuck on the edge of nowheresville, besieged by rubes bent on driving them out of town. *Hey Rube!* was a show that George returned to several times in his career, always retooling it for a new audience, who periodically needed to be reminded of where we really live. It was his own ongoing epitaph.

George's death this past February came as a hard blow to many, but to his former colleagues at Guelph it was a particularly sad occasion. After his (forced) retirement following the purge at Toronto Workshop Productions, we invited George to teach acting for us. I spent many hours sitting in George's office, listening to his stories—tales of the fit-up company in Wales where he serves his apprenticeship (and discovered that he had been hired as a potential husband for the manager's daughter), memories of the great move to Stratford East with Joan Littlewood; stories of the epic struggle to bring the fire of political theatre to Toronto the Good in the '50s. George was a raconteur who led an epic theatrical life.

My most vivid memory is not of his stories however, but his passion. One day I was passing through the acting studio where George had just taught a second-year class. He was standing transfixed by some inner joy, and it is not an exaggeration to say he glowed. I said some commonplace thing in greeting, and he responded with excitement, "Finally, finally, I've figured it out, I finally understand the magic If!" I was humbled: here was a man who had been working on Stanislavsky for more than four decades as an actor, director and teacher, and he was jumping with happiness. I suspect that George discovered something new in every class he taught. He was a brilliant teacher.

He was also as tough as they come. When we invited him to direct a show for us, he declined, because he felt the students were not nearly ready to appear on a stage. His great dream was to open his own acting school. He deserved it, but because he was an iconoclast, a contrarion and an outspoken leftist, there was no way the cultural establishment in this country would support his vision.

George was deeply proud of his working class roots, and he believed strongly that working class art must claim as its own the entire heritage of theatre history. Like Brecht, he believed that theatre was work, not magic—but he also knew that the bloody hard work of theatre is the making of magic. To the rest of my days I will remember the stunning force of his imagery: the hobos jumping trains in *Ten Lost Years;* the dehumanized mill in *The Wobbly*; the battlefields of Spain in *The Mac Paps.* All done on a bare stage, with actors who moved with clarity, purpose and passion.

George Luscombe more than any other figure was the leader who gave English Canada a theatrical voice and vocabulary. He collected some honours: the Order of Canada, honourary doctorates from York and Guelph. But after he was ruthlessly ditched by the theatre he founded (a scandal described in detail in Neil Carson's excellent critical biography, *Harlequin in Hogtown*), he never again directed. What a damning statement that is on our cultural "ecology" (to borrow the Canada's Council's current buzzphrase). And yet George didn't complain. Like the man of the theatre he was, he lived in the present passion. He always seemed to know the rubes wouldn't catch up.

Newletter of the Association for Canadian Theatre Research.
Toronto: Spring 1999.
reprinted by the kind permission of Alan Filewod

In Memoriam
George Luscombe 1926-1999: The Virtue of Intolerance

by Steven Bush

George Luscombe was co-founder and for almost three decades Artistic Director of Toronto Workshop Productions. Among the many productions he directed, and helped to create, were *Hey, Rube!*, *The Mechanic*, *Mr. Bones*, *Chicago '70*, *Ten Lost Years*, *You Can't Get Here from There*, *Summer '76*, *Les Canadiens* and *The Mac Paps*. Although he was not fond of the term, George was, effectively, the dramaturg and, sometimes, the (usually unacknowledged) co-author of several productions. In addition to his inspirational teaching at the University of Guelph and other institutions, George served as mentor, rival and infuriator to many theatre practitioners who subsequently formed, or came to head up, their own companies.

Arriving in Canada in the winter of 1969, fleeing Richard Nixon's Amerika and the Pentagon's ferociously escalating adventure in Vietnam, I was given warm and friendly refuge by George Luscombe and his co-workers at Toronto Workshop Productions. From the first show I saw there—*The Good Soldier Schweik*—I felt a strong and immediate kinship with the TWP vision. Here was a company politically and aesthetically much closer to the kind of theatre that I wanted to do than most of what I had encountered in my previous five years of professional work in the States. This was a company that I wanted to be a part of. I spent a year and a half with TWP as an actor and returned, at later dates, to do other work.

When I left the company later in the summer of 1970 to co-found what become THOG, my work was both inspired by and in reaction against my experience with George. It could be argued that a lot of Toronto theatre that followed would not have happened but for

George Luscombe's pioneering work; certainly, it would have been very different. We who started companies in the first half of the seventies were lucky; whether we liked George's work or not, whether we liked *him* or not, his theatre was there and occupied a space, both politically and aesthetically, quite far to the left of whatever passed for "the mainstream" in those years. His presence forced us to define ourselves more clearly, often more radically. His company also provided an encouraging local example: If a theatre can be built in a city which didn't seem all that interested in theatre ... *and* if it's possible for it to have survived (at that time) for over ten years *and* get sizeable audience by doing work that was theatrically bold and politically responsive ... *and* to do this without an enormous amount in the way of resources ... *then* others can build other companies or do productions that would rock this town. We weren't, of course, thinking of TWP every minute, or analysing its historical importance, *but* George and his company were *always there as a standard*, to be emulated and/or repudiated. Whatever else, better or worse, that followed, George Luscombe and TWP were there first: They were the shock troops.

In my reflections subsequent to George's death in February, I've been wondering why it was, exactly, that his work imprinted so strongly on those who had contact with it. Was it simply because TWP was *the first* "alternative" theatre in Toronto to last more than a short while? Was it because of George's lifelong commitment to ensemble and to the necessity of *ongoing actor training* in conjunction with the public work of a professional company? Was it because of his *theatricalist* sense of design and stage movement? Because he put on plays that did not look *at all* like TV? Because he attacked head-on *burning issues of the day* that many theatres avoided?

"Yes" is the answer to all these questions, I believe, but another feature that made George's theatre so distinct and engaging had to do with *the virtue of intolerance*. And that's what I'd like to honour here.

Shortly after joining the TWP company, I was puzzled to hear George talk about "the other theatre." After a while the naive newcomer found out George wasn't referring to some rival company down the street actually named "The Other Theatre": TWP was "Theatre"; everything else was "the other theatre."

Well, that sounded pretty snooty and exclusionist. Why did he make such a point of separating *his* work from that of "the other theatre"? Over time I started to get the picture and, yes, appreciate his perspective.

What was George intolerant *of*? and *why?*

1. "Shoddy work": George was very big on the conscious craft of the actor. He had great respect for *the actor as a skilled worker* and for the necessity of *high standards* with regards to training and rehearsal process.

2. Theatre that looked like TV: Like Vakhtangov and other giants before him, George wanted "the theatre theatrical"—expressive, imaginative and playful theatrical form.

3. The small-cast "chamber plays" that have progressively dominated the English Canadian stage since the mid-seventies. Readers who were privileged to see his work will recall that there were rarely fewer than ten people onstage, and, when the budget could bear it, there were more. George's stage was alive with vibrant life, with actors who (more often than not) knew how to move.

4. "Artistic" decisions made for non-artistic reasons, reasons lacking in integrity. Clearly, George resisted commercially based or market-driven influences; but he was equally opposed to certain kinds of Drama-in-education or Popular Theatre which he tended to see as "social work" and not as art.

5. Social injustices. While he would be accused—sometimes with good reason—of injustices in his own workplace, his public work—what he offered the world through his stage creations—was invariably intolerant of racism, fascism, classism and all other forms of socio-political cruelty.

As well as being a visionary theatre director and auteur, George was a superb public speaker, a great *ranter.* Again, his intolerance of social evils gave his speech high definition. In the last public addresses I heard him deliver George spoke from a very strong and fearless place. He never flinched at naming problems in language that was bold and clear. In an era when circumstances have encouraged artists to talk (and think?) in timid tones, with carefully chosen words designed not to offend anyone in power, at the World Stage last April George railed eloquently against the fascist tendencies of the Mike Harris government. George was a *voice*—an often intolerant voice—a voice that inspired many even as it alienated and infuriated others. George believed, with Brecht, that part of the job of theatre is to "change the world: It needs it." To a great degree, through four decades of very public activity, he lived this belief.

In retrospect, the closing of Toronto Workshop Productions in 1988—and the discarding of George Luscombe as its Artistic Director—can be viewed as "the canary in the mineshaft," foreshadowing death, not from below, but from above. Now that we're over a decade into the global corporate attack on just about everything except greed, it's easy to see this loss not as some unhappy anomaly, but rather as one of the early warning signals of the *muting of political space* in the New World Order. "Ten lost years" since the forcing-through of the Free Trade Agreement and the progressive abandonment of government responsibility for social welfare. "Ten lost years" of participating in discussions about *how to implement cuts* rather than *fighting cuts altogether.* "Ten lost years" in which Canada has been sold out and the arts, education, health, labour and the environment (just to name *a few* of the victims) have been left bleeding by smug muggers in high places.

OK, I'm ranting. But I'm ranting in the spirit of rants I've heard George Luscombe deliver. And remembering George provides an occasion for all of us who toil, suffer and rejoice in the theatre to reflect not only on George's life and work, on his great achievements and great failures, but also *upon our own.*

In the breathless mad scramble to survive *at all,* are we holding fast to our visions and our own integrity? Or are we caving in to hegemonic pressures, wimping out, betraying our cultural achievements and ultimately, in the process—like Fassbinder's Effi Briest—*collaborating in our own oppression*?

Rigorously pursuing his own path—sometimes obsessively, sometimes without due respect for the needs and feelings of others—George Luscombe made theatre that left indelible imprints on the memories of those who were there... theatre that was bold, strongly shaped, unashamedly partisan, unafraid to stand, never mealy-mouthed. Ultimately, George paid a big price for the virtue of intolerance that helped make his work so distinctively his own. And from this distance it's easy to say that he made too many enemies, and not enough allies to oppose them, when the final crunch came at TWP. But, as far as I know, George never knowingly collaborated in his own oppression. And I am honouring George when I ask the tough question: "How many of us who survive can say the same?"

Steven Bush.
Canadian Theatre Review CTR 99
UT Press: Toronto. Summer 1999

George in front of his theatre, circa 1974 / *photographer James Lewcun*

Excerpts from George Luscombe's address upon receiving an honourary degree from University of Guelph, June 5th 1996

"'In the beginning was the word.' (*Pause*) Bullshit. In the beginning was the experience which produced the sound which became the word."

The proceeding is a quote from *Black Bible*, which I used in an introduction to a play I produced in 1969 called *Mr Bones*. I always thought it was revealing in its contradiction of the Judaeo-Christian admonition. The original biblical quote establishes the primacy of the word in an act of creation, whereas it is the actor's belief through experience that the imagination supersedes all. To believe that, and practice it, you don't have to start with a script to create a play; an idea will do, born out of an irritant and an injustice. A little imagination and the work is begun. Then eventually you bring in the writer and the words become the script *based upon* the work of the actors. Many of my plays were created in just such a way: *Hey Rube!*, *Mr Bones*, *The Golem of Venice*, *The Mac Paps*. It's not the only way to work, but to ignore such an approach is to ignore the potential of the creative process.

In the preparation to bring a new musical to Toronto, the producers of a particular show built a new and bigger theatre building, so—according to them—they could land a helicopter on the stage. (*Pause*) When visiting my theatre TWP, The Market Place Theatre from South Africa, in their original work *Asinimali*, also had occasion to simulate a helicopter. The actor sat himself backwards on a chair and waved his arm around in circles above his head. The beauty of it was ... when he stopped, the helicopter was gone.

In the same production the actors wore white ping-pong balls on their forehead, and when they wanted to assume the role of a white man they just slipped the ping-pong ball on their nose.

Another time, while preparing my production of *Ain't Lookin'*, I asked the designer, who was new to me, to give me a baseball diamond and a bus. He came back with a design that would have cost me a fortune. The baseball diamond was all right, but he was ready to have us build a full-size bus. We finally built the bus with the actors simply placing the suitcases and hand-luggage in the appropriate places to form the inside of the bus. When the players arrived at the destination, the actors picked up their luggage and left. The bus was gone.

Many years ago I improvised the ending of a play we performed called *Woyzeck*, by Büchner. Woyzeck had murdered his woman and was trying to rid himself of the weapon. He throws the knife into the lake; then, fearing it hasn't gone far enough, he wades out into deeper water to retrieve it, and throws it further. As he goes, he quietly slips below the surface and drowns. Of course, we never considered flooding the stage to furnish a lake. The actors became the water, and Woyzeck joined them in movement as he got further out into the lake until he floated under. The other actors floated his hat, then his coat and finally Woyzeck was floating as part of the water in which he drowned. No annoying blackouts, no scenery. The actors stood quietly and took their bows for it was the end of the show.

Since my enforced stay in hospital last year I've been watching more television than I care to admit. The other afternoon I watched what looked like a seminar on saving Canada, entitled *Conference 2000*. There were speakers from all walks of life: politicians, ex-politicians, university professors, representatives of the chamber of commerce, from across the country. I stayed with the conference all afternoon, curious as to who would represent the artist. Who would speak with imagination to help solve our problems? Would we hear from Gordon Pinsent? Perhaps Margaret Atwood would offer a solution. But no. No artists were present, no musicians, no painters, no actors of course, no writers, and of all things, no poets. The representatives of our cultural community were conspicuous by their absence. This was a conference convened for the purpose of stimulating ideas on how to hold this country together, but the people trained and practiced in the use of imagination were nowhere present.

It probably never occurred to the organizers to include {these} people into the discussion. The conference was dealing with political, practical measures. The artists might amuse us after the deliberations have come to an end but they are not expected to contribute to our serious work. We believed ourselves to be a part of our society, but in practice the movers and shakers, the ones who form policy, had very little time for our values.

You—and I talk now to the graduates—you are a new generation, trained and practiced in the use of imagination. Determine now that you will not be shut out. The artists, the writers and poets, yes, even the actors will be heard from. *You are not the afterthought of our society, you are the core. You are not the icing on the cake, you are the bread of life.* You will make your full contribution to this country, and *Conference 2001* will include you.

I became a professional in 1948, as you've been told. 1948. The New Play Society: Mostly radio-actors who felt the need to work on the live stage. The Royal Alexandra Theatre opened on a casual basis with American touring shows. And that was it. It was a very desolate picture for a young person who wanted to make theatre his life. In 1948 I joined a brave little group that toured Ontario with three plays and lasted a few months, but then collapsed. In order to learn and experience a full life in the theatre I had to leave the country. That's no longer necessary and thank god it isn't. There's plenty of opportunities even though they're tough. They will always be tough in theatre. Some would say they should be, but I'm not sure. Certainly the education in this country is there, as at places like Guelph, and the drama program which I was a part of, and proud to be. It was an exceptional one.

The next few years I spent in England and Europe in weekly rep, fortnightly rep and "*fit-up*." Yes I started that way: *fit-up*. "All men help with the fit-up"—that was in the contract. Actually, my contract was a telegram that said: "Come to Nayland, Wales by Friday. Open *See How They Run*, Saturday, in the part of Clive. Do not consider this a contract. Jimmy James, Nayland Repertory Company."

I guess he wasn't quite sure of me. I wasn't quite sure of myself, I'll tell you. It was a long trip. From London to Nayland, Wales is an overnight journey. I spent all night studying the part of Clive, wondering why a novice would be given the lead role. When I met the boss the next morning, he offered me a cup of tea and asked me how was the part of Lionel coming along. (*Audience laughter; George chuckling*) My career couldn't have got off on a (*pause*) better start I suppose. It could only go up from there.

My real education began when I joined Joan Littlewood's Theatre Workshop. For five years as an ensemble member we went from the classics to new plays every two weeks. Then I came home to Canada in 1957. It was two years later that I started Toronto Workshop Productions. TWP, as it came to be known, was the longest running theatre company in the country other than Stratford Festival. From 1959 to 1989, when TWP finally closed, we trained hundreds of actors, a few playwrights, many theatre workers and a number who went on to form their own theatre companies.

Why, why do we do it? You will have read in your theatre history books, theatre began in the churches and moved onto the steps of the church, when it became a bit risky. Or the Greek theatre that finally introduced the first actor. I tell my students, it began in the cave. They had brought home the meat and fed on it, then sat back and started to tell the tale of the hunt. But one told it better than the others, and got to his feet to help better explain, explain the excitement of the kill. The meat had nourished us for the moment; soon we'll need another meal. But the story, if well told, will live forever. That's why we were artists.

Thank you very much, and thank you to Guelph for this great honour.

reprinted by the kind permission of Karen Luscombe

Thanks to Simon Gleave for transcribing the memorial tributes and George's speech

SOURCES FOR FOOTNOTES

1. Laban, Rudolf von and F. C. Lawrence. *Effort: Economy of Human Movement*. London: Macdonald & Evans, 1979. See also Newlove, Jean. *Laban for Actors and Dancers*. London: Nick Hern Books, 1993. Print.
2. Melvin, Murray. *The Art of the Theatre Workshop*. London: Oberon Books, 2006. Print.
3. Newlove, Jean, and John Dalby. *Laban for All*. New York: Routledge, 2004. Print.
4. Breon, Robin. "The Crest Theatre." *The Canadian Encyclopedia*. Historica Foundation of Canada. 1999, Web. 2005. See also Illidge, Paul. *Glass Cage: The Crest Theatre Story*. Toronto: Creber Monde, 2005. Print.
5. Carson, Neil. *Harlequin in Hogtown: George Luscombe and Toronto Workshop Productions*. Toronto: University of Toronto Press, 1995. Print.
6. Ibid.
7. Johnston, Denis. "Newton, Christopher." *The Canadian Encyclopedia*. Historica Foundation of Canada, 1999. Web. 2005.
8. "Moscow Art Theater." *Columbia Encyclopedia*, 6th ed. 2001. Print.
9. "Bertolt Brecht." *Columbia Encyclopedia*, 6th ed. 2001. Print.
10. Moore, Sonia. *The Stanislavski System: The Professional Training of an Actor*. New York: Penguin Books Ltd., 1960. Print.
11. "Danforth's History." *Danforth Collegiate & Technical Institute*. Toronto District School Board. Web. July 4, 2011.
12. Morley, J.T. "Co-operative Commonwealth Federation." *The Canadian Encyclopedia*. Historica Foundation of Canada, 1999. Web. 2005.
13. Newlove, Jean, and John Dalby. *Laban for All*. New York: Routledge, 2004. Print. See also "Gallerie Dell'Accademia." *Home—Polo Museale Veneziano*. Web. July 4, 2011.
14. Gardner, David. "Sir Tyrone Guthrie." *The Canadian Encyclopedia*. Historica Foundation of Canada, 1999. Web. 2005.
15. Carson, Neil. *Harlequin in Hogtown: George Luscombe and Toronto Workshop Productions*. Toronto: University of Toronto Press, 1995. Print.
16. Holgerson, Ron. "Arturo Ui—Authentic Brecht from TWP." Rev. of *Arturo Ui by TWP. Pro Tem* [Toronto] 17 Nov. 1971: 7. *Pro Tem: Glendon's Bilingual Newspaper*. York University. Web. 4 July 2011.
17. Doucette, L.E. "Robert Lepage." *The Canadian Encyclopedia*. Historica Foundation of Canada. 1999, Web. July 4, 2011.
18. Howe-Beck, Linde. "Carbone 14." *The Canadian Encyclopedia*. Historica Foundation of Canada, 1999. Web. 2005.

19. Howe-Beck, Linde. "Édouard Lock." *The Canadian Encyclopedia*. Historica Foundation of Canada, 1999. Web. 2005.
20. "History Carlo Mazzone-Clementi." *Dell'Arte*. Dell'Arte Company. Web. July 19, 2010.
21. "Jordan, Charles." *The Canadian Encyclopedia*. Historica Foundation of Canada, 1999. Web. 2005.
22. Carson, Neil. *Harlequin in Hogtown: George Luscombe and Toronto Workshop Productions*. Toronto: University of Toronto Press, 1995. Print.
23. "Kristin Linklater." http: //www.kristinlinklater.com/. Web. 2008.
24. "David Smukler." http: //www.yorku.ca/finearts/faculty/profs/smukler.htm. York University: Toronto. n.d.
25. "Michael Connolly." *University College Drama Program*. University College—University of Toronto. Web. July 4, 2011.
26. "Jones, Inigo." *Columbia Encyclopedia*, 6th ed. 2001. Print. *See also* "JONES, Inigo." *Chambers Biographical Dictionary*, 5th ed. 1990. Print.
27. "Ewan MacColl." *BBC Music*. British Broadcasting Company, n.d. Web. July 19, 2010.
28. Carson, Neil. *Harlequin in Hogtown: George Luscombe and Toronto Workshop Productions*. Toronto: University of Toronto Press, 1995. Print.
29. "Ginsberg, Allen." *Columbia Encyclopedia*, 6th ed. 2001. Print.
30. "Kerry Feltham." *IMDB*. Internet Movie Database, 1990. Web. July 19, 2010.
31. Carson, Neil. *Harlequin in Hogtown: George Luscombe and Toronto Workshop Productions*. Toronto: University of Toronto Press, 1995. Print.
32. Ibid.
33. Ibid.
34. Ibid.
35. Ibid.
36. Ibid.
37. Ibid.
38. Morrow, Martin. "R.H. Thomson." *The Canadian Encyclopedia*. Historica Foundation of Canada, 1999. Web. June 2011. See also Thomson, R.H. *The Lost Boys: Letters from the Sons in Two Acts 1919-1923*. Toronto: Playwrights Canada Press, 2002, 2001. Print.
39. Carson, Neil. *Harlequin in Hogtown: George Luscombe and Toronto Workshop Productions*. Toronto: University of Toronto Press, 1995. Print.
40. Ibid.
41. "Harry H. Corbett." *Steptoe and Son – A Tribute to Wilfrid Brambell, Harry H. Corbett, Ray Galton and Alan Simpson*. Web. July 4, 2011. <albertandharold.co.uk>.

42. Goorney, Howard. *The Theatre Workshop Story.* London: Eyre Methuen. 1981. Print.
43. "Winter, Jack." *Canadian Theatre Encyclopedia.* Athabasca University, 2002. Web. July 20, 2010. See also Winter, Jack. "Epitaph for George," *Canadian Theatre Review, 138*: 96-101. Guelph: University of Toronto Press, Spring 2009.
44. "Biography." *John Wayne.* Wayne Enterprises. Web. July 20, 2010.
45. Carson, Neil. *Harlequin in Hogtown: George Luscombe and Toronto Workshop Productions.* Toronto: University of Toronto Press, 1995. Print.
46. "*Second City.*" *Canadian Theatre Encyclopedia.* Athabasca University, 2002. Web. July 22, 2010.
47. "Olivier, Laurence Kerr, Baron Olivier of Brighton." *Columbia Encyclopedia*, 6th ed. 2001. Print.
48. "Fit-up." *Merriam-Webster Dictionary.* Web. 2011.
49. "Duse, Eleanora." *Columbia Encyclopedia*, 6th ed. 2001. Print.
50. "Peking Opera." http: //www.beijingtrip.com/feature/opera.htm, n.p. n.d. See also Siu Wang-Ngai, with Peter Lovrick. *Chinese Opera: Images and Stories.* Vancouver: UBC Press; Seattle: University of Washington Press, 1997. Print.
51. "Movies and TV: Hume Cronyn." *New York Times.* New York Times Company, 2010. Web. July 22, 2010.
52. "Movies and TV: Lee Strasberg." *New York Times.* New York Times Company, 2010. Web. July 22, 2010.
53. Mitchell, Glenn. *The Chaplin Encyclopedia.* London: Batsford, 1997. Print.
54. "Donald Meyers." http: //www.imdb.com/name/nm0583526/. Web. n.d.
55. O'Neill, Patrick B. "Whittaker, Herbert William." *The Canadian Encyclopedia.* Historica Foundation of Canada, 1999. Web. July 26, 2010.
56. "Len Doncheff." http: //www.imdb.com/name/nm0232338/. Web. n.d.
57. Rewa, Natalie. "Janson, Astrid Dora." *The Canadian Encyclopedia.* Historica Foundation of Canada, 1999. Web. July 26, 2010.
58. Carson, Neil. *Harlequin in Hogtown: George Luscombe and Toronto Workshop Productions.* Toronto: University of Toronto Press, 1995.
59. Ibid. See also "Negro Leagues History." *Negro Leagues Baseball Museum.* Web. July 5, 2011.
60. Carson, Neil. *Harlequin in Hogtown: George Luscombe and Toronto Workshop Productions.* Toronto: University of Toronto Press, 1995. Print.
61. Ibid.
62. Ibid.
63. "Past Productions: *The Three Lives of Lucie Cabrol.*" *Complicité.* Theatre Complicite, 2010. Web. July 26, 2010.

64. Brecht, Bertolt. *Brecht on Theatre.* New York: Hill and Wang, 1964. Print.
65. Brecht, Bertolt. Ibid.
66. "Georg Büchner." *Encyclopedia Britannica Online.* Encyclopedia Britannica, 2011. Web. June 2011.
67. Carson, Neil. *Harlequin in Hogtown: George Luscombe and Toronto Workshop Productions.* Toronto: University of Toronto Press, 1995. Print.
68. "Bob Rae." http: //bobrae.liberal.ca/. Web. June 2011.
69. "David Archer." http: //ofl.ca/index.php/about_officers/. Web. June 2011.
70. "Leon Major." http: //leonmajor.com/ Web. June 2011.
71. "Mary Durkan." http: //www.imdb.com/name/nm1220086/bio. Web. 2010.
72. Brendan Behan. http: //www.kirjasto.sci.fi/behan.htm. Web. 2008.
73. "John Major." http: //www.johnmajor.co.uk/. Web. 2010.
74. "Tommaso Salvini." *Library of Little Masterpieces: 19th Century Actor Autobiographies.* Ed. George Iles. *Authorama—Public Domain Books.* Web. July 5, 2011.
75. "John Barrymore." *IMDB.* Internet Movie Database, 1990. Web. July 26, 2010.
76. See also Stanislavsky, Konstantin. *An Actor's Work on a Role.* Trans. Jean Benedetti. London: Routledge, 2010. Print. (This is "a contemporary translation of *Creating a Role.*")
77. Carson, Neil. *Harlequin in Hogtown: George Luscombe and Toronto Workshop Productions.* Toronto: University of Toronto Press, 1995. Print.
78. Behan, Brendan. *The Complete Plays,* London: Eyre Methuen, 1978. Print.
79. "The Reform Party." *The Canadian Encyclopedia.* Web. 2011.
80. "The My Lai Cases." William George Eckhart. University of Missouri-Kansas City Law School. Web. 2009.
81. "The Chicago Seven." Douglas Linder. University of Missouri-Kansas City Law School. Web. 2011.
82. "About Us." IATSE Local 891. International Alliance of Theatrical Stage Employees, 2010. Web. July 26, 2010.
83. Carson, Neil. *Harlequin in Hogtown: George Luscombe and Toronto Workshop Productions.* Toronto: University of Toronto Press, 1995. Print.
84. Gould, Allan M. "Don Harron." *The Canadian Encyclopedia.* Web. 2011.
85. Carson, Neil. *Harlequin in Hogtown: George Luscombe and Toronto Workshop Productions.* Toronto: University of Toronto Press, 1995. Print.
86. Rother, Rainer. *Leni Riefenstahl: the Seduction of Genius. Leni Riefenstahl Die Verführung Des Talents.* Trans. Martin H. Bott. Berlin: Henschel, 2000. *Google Books.* Web. 06 July 2011.
87. "Terrorism: Horror and Death at the Olympics." *Time.* Time Inc., September 18, 1972. Web. July 26, 2010.

88. "The Days of Action Campaign." *Canadian Auto Workers*. Canadian Auto Worker's Union, June 19, 1998. Web. July 26, 2010.

89. Bourassa, André G. "Roux, Jean-Louis." *The Canadian Encyclopedia*. Historica Foundation of Canada, 1999. Web. July 26, 2010.

90. "FRANCO (BAHAMONDE), Francisco." *Chambers Biographical Dictionary*, 5th ed. 1990. Print.

91. Carson, Neil. *Harlequin in Hogtown: George Luscombe and Toronto Workshop Productions*. Toronto: University of Toronto Press, 1995. Print.

92. "Mixed Company Theatre." www.mixedcompanytheatre.com. Web. 2011.

93. Bush, Steven and Allen Booth. *Life on the Line*. Playwrights Toronto: Canada, 1984.

94. "Ground Zero Productions: Edmonton." www.gzpedmonton.org/. Web. 2011.

95. "Old Vic." *Columbia Encyclopedia*, 6th ed. 2001. Print.

96. Littlewood, Joan. *Joan's Book: Joan Littlewood's Peculiar History As She Tells It*. London: Methuen, 1994. Print.

97. Melvin, Murray. *The Art of the Theatre Workshop*. London: Oberon Books, 2006. Print.

98. Crew, Rob. "Neville, John." *The Canadian Encyclopedia*. Historica Foundation of Canada, 1999. Web. July 26, 2010.

99. Zuckmayer, Carl. *The Captain of Köpenick, a modern fairy tale in three acts*. London: G. Bles, 1932

100. Brooks, Daniel and Guillermo Verdecchia. *The Noam Chomsky Lectures*. Toronto: Coach House Press, 1991.

101. Carson, Neil. *Harlequin in Hogtown: George Luscombe and Toronto Workshop Productions*. Toronto: University of Toronto Press, 1995. Print.

102."Archives and History." *Stratford Shakespeare Festival*. Stratford Shakespearean Festival of Canada. Web. July 26, 2010.

103."UNICEF People: Sir Peter Ustinov." *UNICEF*. United Nations International Children's Emergency Fund, April 29, 2010. Web. July 26, 2010.

104. *PACT*. Professional Association of Canadian Theatres, 2004. Web. Aug 15, 2010.

105. D'Ermo, Delia. "George Luscombe : his life and art, 1926-1989." http://www.mcgill.ca/library/library-findinfo/escholarship. diss., McGill Univesity, Montreal. 1993.

106. Carson, Neil. *Harlequin in Hogtown: George Luscombe and Toronto Workshop Productions*. Toronto: University of Toronto Press, 1995. Print.

107. Ibid.

108. *Evgeny Vakhtangov*. Compiled by Lyubov Vendrovskaya and Galina Kaptereva; trans. Doris Bradbury. Moscow: Progress Publishers, 1982.

109."About Us." *Contrary Company.* Contrary Company, 2010. Web. Aug 15, 2010.

110."The Red Barn Murder." *St. Edmundsbury Borough Council.* St. Edmundsbury Borough Council. Web. Aug 15, 2010.

111. Johnson, Brian D. "Drabinsky, Garth Howard." *The Canadian Encyclopedia.* Historica Foundation of Canada, 1999. Web. 2005.

FOR FURTHER READING

Carson, Neil. *Harlequin in Hogtown: George Luscombe and Toronto Workshop Productions*. Toronto: University of Toronto Press, 1995.

Filewod, Alan. "Documentary and Popular History: *Ten Lost Years*." *Collective Encounters: Documentary Theatre in English Canada*. Toronto: University of Toronto Press, 1987.

Goorney, Howard. *The Theatre Workshop Story*. London: Eyre Methuen, 1981.

Littlewood, Joan. *Joan's Book: Joan Littlewood's Peculiar History As She Tells It*. London: Methuen, 1994.

Melvin, Murray. *The Art of the Theatre Workshop*. London: Oberon Books, 2006.

Newlove, Jean. *Laban for Actors and Dancers*. London: Nick Hern Books,1993.

Stanislavski, Konstantin. *An Actor Prepares*. Transl. Elizabeth Reynolds Hapgood. New York: Theatre Arts Books, 1948.

Winter, Jack."Epitaph for George." *Canadian Theatre Review* 138 (2009): 96-101.

Winter, Jack & Cedric Smith. *Ten Lost Years*. *The CTR Anthology: Fifteen Plays from 'Canadian Theatre Review'*. Ed. Alan Filewod. Toronto: University of Toronto Press, 1993. 133-189.

CREDITS & THANK-YOUs

Regarding Preface and Tributes:

Thanks to all the copyright holders for permission to reprint.
Copyright remains with the authors or their estates.

Photography credits:
Cover photo by James Lewcun.

Thanks to all the photographers who have generously allowed us to reproduce their photos in this book. Where they are known to us, their names appear with their photos. And where they are not known to us, we also thank them. This is a better book because of their work. Every effort has been made to trace copyright holders for all photographs. However, if anyone picks up this book and says "Hey, I took that picture!" please contact the publisher. The co-author and the publisher stand ready to rectify any omissions in future editions.

And thanks to all the actors who appear in the photos.

Conversations with George Luscombe has been completed with the generous assistance of Ontario Arts Council Theatre Initiatives. OAC is an agency of the Government of Ontario.

For what was to have been a simple book of two men talking about theatre, there are a lot of people to thank. Indeed, *Conversations with George Luscombe* would never have made it into print but for the generous assistance of many individuals and several institutions.

Mona and Karen Luscombe... for supporting George in major ways over many years (and myself in less major—but still crucial—ways in the course of preparing this book)

Howard Aster... for recognizing that this is "an important book for Canada"... and for making the trip to Guelph to help me select photos from the Toronto Workshop Productions Collection

Don Bouzek... for generously providing an excellent-quality tape-recorder and microphone

R.H. Thomson for his preface and Alan Filewod and Ken Gass for permission to reprint their tributes to George; and Shelagh Hewitt-Kareda for permission to reprint Our father by Urjo Kareda

and for extremely insightful dramaturgical/editorial advice… J. Douglas Campbell, BA (U. of A., 1957), MPhil (U. of T., 1969), TWP (47 Fraser, 1959-61). (What a laugh George must have had, overhearing from the astral plane our chat about footnotes vs. endnotes!)

For editorial assistance (2005-2011):
In the preliminary phase of analysis, organizing and editing, I was helped enormously by Amanda Montague, Research Opportunity Program student at the University of Toronto. Throughout later stages of editing I frequently referred to Amanda's astute 'reflection paper' which summarized our Analysis and the organization of Units that came out of that process.

Annie Huang… for helping to move earlier edits along: proofing, researching and creating footnotes and making a list of 'searchables' for the index Simon Gleave… for some very heavy lifting in the final push up the hill towards the publication-ready text: finding and scanning photos, fact-checking, tracking down missed index topics and correcting footnotes and endnotes and Kathryn Binnersley… for very thorough last-minute trouble-shooting on all notes.

Juana Awad (for transferring original cassette recordings to CDs) and Peter Freund, Technical Director at UC Drama, University of Toronto (for arranging to get Juana on this task) … and to Juana again for producing the audio CD, *Conversations with George.*

For transcribing the recordings to print (2002-2005):
Henriette Palffy, Ryan Purdy & Trevor Jablonowski

Robin Breon… for suggesting that I engage students to transcribe the tapes and that I exploit ('only in the correct sense') this wonderful resource provided by the University of Toronto Work-Study Program.
Edith Tveit & the Research Opportunity Program, Faculty of Arts & Sciences, University of Toronto … for the services of Annie Huang and Amanda Montague and to UC Drama, University of Toronto and to the Directors we've been lucky enough to have steering the ship during my time there: Prof. Pia Kleber, Ken Gass and Prof. Tamara Trojanowska and Prof. Stephen Johnson.

Photo credits:
Calvin Butler… for the use of images from his important documentary film *Hey Rube!* (May it become more readily available!)

Jeff Braunstein ... for loan of his sizeable collection of TWP documentation
Richard Payne (sorely-missed "brother artist") ... for tipping me off that Jeff had this collection

Astrid Janson ... for slides from her work at TWP

Karen Luscombe ... for generous access to Luscombe family photos

Maja Ardal and Diana Belshaw ... for photos and information about Humber Theatre's superb production of *The Threepenny Opera*

Simon Malbogat & Mixed Company Theatre ... for *Life on the Line* production shots

Deanne Taylor and Adam Barrett ... for production shots from the Videocabaret and Hummer Sisters archives

Simon Gleave, Khamla Sengthavy, D.J. Sison and Amanda Wagner (Digital Designer, Information Commons, University of Toronto) for their generous assistance in scanning photographic originals

Theatre Royal Stratford East Archives Collection (Murray Melvin, Archivist, and Karen Fisher, Associate Producer) for use of the photo from the Theatre Workshop production of *Mother Courage and Her Children*

Archival and Special Collections, University of Guelph Library ... for making George's 1996 Convocation Address available and for giving me access to, and scanning images from, the Toronto Workshop Productions Collection ... with personal thanks to Jan Brett, Bev Buckie, Dave Proctor and Darlene Wiltsie ... and all the performers and other artists for the use of images of their work.

Very grateful nods for responding to my calls for help re: performer ID and other questions ... to François-Regis Klanfer who has a wealth of narrative and information about several stages in TWP's history ... to Sandi Ross, 1984 TWP company member, who—at the suggestion of Maxine Schacker, Director—now teaches Laban's 'Efforts' to a younger generation at Max the Mutt Animation School in Toronto ... to Ross Skene ("honourary uncle to Karen Luscombe's children") whose 14 years of experience with George and several TWP 'companies' positioned him to provide perspective and great assistance identifying actors ... and to Jack Winter who was there for so much of it, and so central, to the creative work of TWP. (As with other TWP veterans, these all have great stories to tell and I urge them to write up their recollections of days with George. May they be inspired to do so!) ... and to M.T. Anderson, Vladimir Bondarenko and Arla-Jean Sillers (for getting Len to call me), Mary Durkan, Caryn Green, Bob Greene, Camilla Holland, John Macfarlane, Michael Marshall, Aaron Shepard, Cedric Smith, Justin Struss, Ray Whelan, Matthew Wiesblatt (for saving Simon's work on very short notice) ... and to Zoia Horn for strongly reinforcing my intuition that this book should have an index; to Pat Horn Fell for invaluable indexing advice; and to Terry Binnevsley for rescuing me from "indexing hell" with her clarity and professional experstise.

For tips on publishing and/or important letters of support: Howard Aster, Chris Brookes, Prof. Alan Filewod, Cynthia Good, Astrid Janson, Prof. Ric Knowles, Prof. Alexander (Sandy) Leggatt, Simon Malbogat, Leonard McHardy of Theatrebooks, Rick Salutin & Lib Spry

Lisa Cristinzo, Ray Stedman & Artscape Lodge, Gibraltar Point Centre for the Arts for several quiet retreats in which to edit the transcripts and shape them into a book. It is a blessed haven for artists in this 'fast forward & out of control' world.

All the folks who collaborated with George at Toronto Workshop Productions throughout the course of its thirty-year history

and finally, to Catherine Marrion ... for persistent love, support & the sane perspective of laughter over the extremely long 17-year haul bringing this project to publication

Index

STEVEN BUSH (B.1944) got imprinted by George Luscombe while working as an actor on five TWP productions in 1969-70. He has never 're-covered' and since 1993 has taught a Luscombe-inflected Stanislavski curriculum at UC Drama (University of Toronto). With over 45 years professional theatre experience, Steven has written *Beating the Bushes* (Talonbooks, 2010) and co-authored *Available Targets*, *Life on the Line* and *Richard Thirdtime* (all published by Playwrights Canada). *Richard Thirdtime*, directed by George, premiered at Toronto Workshop Productions (1973-74).